A Serial Killer's Daughter

MY STORY OF FAITH, LOVE,
AND OVERCOMING

Kerri Rawson

NELSON
BOOKS

An Imprint of Thomas Nelson

Published in Nashville, Tennessee, by Nelson Books, an imprint of Thomas Nelson. Nelson Books and Thomas Nelson are registered trademarks of HarperCollins Christian Publishing, Inc.

Published in association with the Doug Grad Literary Agency, Inc., 156 Prospect Park West, #3L, Brooklyn, NY 11215, www.dgliterary.com.

All photos are from the Rader family's personal collection.

Thomas Nelson titles may be purchased in bulk for educational, business, fund-raising, or sales promotional use. For information, please email SpecialMarkets@ThomasNelson.com.

All Scripture quotations, unless otherwise indicated, are taken from the Holy Bible, New International Version®, NIV®. Copyright © 1973, 1978, 1984, 2011 by Biblica, Inc.™ Used by permission of Zondervan. All rights reserved worldwide. www.zondervan.com. The "NIV" and "New International Version" are trademarks registered in the United States Patent and Trademark Office by Biblica, Inc.™

Scripture quotations marked ESV are taken from the ESV® Bible (The Holy Bible, English Standard Version®), copyright © 2001 by Crossway, a publishing ministry of Good News Publishers. Used by permission. All rights reserved.

Scripture quotations marked NASB are taken from the New American Standard Bible®, Copyright © 1960, 1962, 1963, 1968, 1971, 1972, 1973, 1975, 1977, 1995 by The Lockman Foundation. Used by permission, www.lockman.org.

Scripture quotations marked NLT are taken from the Holy Bible, New Living Translation. © 1996, 2004, 2007, 2013, 2015 by Tyndale House Foundation. Used by permission of Tyndale House Publishers, Inc., Carol Stream, IL 60188. All rights reserved.

Scripture quotations marked PHILLIPS are taken from J. B. Phillips: THE NEW TESTAMENT IN MODERN ENGLISH, Revised Edition. © J. B. Phillips 1958, 1960, 1972. Used by permission of Macmillan Publishing Co., Inc.

In rare instances, a name was changed to protect the privacy of the person described. Events and conversations have been constructed from the author's memory. Dennis Rader gave permission to use the contents of the letters from Dennis Rader to Kerri Rawson.

ISBN 978-1-4002-0176-1 (eBook)
ISBN 978-1-4002-0175-4 (HC)
ISBN 978-1-4041-0855-4 (IE)

Library of Congress Cataloging-in-Publication Data

Library of Congress Control Number: 2018957741

Printed in the United States of America

19 20 21 22 23 LSC 10 9 8 7 6 5 4 3 2 1

To Darian, for loving me without fail.
And to Emilie and Ian: when you're old enough,
I will hand you this story—to tell you my story.
No, you're not old enough yet, so stop asking. And
yes, Mom is finally done with her book.

Contents

Contents

Part III: Love Will Never Fail You

Part IV: When All Else Has Fallen Away

Part V: Seek Refuge

Part VI: Stand on Your Rock

Contents

Author Note

My family and I owe a great debt of gratitude to the following organizations and the people who serve and work for the better good. There are hundreds of people who aided and assisted us over the past four decades, including the Wichita Police Department, the Federal Bureau of Investigation, the Kansas Bureau of Investigation, the Sedgwick County Sheriff and the Sedgwick County Detention Facility, the Park City Police Department, the El Dorado Correctional Facility, the Sedgwick County District Attorney's Office and the Sedgwick County Public Defender Office, the city and community of Wichita, the *Wichita Eagle*, and Christ Lutheran Church.

Any and all mistakes in the text are mine.

Stubbornness Might Be Enough

On February 25, 2005, my father, Dennis Lynn Rader, was arrested for murder. In the weeks that followed, I learned he was the serial killer known as BTK (Bind, Torture, Kill), who had terrorized my hometown of Wichita, Kansas, for three decades. As he confessed on national television to the brutal killings of eight adults and two children, I struggled to comprehend the fact that the first twenty-six years of my life had been a lie. My father was not the man I'd known him to be.

Since his arrest, I've fought hard to come to terms with the truth about my dad. I've wrestled with shame, guilt, anger, and hatred. I've accepted the fact that I am a crime victim, dating back to the days my mom carried me in her womb.

I no longer fight the past nor try to hide it. It just is. It happened and it's terrible. Terrible to dream about, terrible to think about, terrible to talk about. Incalculable loss, trauma, emotional abuse, depression, anxiety, posttraumatic stress—these things leave scars.

I've struggled with forgiveness, fought for understanding, tried to put the ruptured pieces of my life and my family's life back together. It's an ongoing battle. But hope, truth, and love—the things that are good and right in this world—continue to fight through the darkness and overcome the nightmares. I am a survivor who has found resilience and resistance in faith, courage, and my sure stubbornness to never give up.

—KERRI RAWSON

PART I

Hold On to Your Foundations

Therefore we will not fear, though the earth give way and the mountains fall into the heart of the sea.

—Psalm 46:2

CHAPTER I

What Doesn't Kill You . . .

On the day the world dropped out on me, I woke up late. I had pulled my dark brown hair back in a loose scrunchie, and at noon, I was still in my mint-green fleece pajamas. They'd been a gift from my parents on Christmas morning two months earlier, when I was home in Kansas with my husband, Darian. This was our second winter living in Michigan, and I'd taken the day off from substitute teaching. I'd been staying home a lot because driving on snow and ice set me on edge.

Friday, February 25, 2005, had begun as just another cold day, with snow on the ground and in the air. About 12:30 p.m., I glanced out our picture window to see how much snow had fallen the night before. Not that anyone could tell by late February—it was just a heap of white upon white.

I noticed a maroon car, slightly rusted and beat up, parked next to the green dumpster behind our apartment building. A man sat behind the steering wheel and seemed to be glancing up at our window on the second floor.

My internal alarms buzzed. *Stranger danger.*

I wasn't expecting Darian to be home until later for lunch, if at all.

As it neared one o'clock, I looked again.

The man was still there.

All right, that does it. I'm calling Darian.

"Hey, when are you coming home for lunch?" My voice was calm enough to fool him.

"Not sure. Want me to bring you something? Taco Bell?"

"Nah." I paused. "I'm calling because a strange old beat-up car is parked by the dumpster. A man is sitting in the car, and I swear he's looking into our window." I was beginning to sound a little panicky, but Darian was unfazed.

"Hmm, our window? Upstairs?"

"Yeah, looking right in it."

"Um, that's really not possible. But if he's giving you the creeps or something, call the cops."

"Nah. Well, maybe. Yeah. If he doesn't leave soon."

"Okay. I'll be home in a while to eat if I can get away. Swamped here today."

We said goodbye, and I looked again, this time peering through the corner of the blinds, like my dad might do.

My dad repeatedly taught us to be fearful of strangers, not to open doors to people we didn't know, to be extremely cautious. When I was younger, he'd worked as a security alarm installer, and I'd always figured that's where he picked up this bit of paranoia. Still, nothing wrong with being smart. Being safe. Better than sorry.

I peeked again.

The car was still there. The man was not.

Clank, clank, clank.

What happened to the intercom, a visitor buzzing to be let in? Someone must have propped the front door open again.

Now my alarms were sounding full force. My heart was speeding up; my skin was growing hot.

I was sure the man in the car was now on the other side of the door, which only had a simple lock on it, no deadbolt. The house I grew up in had deadbolts, which were always kept locked. No matter the time of day.

I'll pretend I'm not home.

Clank, clank, clank.

Okay. Be brave. It's nothing.

I propped my wire-rim glasses on my head and squinted through the peephole to see a man in his fifties wearing a dress shirt. Tie. Glasses.

I twisted my glasses in my hands and placed them back on my face.

"Hello? Can I help you?" I called from my side of the subpar door.

"Yes. I'm with the FBI. I need to speak with you."

Me? The FBI?

"What about?"

"I need to speak to you. Can you let me in?"

I'm still in my pajamas, in my bare feet.

Dad always said, "Make them show you a badge. Make them prove to you who they are." Not that anyone, ever, had approached my door with a badge, but I guess there was a first time for everything.

I opened the door a bit, putting my foot next to it. If he was FBI, he might or might not push his way in. Hard to say, based on what I'd seen in movies.

He didn't look like FBI. He looked like someone who might do my taxes.

"So, uh, can I see your ID?"

"Yes." He flipped opened his badge and let me study it for a bit, then asked more softly, "Can I come in? I need to talk to you."

Okay . . . but what the heck?

"Sure. My husband will be home soon. He's on his way. You know, for lunch?"

That's another trick Dad taught me long ago: tell the stranger in your house someone is on the way, even if it's not true.

"Okay, good. I need to talk to him too."

Standing with this guy in my apartment's foyer, I decided he seemed all right. He wasn't even carrying a gun, just a yellow legal pad and a pencil.

So much for the movies.

"What do you need to talk to me about? You've got the right person, right?"

He glanced down at his notepad and then back up at me.

"Yeah, think so. Are you Kerri Rawson? Maiden name Rader? Twenty-six years old?"

I nodded.

"Originally from Wichita, Kansas? Your father is Dennis Rader?"

"Uh, yeah. That's me." My mind was scrambling. *Why is this man here? What does he want?*

I turned to walk toward the kitchen, but the hallway was so narrow only one person could walk through at a time. I didn't like him behind me, so I stopped and stepped back, allowing him to go in front. My mind tried to find some reason for this man's visit and came up with nothing but sharp white noise. And *fear.*

I focused instead on tiny details: the cornflower-blue dish towels with bright sunflowers hanging in my white-on-white kitchen, color brought from Kansas to Michigan eighteen months before when Dad had helped us move after the wedding. A chocolate Bundt cake with powdered sugar icing sat on the counter; I'd made it the night before.

My keys and navy-blue purse were next to my cookbooks. A red spiral-bound Betty Crocker was propped up by a box of handwritten recipe cards, favorites from friends and family back home.

The man from the FBI was now facing me, his back to the microwave.

"Have you heard of BTK?"

Wha—?

6

The room brightened then narrowed, intensified.

"Um, you mean that guy they are looking for in Wichita? In Kansas?"

"Yes."

I hit the panic button. "Has something happened to my grandma? Has my grandma been murdered?"

"Your grandma? No. She's fine."

"Grandma is frail," I said. "Keeps falling. My folks have to help a lot. She's been to the hospital this week. BTK murders women."

"No. It's your dad."

"What is my dad?"

"He's been arrested."

"My dad has been what?"

"Arrested. Your dad is wanted as BTK. Wanted for murders in Kansas."

"My dad is wha—?"

"BTK. Wanted. Arrested. Can we sit down? I need to ask you some questions."

"My mom? Is my mom, Paula, okay? Has my mom been murdered? By my dad?"

"No. She's all right. Safe. She's being picked up right now for questioning."

"Who? Who is picking her up?"

"The police. They're questioning her. She's okay."

"My brother, Brian? Is my brother okay? He's stationed at Groton, Connecticut, with the United States Navy."

"Yes. We are notifying him right now."

"Who is?"

"The FBI." The man lifted a page on his notepad. "I need to question you. It's important. When did you say your husband will be home?"

The room was spinning.

I grabbed at the wall jutting out near the stove. My hand

brushed against the smooth stained-glass picture hanging there—it was made of vivid purples, pinks, greens, an etched butterfly, and the words *Love Never Fails*.

I'd heard: *Your dad is BTK.*

I was shaking all over. "I think I'd better sit down. I'm not feeling well."

The room turned red. Dark splotches came into view.

I was falling into a black hole, with no idea of how I was ever going to get out.

CHAPTER 2

Believe in Good Beginnings

JUNE 1981
WICHITA, KANSAS

People who knew my parents before February 25, 2005, would have told you this: Dennis cherished Paula. My dad would tell you the same—still to this day. But he should have known it wasn't going to be forever.

Some of my earliest memories are of music filling the house, spun out from the turntable Dad shipped home from an overseas air force deployment years before. As the Carpenters harmonized on "We've Only Just Begun," Dad would pull Mom close and she'd laugh, and they would spin together for a minute or two in the living room, lost, remembering the good times spun early around their song. As a toddler, I'd twirl and clap and wait my turn. When Dad and I danced to "(They Long to Be) Close to You" with my little feet on top of his white socks, I was certain my dad's love for me knew no bounds.

Those hit singles came out in 1970, shortly before my folks met. Dad, the oldest of four brothers, was the last of them to meet Mom, the oldest of three sisters. At Christ Lutheran Church, my grandma, Dorothea, would say to my mom, Paula, "I've got one more son. You haven't met Dennis yet. Just wait, he will be back home soon."

In the summer of 1966, Dad enlisted in the military on his own

9

terms before the draft got him. He traveled happily for four years as an air force communication linesman to assignments that kept him out of Vietnam: Greece, Turkey, South Korea, and Okinawa, Japan.

Dad could shimmy up a power pole effortlessly, installing antennae, wires, and whatever else he needed to rig up with a few flicks of the wrist, a bit of tinkering, and patience. He came home with stories and a box full of photos and souvenirs, his time abroad spent more like a tourist than a sergeant serving in wartime.

Two of Dad's brothers fought in the jungles of Vietnam: Paul as a sailor on a navy PT boat, Bill as a marine walking the bush. My uncles didn't talk much about their tours of duty, but it was clear: they sure didn't feel like vacations. Dad's youngest brother, Jeff, was spared from having to go to Vietnam.

My dad's father, William Rader, grew up in Rader, Missouri, a town founded by my ancestors in the 1800s. His family later settled in Pittsburg, Kansas, where he and his siblings worked the family farm. In February 1943, my twenty-year-old grandpa joined the Marine Corps. Two months later, my seventeen-year-old grandma, who lived in Columbus, Kansas, rode trains out to San Diego, California, to marry her high school sweetheart on his day off from aircraft mechanic training.

I always imagined my grandparents dancing to "Moonlight Serenade" by the Glenn Miller Orchestra, a favorite of Grandma Dorothea's and mine, although the timeless swing tune "In the Mood" might have been more their speed. They had one night together; then it was back to the realities of World War II.

Grandpa soon ended up in the Pacific, repairing B-25 bombers that survived enemy fire and somehow made it back to Midway Island. He came home full of stories about crash landings, airplanes full of bullet holes, and life on a two-square-mile atoll in the middle of the ocean.

A shore leave rendezvous netted the birth of my dad nine months later in March 1945. Grandma and my infant father stayed with family in Columbus for a year until Grandpa made it back home in March 1946. Grandpa cooked in the mess on the ship as they crossed the Pacific, peeling mountains of potatoes, saying later, "It sure beat swabbin' decks."

When Dad was little, my grandparents moved to the Riverview area of north Wichita for Grandpa's new job working the graveyard shift at the Ripley plant for Kansas Gas & Electric (KG&E). The red brick smokestacks, standing tall across the Little Arkansas River, could be seen from the street where Dad's family settled in a sharp white bungalow with black trim.

Dad and his three younger brothers slept in bunk beds in one room, where Dad spun stories of cowboys and Indians or cops and robbers as the younger ones drifted off to sleep. The boys walked to Riverview Elementary down a street lined with arching trees, and every autumn they each got a new pair of jeans Grandma patched again and again before she turned them into shorts for summer break. Growing up, the boys spent a lot of time outdoors, roughhousing, fishing, and shooting around the river.

In 1960, Grandma took on a calmer day job as a bookkeeper for Leeker's Family Foods. My fifteen-year-old dad soon joined her as a grocery bagger and stocker.

Later, when we all gathered in the fall for Rader family campouts, my dad and uncles would spin story after story from their own boyhood while my cousins and I drifted toward sleep next to a blazing orange campfire. There were war stories and ghost stories, tall tales and humdingers.

———

My mom's mother, Eileen, graduated from Plainview High School in south Wichita in 1944 and went to work at Boeing. She drove a Cushman cart on the factory floor, delivering parts as B-29 bombers churned out overhead.

My mom's father, Palmer, grew up in WaKeeney, Kansas, and served two years in the Pacific as a radioman and Morse code operator with the army air forces. He told us, "Eggs never go bad—we ate two-year-old eggs on those troop ships and we were happy to have them."

After the war, Grandma had her eye on a checker at the Safeway grocery store. Granddad had his eye on her, too, declaring, "That's the girl I'm going to marry" the first time he saw her in his checkout lane. It still seems up for debate who was chasing whom, but after a few dates, it was all settled. They married three months later in 1946.

Mom was born in 1948, lived in Plainview her first few years, then moved to Park City, a northern suburb of Wichita, growing up three miles from Dad. As teenagers, Mom and her sisters, Sharon and Donna, helped out at my grandparents' bakery in Wichita and ran the Park City Pool with Grandma.

In August 1970, Dad, twenty-five, was just back from the air force. He was handsome and sleek in his dress blues, his dark hazel-green eyes crinkling when he smiled. Mom, twenty-two, was a long-legged looker in a go-go dress with dark brown eyes and cropped dark brown hair. They caught each other's eye while standing in the fellowship hall after church let out.

Mom would tell me, "When you know, you know."

Dad would say, "It was love at first sight, plus she drove a hot car."

Dad lived with his folks the next several months, attended Butler Community College, and worked part-time at Leeker's. Mom lived with her folks and worked as a secretary at the Veterans Administration.

My parents got engaged shortly after Christmas 1970, out in the middle of the frozen Arkansas River in downtown Wichita. Two months later, Mom's red '66 Chevelle, nicknamed Big Red, slid on an icy bridge a block from church and slammed into another vehicle. Mom broke her back, and Dad rushed to her side at Wesley Hospital, helping her through the recovery.

In May 1971, friends and family gathered for my parents' wedding. Mom's sisters stood up with her, wearing sky-blue dresses and matching pillbox hats, holding white daisies. Dad's brothers stood up with him, wearing ties and suit coats.

Standing before the altar in the church where they met, my mom's aunt sang "We've Only Just Begun." Dad wore a white suit coat and flubbed the traditional vow of faithfulness, saying, "I plight me your troth." After hearing the story so many times, I still don't know the right way to say it. Mom recited her vows perfectly, standing ramrod straight, her high-collared white lace dress hiding a back brace.

On the evening my parents wed, the sky grew dark and their wedding cake with blue and yellow flowers almost toppled over in the parking lot. The cake was saved from disaster and during the reception, Dad, with a mischievous glint in his eye, fed Mom too big of a bite. Mom, with bright, smiling eyes, politely covered her mouth with her hand and then returned the favor.

Standing in the doorway of the church, Dad and Mom bid farewell to their friends and family with a wave. Then, hand in hand, they ran laughing through a shower of rice and rain out to Big Red, decorated with flowing streamers, trailing cans, and handwritten signs in white shoe polish, wishing love, luck, and happily ever after.

CHAPTER 3

Hope for Happily Ever After

JUNE 1971

After their honeymoon, my folks bought a nine-hundred-square-foot, three-bedroom ranch—white with yellow trim—that was a block away from Mom's parents. A mid-1950s brick home, it had an identical floor plan to the house Mom grew up in.

Well on their way to the American dream, my parents tucked away their bone-white wedding china in paper-lined cabinets and bought kitchen appliances in the shade of avocado. Mom hung brown-and-cream wallpaper in their kitchen and sewed light-blue curtains out of durable fabric for their big picture window in the living room. Blue pitchers, handed down from Dad's grandmother, Carrie, decorated end tables; records were stacked together next to Dad's turntable. Mom was glad to have her parents so close and wistfully hoped to have children toddling around on her hardwood floors.

While finishing college, Dad took a second-shift plant job at the Coleman Company. He quit after graduating with an associate's degree in electronics from Butler in the summer of 1972. He started at the Cessna Aircraft Company in early 1973, working in the electrical tool-and-die section, a job he enjoyed and that fit his growing skill set. Mom kept working at the VA as a secretary, her nimble hands flying over her typewriter and taking dictation in precise shorthand that would require an expert code breaker to crack.

14

After work, Angelo's became a favorite place to split a pizza, followed by a movie at the Crest. The first and last scary movie Mom saw with Dad was a rescreening of the 1967 film *Wait Until Dark*. I can imagine Mom, holding tight on to Dad's arm, saying firmly, "From now on, I pick the movie."

Dad also learned Mom wasn't into camping after a night trying to weather a thunderstorm at Wilson Lake. Mom tells the story of huddling together in an army-green canvas tent that smelled like "a mangy ol' mutt," when a park ranger shone a flashlight on them, warning of an approaching tornado. She still says about that night, "I told your dad that was it. He was on his own to camp from then on."

———

I grew up on these stories: how my parents met, married, and spent their early, happy life together. These stories became canon in my life—solid ground I would anchor my own beliefs of the world on. I wish I could continue telling just these stories, right up to the ever-after. It's what I was expecting, depending on.

Dad desired his "good side, white hat life," but he also wanted his "dark side, black hat life."[1] He went to great lengths over the next three decades to maintain these two lives next to each other, hiding his second life from everyone. Eventually, though, his second life caught up with his first, exposing its own terrible truths.

Dad didn't just decide one day to commit murder. The decision would build in him, growing over the course of his first twenty-nine years of life. After he was arrested, Dad spoke of hidden deviant behavior dating back to his early years: spying, stalking, breaking and entering, theft, animal torture. He told of an immense fantasy world built around violence, bondage, and sadism. He read about notorious criminals and idolized them—adding their narcissistic, murderous actions to his own evil ideals. He twisted all this together in his head: fact, fiction, half truths, downright lies. And out of it came his "Factor-X."[2]

He thought he could control it, stop it at any time, but he couldn't have been more wrong.

NOVEMBER 1973

In the fall of 1973, Dad was laid off from the Cessna Aircraft Company. He liked his job. It paid well and losing it started a downward spiral within him that would lead to immense outward devastation. Angry, idle, and antsy, he escalated, breaking into area homes and attempting to kidnap a woman at the Twin Lakes Mall.[3]

In January 1974, Dad murdered Joseph and Julie Otero and their two youngest children, Josie, age eleven, and Joey, age nine. The three older Otero children found their family's bodies after walking home from school. Dad then became a wanted man who lived every day of the next thirty-one years as a betrayal—as a lie.

After the Otero murders Dad started classes at Wichita State University (WSU), pursuing a bachelor's degree in administration of justice. Studying law enforcement, Dad kept his own ironic, nefarious agenda hidden. Attending college became a cover story for Dad at times. He'd tell Mom he was headed to the campus library to study—while he was actually out trolling for victims.

In April 1974, Dad murdered Kathryn Bright, a twenty-one-year-old, who lived near the WSU campus, and he fought with her nineteen-year-old brother, Kevin, shooting and almost killing him.

That fall, Dad, seeking notoriety, contacted the *Wichita Eagle*, claiming responsibility for the Otero murders and calling himself BTK, for bind, torture, and kill. He also started working at ADT installing security systems, capitalizing on the fear and opportunity he created, and giving himself access and cover because no one pays attention to utility vans and work uniforms. Working days and attending evening classes, Dad was gone long hours and late nights.

To get him through college, Mom often typed and sometimes even helped write his thesis papers.

As my father studied justice and worked in security, he stole those very things from the Otero and Bright families. He also grew overprotective of his own family. Dad's self-induced twisted insanity of overcaution and suspicion permeated my home for the next decades. We never had a security system, but we did have ADT stickers on the doors and thin metallic tape outlining our back door's window—which Dad told me was enough to fool the bad guys. After his arrest, Dad said about this time, "I became overly defensive. I watched the road outside and had a loaded gun ready. I made sure our locked windows were secure, probably like everyone else in Wichita."[4]

My green-eyed, blond-haired brother, Brian, arrived on a July evening in 1975. After struggling for three years to conceive, my folks were thrilled to be parents. Mom named Brian after the pro football player Brian Piccolo, who fought a cancer diagnosis in the 1960s and who James Caan played in the 1971 tearjerker *Brian's Song*. A few weeks later, my brother was baptized at the wooden baptismal font that stood in the same place my parents had wed four years before. My parents settled into family life as Mom left the VA to stay home with him.

Decades later, Dad commented about the gap in murders that began after my brother's birth, saying, "We were now a family. With a job and a baby, I got busy."[5] Dad continued to stalk potential victims, though, and in March 1977, Dad murdered Shirley Vian Relford, a mom to three young children. In December 1977, when Mom was three months pregnant with me, Dad murdered twenty-five-year-old Nancy Fox. My dad was raising children, yet he chose to take another mother away from her own children. He was about to have a daughter yet took two more daughters away from their families.

I was born early in the morning in June 1978 and baptized not long after. My name came from Dad's grandma, Carrie, and I shared his middle name, Lynn.

Dad continued to play games with the police and media as BTK—leaving my hometown and my mom fearful. Then he went silent, ceasing communication the day after my first birthday. He graduated from WSU and said after his arrest, "I got busy, being a family man, raising kids."[6]

But his Factor-X wasn't ever that far from him.

NEWS BULLETIN

JUNE 1979

Today, the man who calls himself BTK—for Bind, Torture, Kill—dropped off a letter at a post office in downtown Wichita.

At 4:00 a.m., a man approached a clerk who was arriving to work. He handed her a letter and told her to put it in the box for KAKE, a local TV station. The clerk reported the man was around the age of thirty, clean-shaven, with his hair cropped short above his ears. He was in an odd outfit for summer, wearing a jean jacket, jeans, and gloves.[1]

BTK is wanted for seven murders dating back to 1974.

If you have seen this man, please contact the authorities immediately.

CHAPTER 4

Weave Among the Pines
Like a Tomboy

MAY 1980

Patches, a wiggly orange-and-white Brittany spaniel puppy, arrived on Mother's Day when I was near the age of two. She followed my dad all over our yard with me trailing right behind, and Dad would work to keep us both out of trouble. He'd lift me up, dust off my knees, and brush my face with his dark mustache, making me squeal, "Daddy, you're bristly."

In the mornings, I'd stand in our hallway, peering into the bathroom, watching Dad shave off his overnight whiskers. Sometimes, seemingly abruptly, he would shave off his mustache or grow out his beard, and when I was very little, I'd wonder where my father had gone.

When Dad's eyes were the color of grass in the spring, it was easy to tuck up next to him while he answered my myriad questions. But as early as I can remember, being around Dad could be complicated. When his eyes turned dark—stormy like the unsettled sea—it was wise to stay clear till he was himself again.

It could be hard to know *who* was coming home at six o'clock, who was driving up in the white van with the red ladders and the letters *ADT* on the side. When Dad was gruff and sullen, it was best to have your shoes put away and to mind your p's and q's. After my dad's arrest, my mom said, "Near Dad, it could often feel like we had to walk on eggshells."

Mom knew how to gently send Dad along, saying, "I'll clean up dinner. Why don't you go take care of the outside chores? Maybe Patches would like to go on a walk. Weather looks nice this weekend, might be a good time to fish."

I learned at an early age that if you could get Dad outside, his shoulders would straighten, the haunted look in his eyes would fade, and he would just be *Dad* again.

When I was around the age of three, Dad temporarily turned my corner bedroom into a greenhouse. Over the winter, I helped Dad pick out seeds from the Burpee's catalog, and in the spring, he set mint-green trays with speckled soil under fluorescent lights in my room. He rigged smaller lights in the attached shed, where I stood on my tiptoes on his small wooden ladder, peering into the trays to see what had sprung to life.

As Dad's garden continued to expand in one corner of our yard, he drew up blueprints for a treehouse in the opposite corner. On top of four redwood poles, a wooden platform slowly emerged, and we kids dangled our feet off it as Dad added walls and windows. Once it was tall enough for even Dad to stand in, he topped it with a slanted shingle roof, propped a tall wooden ladder in the doorway, and turned it over to my brother and me.

I often tagged along with Dad on Saturday mornings to Payless Cashways, wandering up and down the aisles of tools, gadgets, and good-smelling lumber. Dad would select what he needed, lay it in the back of the car, and tie a red warning flag off the end. We'd drive home and get to work.

MAY 1982

When I was almost four, my dad's parents—Grandpa Bill and Grandma Dorothea—arrived at our home, towing a small yellow-and-white trailer with their large, gold Oldsmobile Cutlass Supreme. We loaded the car up in the faint gray predawn light and headed south.

In Texas, we stopped at Goose Island State Park, to visit the Big Tree, a massive oak whose arms twisted to the sky, and tossed a bit of Grandma's Chex Mix up to the swirling gulls.

We crossed over to Padre Island via a ferry at Port Aransas and spent the next several days parked right up next to the beach. Dad carved a large birthday card for Mom in the sand and helped us kids build elaborate castles, finding the just-right shells to decorate our fleeting dwellings with. I squealed as the tide came in and broke apart our creations, carrying them back to the ocean.

Dad inadvertently ran into a Portuguese man o' war one morning in the surf and came back to the trailer, jumping and yelling, with a bright purple, angry mark stretched over his foot. Dad's hooting and hollering gave me the giggles.

The seashore cemented in my heart on that magical trip, but I was so young that as I grew up, I'd ask Mom again and again, "Did we really visit the Big Tree, feed the gulls, and stay on the beach for days?"

She would say, "Don't you remember?"

While my brother was in school, I'd tag along with Mom to church, where she worked as a part-time secretary. Sometimes we would run into Grandpa Bill, who would wave as he drove a riding lawnmower over four acres that jutted up against fields. I liked playing out back near the white shed; there was often a horse to pet carefully over the barbed wire fence and an old pile of boards to get into trouble on.

On Sundays, Mom sang in the choir and Dad ushered. While my parents were busy during the service, my brother and I sat next to my grandparents in a wooden pew. I often sat between my grandmas, fidgeting in frilly dresses with lace petticoats, scuffing my black patent Mary Janes on the tile. Grandma Dorothea's offer of yellow-wrapped Juicy Fruit gum and Grandma Eileen's offer of green Echo Hills golf pencils to doodle with on the bulletin usually kept me busy. Granddad Palmer helped by giving me the giggles and Grandpa Bill sometimes offered to take us all out for brunch at Furr's Cafeteria afterward.

Sunday after Sunday, I wistfully daydreamed as I stared out the stained-glass windows, wishing I could weave through the towering pine trees swaying in the wind. But if I fidgeted too much or caused a disturbance, Dad would haul me out of church, and I'd get stuck sitting in our tan, two-door hatchback Chevy, with its sticky, too-hot-in-the-summer leather seats. Dad would loosen his tie and, with his sleeves rolled up, prop up his arm on the open windowsill and read the thick Sunday edition of his beloved *Eagle*.

If he wasn't fuming too much—if I'd gone out in his arms willingly, not kicking and screaming—Dad would pass me the comics with a grin or let me run around the grounds, zigzagging through the pines, kicking up needles, no matter how I might scuff up my fancy shoes, tear my tights, or dirty up my nice dress. Mom would shake her head and ask, "Can you at least act like a lady on Sundays?"

I'd simply reply, "Nope."

And Dad would say with pride, "That's my tomboy."

———

Dad committed murder three more times after I was born. Even now, it's not possible to reconcile the man and life I knew with the other man—and his other life.

After his arrest, Dad talked about his ability to "compartmentalize" his two sides.[1] It was his way of separating the dark from the light. Since his arrest, I've fought to hold on to the man I knew and the places we loved, but the truth is, he continued to inflict devastation, taking other lives and ruining more families, while living with and caring for his own family.

APRIL 1985

Dad murdered Marine Hedge, a grandmother and widow, at the end of April 1985. She lived down the street from us, and Mom and I would wave hello to her on our way to my grandparents'.

Mrs. Hedge went missing on a stormy night. When I heard the police were searching for her, I felt scared. I was six years old, and only Mom and I had been home that night—how did I know if we were safe?

A few days later, a police officer walked up our driveway. He was out canvassing the neighborhood and stopped to ask Mom some questions. I grew even more frightened when they found Mrs. Hedge's body in the country a week later—she had been strangled. I don't know how I knew this at my young age, other than overhearing the TV news or my folks talking. At the time, Dad had reassured me: "Don't worry, we're safe."

A few weeks after Mrs. Hedge's body was found, I was climbing the huge pines at church and Mom yelled, "Get down before you break an arm!"

Minutes later, running inside, I fell—and broke my arm. Dad rushed to my side, rigged up a splint, and placed me in the back of our new silver Oldsmobile station wagon. He drove me to Wesley, where I had surgery on a compound fracture of the elbow. Doctors put my bones back together with pins and placed my arm in a split-cast. Due to complications, I ended up staying five days in the hospital. Mom rarely left my side.

Because my injury was so severe, I wasn't able to finish first grade, and we weren't able to go on vacation to Padre Island. I felt awful about missing the beach, and I could tell Dad was disappointed—he was really looking forward to our trip.

My young mind tied everything together: the shock of my broken arm, my guilt over our canceled vacation, and my fear when learning that our neighbor who had gone missing was found murdered. It would be thirty years before I fully faced these events, attempted to understand their traumatic impact, and began to recover.

Best I can figure, my night terrors began around this time. When Mom heard me scream, she would quickly come to my side, sit on the edge of my bed, and try to soothe me back to sleep. Half-awake, I'd often argue with her, sometimes belligerently, saying, "There's a bad man in the house—in my room."

She would gently reassure me, "No, you're dreaming, you're safe—go back to sleep."

I'd drift back off because my mom was right there and my dad was right across the hall—and he'd never, ever let anyone or anything hurt us.

That summer, because we weren't able to go to the beach, my mom and her sister, my aunt Sharon, took the kids to FantaSea in Wichita. My cousin Michelle was nine, I was seven, and we were quite the sight. She had jumped out of a swing and broken both her wrists around the same time I broke my arm. With plastic bags around our casts, we stood under a waterfall that day, our hair pulled back in ponytails, grinning as we watched our older blond-headed siblings tackle the waterslides. Michelle's older sister, Andrea, and I would later shake our heads and laugh about our moms' attempts at adventure.

That afternoon, Mom and I were out on a raft in a wave pool when a wave came up and tipped us, causing me to fall overboard. As I sank, partly weighted down by my cast, Mom firmly grabbed my good arm and brought me back up. A lifeguard had been ready to jump in and save me, but Mom had me, no problem.

CHAPTER 5

Go Comet Hunting
in the Winter

AUGUST 1985

In 1985, after thirty-seven years with Kansas Gas & Electric, Grandpa Bill retired as a plant operator with a steady pension and a gold watch. He took the cousins on a tour of his plant once, and I remember being in awe of the massive generators he had worked around for decades. Grandma Dorothea joined him in retirement after twenty-five years with Leeker's. Mom had worked alongside my grandma as a bookkeeper for a few years before she accepted a job with Snacks convenience store. I liked visiting them in their wood-paneled office, watching long, thin strips of white paper curl as their fingers flew on their adding machines.

After my grandparents retired, my brother and I and my cousins, Lacey and her younger sister, Sarah, sometimes stayed for days at a time with them. We were known to wreak havoc and were often sent downstairs to the wood-paneled family room or outside to run amuck. We liked playing hide-and-seek downstairs; the unfinished part of the basement was a great place to hide. Outside, you could crouch down behind the garden tools in the old white shed that smelled of machine oil and dirt.

In the evenings, with Grandma, we would watch old black-and-white movies with smartly dressed, mouthy heroines who solved mysteries. We also played Uno at the dining table while passing around popcorn and drinking RC Cola. Grandpa would accuse us kids of holding a Pick 4 card up our sleeves. We'd shake out our arms and say, "Nothing's here, dude." He'd raise one eyebrow and chuckle.

We girls, who shared the same color hair and eyes, sometimes slept in my grandparents' king bed in our dads' old bedroom. Photos of my dad and uncles rested on a white shelf above my grandparents' bed, and we giggled over what they used to look like. I'd drift off to sleep, listening to the wind chimes that hung on the back porch gently sounding with the breeze.

In February 1986 I stayed up all night comet hunting, alongside Grandpa Bill, Dad, and Brian, parked on a dirt road. We were some of the lucky ones to finally catch a glimpse of Halley's Comet in the bone-chilling, hazy blue-gray dawn. It passed by quickly, and I wasn't even sure I'd seen it. But the guys all agreed the slight, fast-moving round object streaking across the sky was indeed Halley. After it went by, as the sun was beginning to show, Grandpa said, "Well, that was something. Now, who's hungry?" And he proceeded to take us out to a breakfast of biscuits and gravy at Grandy's.

AUGUST 1986

Dad was a blast to adventure with, splashing cannonballs in motel pools, running down sand dunes in thunderstorms, and yelling right alongside us on Space Mountain. But in August 1986, while we were vacationing in Southern California, my dad flipped out early one evening.

Noticing dusty footprints on top of a van parked under our motel balcony, he was convinced someone had climbed onto the van and broken into our room while we were gone. I'd never seen him that on edge before: bug-eyed and sweaty, pacing back and forth, ranting like a lunatic. He even made our family use a password to answer the door, even though he was the only one coming and going with bags from the car.

I learned how to navigate around my dad during these trickier times by watching my mom. It was best to go along with him; he'd settle down soon enough.

Despite my dad's irrational behavior that night, we had an unforgettable vacation. We stopped at sites along our route between Kansas and the Pacific Ocean. In California, we went to Sea World and the San Diego Zoo, and we spent three magical days at Disneyland.

When school started in August, I brought in photos of my vacation, and my third-grade teacher attached them to a bulletin board. I can tell you all about our trip, and I can describe my classroom in detail. What I can't tell you is why, only a month after our return, Dad murdered Vicki Wegerle, a mother of two children. Mrs. Wegerle lived near the Sweetbriar area where my dad and brother went to the barber, around the corner from the library where I spent hours perusing the bookshelves. I can't fully separate out that time period in my life now. I have my memories, and now I know the truth.

JULY 1988

My family continued to attend church almost every week, and around the age of ten, I served as an acolyte. Around that same time, Dad served occasionally as an assistant to the pastor, donning a robe and a colorful vestment, doing his best to chant his way through the Apostles' Creed. Dad and I would sit across from each other when we served together—occasionally catching each other's eyes and silently communicating, *I blame Mom for this—I'd rather be fishing.*

When Dad was laid off from his job at ADT in July, he came home dejected. I remember him opening the kitchen door while holding a typed piece of paper and asking Mom to step outside.

When they came back in, Mom looked worried. Dad had drawn up plans to add on to our home, but those plans were set aside that day and never picked up again.

Dad found a temporary job with the 1990 census, but it required long business trips. He was often gone for days at a time—traveling around Kansas, but also in Missouri, Arkansas, and Oklahoma. I missed him and was glad when he was home. We went on long walks with Patches, stayed up late watching scary movies after Mom went to bed, and shared paperback mysteries—ones Mom didn't necessarily approve of me reading.

Dad was later put in charge of a large office floor of workers downtown, across from the main library branch—one of our favorite places to hang out. I found his temporary office fascinating, with its portable cardboard desks and high-up, important view. And I remember him closing the office for the last time, hauling out boxes of supplies and saying the census was over and the government didn't need any of this stuff.

That winter was terrible for my family. Mom fell ill in December, spending twelve days in the hospital with pneumonia. Dad tried his best to take care of us kids and the house, though he backed the Oldsmobile into our neighbor's car on our way to see Mom at St. Francis.

I ended up with a D in English, even though I'd always been a good student, but I'd never seen Mom ill for more than a day or two. My relationship with Dad seemed to be fraying at times. It felt as if he was pushing me away—he was preoccupied and moody. Life felt unstable and I was fearful our family would crack under the stress.

In January 1991, Dad murdered Dolores Davis, a mother and grandmother who lived a few miles east of us.

APRIL 1991

In the spring of 1991, Dad took up the hobby of stamp collecting. He often spread them all over the kitchen table while Mom was at choir practice. I'd already learned it was better to leave Dad to his own devices. If he was content, he caused less grief in the house and I was in less trouble, owing fewer quarters to the swear jar.

In April, Dad finally found a new job as a Park City compliance officer. His office was in the same building as the police station, just down the hall. He wore a brown uniform, decked to the nines, similar in appearance to a county sheriff's, even including the gold badge over his heart. In his element, he drove around neighborhoods in a marked truck, and had an excuse to snoop in other people's yards. He was happier employed, and life at home settled for all of us.

My father murdered four members of the Otero family in the winter of 1974, and seventeen years later, he murdered Mrs. Davis. He was unemployed both times and stated after he was arrested that he was in similar downtrodden states. I knew when I was twelve Dad wasn't well—but I never would have thought he could commit murder.

Lots of people lose their jobs, experience loved ones becoming ill, go through seasonal ups and downs, or battle mental illness, yet they never cause harm. My father took care of Brian and me, cooking us odd-looking eggs for breakfast when my mom was in the hospital, and then, a month later, murdered a grandmother.

It is truly insane, then, what my father did—taking ten lives over seventeen years and then living the next fourteen as if he hadn't.

CHAPTER 6

Have Adventures,
Because Life Is Fragile

AUGUST 1991
COLORADO

Grandpa Bill and Grandma Dorothea took Brian, Lacey, Sarah, and me to Woodland Park, northwest of Colorado Springs, in August 1991. We towed a long brown-and-white trailer behind the Suburban. My grandma gave us strict orders that all our clothes for the week needed to fit in one sturdy tomato box per grandchild, and we could do laundry at the KOA.

In Colorado we went trout fishing in a bright-blue lake set high in the Rockies. I was always thrilled and tickled that my grandma fished and drank beer out of a can. While riding horses through the red rocks of the Garden of the Gods, Grandma uttered she was getting too old for this sort of thing while Grandpa chuckled and sang, "Whoopie ti-yi-yo, git along, little dogies."

My parents drove out the next weekend and picked us kids up while my grandparents stayed on for weeks more, likely glad to have peace and quiet restored.

Three years later, Grandpa Bill fell ill in Colorado Springs with leukemia. Dad and Uncle Bill drove to the mountains to be with my grandparents and tow the trailer back.

After that, it became routine to visit Grandpa in St. Francis's cancer wing. At first, I was nervous about visiting the hospital, but Grandpa took it all in stride, and his calm acceptance helped the rest of us cope. On our way to the hospital, we'd offer to bring him something decent from a favorite place like Long John Silver's or Braum's, but he'd usually decline. Mom would fetch him Ensure shakes and crushed ice and sit by his bedside while Dad and I took Grandma to dinner.

Grandpa always had a couple of paperbacks stacked on his hospital tray, often from Michener or L'Amour, and we would talk books: Grandpa, Dad, and me. Sometimes Dad would stay the night, but he always made sure to walk us girls to our cars before returning to Grandpa.

MARCH 1995
TEXAS

In March 1995, Dad and I set out on a late Friday afternoon with Brian and my cousin A. D., who was two years younger than me, for a weeklong camping trip on the South Rim of the Grand Canyon. During the drive, the boys conked out in the dark-brown Suburban we had borrowed from Grandpa Bill, but I'd stayed awake to keep my dad company as we headed to Dalhart, Texas, for the night. We drove through the Panhandle, eating Cheez-Its and marveling at the blinking irrigation lights out in the fields; they looked otherworldly.

The next day, Dad and I talked for hours while driving across New Mexico, taking in the stark red-orange mesas that rose on the edge of the rolling yellows and greens of the plains.

I was sixteen years old, a junior at Wichita Heights High School, where I switched between honors classes every fifty minutes. After school, I played golf in the fall and ran track in the spring. Some Saturdays, I would compete with my scholar's bowl team, and on Sundays, I worked an afternoon shift, often by myself, at Snacks.

Heading along I-40 that afternoon, the four of us listened to the trucker line over Grandpa's CB radio and created our own handles as we said things like, "Breaker, breaker." The highway ran parallel in places to old Route 66, and Dad regaled us with tales of the trip he'd taken to California in the mid-1950s with his folks and brothers.

After a long day of driving, we arrived the second night at a roadside motel in Flagstaff that was set alongside railroad tracks. Not long after we'd all fallen asleep, a train went barreling by. I sat straight up in bed and screamed, waking up the boys, who were in sleeping bags on the floor. I looked over and saw my dad's maps and a current *National Geographic* magazine laid out on a small table near the window, illuminated by a hazy yellow streetlight.

Though my mom was the one who usually calmed me down at night, Dad was able to put me at ease, saying, "Kerri, it's okay—just a train, nothing to be scared of. They are going to be running all night—hear the rattles and rumbles on the tracks? It's a good sound to sleep by."

The next morning, we drove to the canyon and set up our tents in a campground surrounded by towering pines near the South Rim. The boys and I tossed a football under the aromatic trees, needles crunching as I hurried to catch their throws. A good climbing tree was in our camp, and each of us kids tried it during the week.

We spent the next four days exploring, covering a good expanse of the rim trail and hiking down the Bright Angel and Kaibab trails. The canyon was a daytime oasis of warmth and color, showing signs of the coming summer. The rim was awash in early spring coolness, still hanging on to winter. At night, I tucked myself into my sleeping bag and rolled up against my dad, trying to stay warm in our forest-green, two-man tent. Our breath froze overnight, crystallizing on the blankets we'd thrown over ourselves.

Ice pelleted our ponchos one evening as Dad and I walked down to the pay phone to call and check in with Mom. We'd been quite cold, freezing in the desert, but even with the rougher conditions for camping, we'd caught the hiking bug. The last trail we went down was Hermit. While eating lunch in Waldron Basin, a mile and a half below the rim, the vastness of the canyon called to us. Majestic expanses, rising high, were just out of our reach for a day trip. We vowed to each other then: we would return.

When I got back home, I quit track. I was suffering from shin splints, and the steep trails in the canyon had aggravated them. Leaving track meant I could go straight home from school and crash on the couch before tackling homework. I expected a lecture for quitting, worried Dad would be disappointed in me, but he just shrugged and said, "That's all right, kiddo. Your studies are more important."

Not long after we got back, Dad started planning our next trip, researching camping overnight below the rim. And then a whole heck of a lot of life—the hard, unexpected kind—happened. Back then, I figured, I was going through the worst days I would ever see.

CHAPTER 7

Allow Yourself to Grieve

On a Wednesday afternoon in August 1996, I was working one of my last days at Snacks when I felt a sudden, sharp stab in my chest. Pressing down on the pain with my hand, I turned toward my mom, who was sitting feet away in her tiny office, and said, "Mama, my heart hurts—something's wrong."

Grandma Eileen's heart had taken on a similar ailing, and late that evening she called to tell us Aunt Sharon's family had been in an accident out in Colorado, where they were vacationing. Mom and I, concerned, hurried down the street to her parents' house where we found Grandma Eileen and Granddad Palmer in the dining room, waiting for a phone call.

Grandma sat with her fingers interlaced around a cup of coffee. Her cloudy blue eyes, tucked behind light-brown frames, searched into the space around us, landing on our worried faces.

Granddad, who still had a head full of hair I thought made him look boyish even though it was silver gray, was sitting ramrod straight in a sleeveless white undershirt. It was hard to see him quiet, pained; he often joshed around, full of life.

I curled up on the floor next to my mom and pressed my head into her side when the phone rang.

Mom answered, speaking to Andrea.

I caught it in Mom's voice, breaking, high: "What, honey?"

Michelle had died.

I crumbled over, screeching out in pain.

Andrea, age twenty-two, told us they were jeeping when a rain-soaked, narrow road gave way under their jeep, which rolled down into a deep ravine. Andrea, injured, climbed out and hiked for help along the road.

They were in such a remote location that it took hours for rescue crews to reach them. Uncle Bob, also injured, did what he could for twenty-year-old Michelle, whose injuries were fatal, and for Aunt Sharon, who'd been airlifted to a nearby hospital and was fighting for her life.

Grandma turned pale, her hands shaking as she grasped my mom's arm. Granddad hunched over, putting his hands on his knees, anguished by the loss of his granddaughter, fearful for the life of his daughter.

When Dad came through the front door, I got to my feet and rounded the hallway corner. Standing in my grandparents' living room, Dad's eyes shrouded in gray, his face darkened, and his countenance broke. I rushed into his arms, so grieved I could barely stand.

I'd never seen the men I loved ever look that way, and I didn't know what to do about it. My heart bottomed out.

The night we lost Michelle was one of the worst nights of my life. Michelle died in an accident, but after my father's arrest, after I learned about his murders, I grieved the sudden, irreplaceable losses that seven families had to go through because of my father.

That night, Dad had walked down to my grandparents'—right by Mrs. Hedge's old house. It's still not fully possible for me to reckon these two sides of the same man.

Back home, I found Michelle's high school senior photo from two years before. She was grinning, her bright blue eyes twinkling, her long, light-brown hair streaked with sun. An abundance of yellow poppies surrounded her under a piercing blue Kansas sky. I ran my thumb across the photo and placed it in a small light-blue frame, setting it on my desk.

I dug around in my desk drawer for a small inspirational book given to me at graduation. It had several Bible verses in it, and flipping through them offered the first small piece of solace. I set it next to Michelle's picture, along with a small wooden angel with twisted metal wings.

Mom came in and sat on the corner of my bed, gently brushing my hair away from my face. We talked softly late into the night, sharing stories about the girl we loved till I fell asleep.

The next morning, there were a few seconds when I didn't remember what had happened. Then the pain came rushing back to my chest, and I cried out.

Coming to my side, Mom stroked my hair again as the dark waves hit. She told me the doctors were able to save my aunt's badly fractured leg and foot in a complicated surgery, and she was now recovering in the ICU from several injuries. It would be some time before she was well enough to travel home to Wichita, so my grandparents were packing to drive out to Colorado to help.

Later that morning, I sat on the couch with my knees tucked under me while Pastor Sally, from our church, tried to offer comfort. I was wearing an old T-shirt and baggy pants I'd slept in and picking at a lemon poppy-seed muffin.

I felt my anger rising. I was having none of it. I didn't want platitudes. I didn't want to hear about God. Michelle was gone.

My faith began to wane in September 1992, a month into my freshman year, when two boys died after their pickup rolled a block from school. That fall, I sat down with Pastor Sally, whom I'd taken confirmation classes with. I told her I couldn't reconcile what happened down the street with God, who I wasn't even sure existed.

My heart was hardening but Mom ignored it, insisting I wear a white dress and take an oath of confirmation. In November 1992, I stood up in front of my family and congregation, appearing obedient, hiding a growing defiance in my soul. No one seemed fazed by my choice of scripture to read: "'Today, if you hear his voice, do not harden your hearts.'"[1]

Even conversations with my family about the Bible were frowned upon. One Sunday, while turning out of the church parking lot, I brought up the sermon, but straitlaced Dad quickly shut it down, declaring curtly, "We don't talk about religion, sex, or politics."

In April 1995 two men blew up the Alfred P. Murrah Federal Building in Oklahoma City, a few hours south of Wichita, killing 168 people, including 19 children. For the next several days, my family and I watched national news coverage of the recovery efforts. *Where was God then?*

Where is God now?

After the pastor left, the phone kept ringing. It echoed from the kitchen and my parents' bedroom, followed by Mom's voice catching.

I told her, "I've had enough," and headed to my best friend Rita's house. We had grown close over the past few years in high school, surviving advanced placement classes during the week and catching the latest blockbusters at the movie theater on the weekend. She greeted me at her door with a big hug, her normally bright blue eyes darkened with concern.

I hid out at her home the rest of the day, watching movies and talking about leaving for Kansas State University soon; we were going to be roommates. I was fighting to numb the sorrow that kept catching in my throat; I'd be able to go a stretch without crying—then the stinging pain would come back and I'd weep again. I was embarrassed by my swollen red eyes and face at dinner that night with her family, but thankful to be included. I didn't want to leave the warmth around their dining table and go back to my house tight with grief.

Four days after the accident, I unfolded our thick Sunday *Eagle* and saw an article about it on the front page. It was surreal to read about those I loved in peril in the mountains. Later I carefully folded the paper and tucked it away to keep.

I spent the next week packing for college in a blur, and on a Friday morning, after Dad and Brian stacked the back of my grandpa's Suburban full, my family set off on a two-hour drive to Manhattan, Kansas. We stood in line at the old Kansas State gymnasium to finish my registration, where my first student loan check was handed to me.

Rita and I were living in Boyd Hall, an all-girls residence beautifully crafted out of limestone in 1951. Our dorm room was in a sizable corner, with a lofted ceiling. It had a good view of Quinlan Natural Area, which sat across a circle drive.

On Sunday, standing in my doorway, my mom was in tears as she said goodbye. She and I'd been at odds that morning and now we were parting ways roughly. I was likely being difficult because it was easier to push her away than be sad over her leaving me. It didn't strike me till later how hard it must have been for her to let me go.

I was on the pre-vet track, hoping to make it into veterinary school in two years. Scrambling between the massive limestone buildings on campus, collecting a pile of syllabi, I began to wonder how I'd keep up with my sixteen-hour credit load. It had seemed like a reasonable number of courses when I enrolled a few months before, after sitting down with my adviser for a few minutes. She'd said, "You seem very capable," as she signed off on my slip, a long line of students waiting behind me.

The first week of college passed by quickly, as I spent time hanging out with old friends and making new ones. On Friday afternoon, I loaded up a basket of laundry, textbooks, black shoes, and dress clothes, and headed home for the long Labor Day weekend. We were having Michelle's memorial on Monday; I knew I needed to be there and wanted to be with my family, but I was dreading facing it too.

For dinner Friday evening, Mom made cheese manicotti, a favorite of our family, putting in a good deal of effort after working all day. I was glad to be home, but when the four of us sat down, tensions from the past weeks boiled over, landing us in an argument. Someone pounded on our old, rickety brown table, one of the metal legs popped out, and the table and all its dishes crashed down.

My dad, red-faced, wound tight, leaped up from his chair, full of rage. Standing in the middle of broken plates, tomato sauce, and noodles, he lunged at my brother. Facing him, putting his hands around his neck, Dad began to choke him.

Dad's eyes and face were blazing, close to manic. My brother, terrified, turned white. Yelling, Mom and I pushed at Dad and were able to break it up.

Dad stepped back and shook his head, and as his eyes began to clear, his shoulders slumped. With his head down, he said, "Ah heck, let's get this mess cleaned up."

With a flash of anger in her eyes and firmness in her voice, Mom said, "We'll handle it. You go outside."

While helping Mom pick up broken pieces of plates and glasses, I glanced at her with uncertainty, my face questioning what had just happened. As she cleaned the floor, she had tears in her eyes. With weariness in her voice, she said, "You haven't been here this past week. It's been a lot. You've been gone."

Dad's temper was unpredictable. He'd threatened us kids before but had never physically hurt us, let alone tried to strangle one of us.

All families get into arguments, but what my father did was inexcusable. Yet, at the time, we dismissed it. It'd been that way as long as I could recall: *Dad is under a lot of stress. He just lost control. He didn't mean it. He will apologize soon.*

On the exterior, our family looked like the American dream, and I'd grown up believing that very thing. I tucked away, deep within me, this outburst of my father's, telling no one till he was arrested. What would have happened if we had called the police that night? Would they have done anything? Would they have questioned him enough to find decades-long terror hiding behind his rage? These questions still haunt me.

CHAPTER 8

Attempt to Outrun What Haunts You

SEPTEMBER 1996

Three days later, my family dressed up and quietly drove to Michelle's memorial. It was held downtown at the Wichita Boathouse, where Michelle had taught kids to row that past summer along the banks of the Arkansas River.

My heart lifted when I saw my grandparents arrive in the family room before the service. I was glad to stand close to Grandma Dorothea, her warm brown eyes looking into mine with concern while holding my hands between hers. It was good to give Grandpa Bill, taller than any of us at six foot one, a big hug—to have his kind, reassuring presence there.

Grandpa's battle with leukemia had taken his hair, but not his inner fortitude. A man of steady faith, I'd never heard him complain once about what he was enduring. Just by being there, he was telling us we'd get through.

How could we have known my high school graduation party, three months ago, would be the last time we would all be together? We had a houseful gathered around folding tables set up in our living room, just as we always did. There was a heap of food, and dessert was Mom's chocolate sheet cake with homemade ice cream churned out on the patio by Dad.

We six cousins on Mom's side, including A. D.'s older brother, Jason, had our picture taken in my family's front yard that day. We were full of smiles, standing shoulder to shoulder in front of our tall pine tree and swaying pampas grass.

The memorial service was held in a large open room, packed with people who knew our family. Granddad Palmer kept patting us kids on the shoulders, and Grandma Eileen kept taking our hands. Both of their faces were shadowed with heartbreak.

As sunlight poured in from the tall windows that surrounded us, Michelle's testimony was shared. She was a Christian; she had accepted Jesus as her Savior in college the year before. Verses from John were read: "My Father's house has many rooms; if that were not so, would I have told you that I am going there to prepare a place for you? And if I go and prepare a place for you, I will come back and take you to be with me that you also may be where I am."[1]

I'd heard about God and Jesus for eighteen years at our church. But I didn't know them. Not the way Michelle did.

Three weeks before she passed away, I stayed a few days with her while her folks were away on a short trip. She slept upstairs and gave me her bedroom downstairs. Her Bible and other books on faith were stacked next to her bed, with prayer notes and bookmarks sticking out.

I didn't even know where my Bible was.

Late on a Sunday morning, I crawled out of bed and walked into her den. Michelle was sitting cross-legged on the floor in her pink PJs with a bowl of cereal, her hair up in a loose ponytail. The funny papers were spread out next to her, her two schnauzers were lying close by, and the Atlanta Olympics were on in the background. She looked right with the world, and I should have asked then about her stack of books and her Bible.

But I hadn't.

Instead I joined her with my own bowl of cereal, and we watched rowing, talking about what it might take to get to the 2000 Olympics.

That weekend was the last time I saw her.

If I'd only known, I would have stayed several more days and asked her about Jesus.

After the service, I hugged Andrea for a long time, her forest-green eyes full of heartache. The two of us looked hard into each other's faces—trying to reassure the other we were going to be okay.

Aunt Sharon, blonde and petite like Andrea, sat in a wheelchair holding a basket of flowers in her lap. Her face was weary, but her sea-green eyes were determined; she was going to get all of us through this. Uncle Bob, slim, near my height, with brown hair and blue eyes that matched Michelle's, was standing quietly behind the wheelchair, holding on to the handles. He'd steadily reply, "We're hanging in there, doing all right," as folks offered condolences and hugs, trying to reassure others they'd be all right too.

On that bright, last summer holiday, the five remaining cousins walked to a nearby bridge and tossed daisies into the river below. On a cool spring day the year before, I'd stood on a bridge a few miles north of there in Riverside, cheering for the girl who'd flown down the river with her college crew. Running across the bridge as they rowed under it, I was able to yell from both sides.

Now that girl was gone, and I watched white flowers float slowly south till I couldn't see them anymore.

That evening, Rita and I rode back to college with A. D. and Jason's mom, Aunt Donna. While heading north on Route 77, a two-lane highway that dips and rises above the western edges of the Flint Hills, I tried to catch a glimpse of the stars through my passenger window. George Strait was singing "Love Without End, Amen" through the tape deck as I placed my head against the cool pane of glass. *Would life ever hurt this much again?*

Back inside my dorm, I felt like I'd aged a decade over the past four days. I set my alarm, wondering whose bright idea it was to schedule a class at seven a.m. (or to sign up for it).

The next morning my alarm blared from the edge of my dresser. I sat up, turned in bed, and swatted at the big gray button on top.

I'll just hit the snooze once.

Eight minutes later, blurry-headed, I reset the alarm for a few hours later.

Forget it. I will skip, just this once.

Right now, you're making the choice to not get up. To screw up.

I was able to quiet the small, persistent voice by rolling over to face the wall, pulling my comforter up to my chin, and squeezing my eyes shut. Sleep alleviated all worry, all pain, all suffering—it wiped out everything.

Instead of beginning to deal with the gaping hole that'd been knocked into me, I threw myself into college life. Weekdays were busy with attending classes, having meals at the dining center with a growing group of friends, and attempting to study in the evenings. On home game Saturdays, I stood for hours with Rita in the student section clad in purple, cheering for our Wildcats. Sundays meant sleeping in, playing Frisbee golf, and eventually getting around to my textbooks.

In early fall, I went with a group of friends to the student union to watch *Phenomenon*, the last movie I'd seen with Michelle. I'd gone to a theater with my family on the Fourth of July and by some quirky chance ended up at the same show as Michelle and her parents. Afterward, our families visited together, standing outside on concrete that sparkled silver under a glowing pink-and-green neon marquee.

A few weeks later I was with Michelle on our long weekend, and she bought the soundtrack to the movie, which led with Eric Clapton's "Change the World." On that shopping trip, we talked about the main character, a brilliant man who leaves a legacy of love before dying way too young.

I cried during the movie in July, and now sitting in the student union, I could barely contain my sorrow. Sobbing, wiping my nose and face on my sleeve, I couldn't understand what was wrong. I felt like the walls of the auditorium were closing in as I tried to tuck up my uncooperative body as small as I could, hoping no one would notice me.

After the show was over, we began walking back to our dorms, but I couldn't stop my tears or the seizing in my chest. Not explaining myself, I took off, leaving the group, trying to flee the sharp, black pain searing my heart. *Why doesn't anyone understand how much this hurts?*

Over the previous weeks while walking on campus, I would find something familiar in a walk, a ponytail of light-brown hair, or a laugh, and my heart would lift. *There's Michelle! She's right here!*

Then—*Oh, that can't be her. She's gone.*

I kept running the day we lost Michelle through my head, picturing jeeps rolling down the sides of mountains, picturing the details of the crash and the terrible hours afterward. I could see it, even though I hadn't been there. It was stuck, replaying over and over. How could I tell anyone? They would think I was going crazy.

After I got back to my room, Rita sat up with me till late, listening and offering her calm presence. She told me she'd been praying for me. As I crawled into bed, my face red and tearstained, I thought more about praying. It sounded comforting, but I was too angry with God. *Where was he that afternoon? Why didn't he save her?*

Michelle believed in him. If anyone were in heaven, she would be. She had to be. I couldn't face it at all if she wasn't somewhere. If she was in heaven, then there had to be a heaven. If there was a heaven—then there had to be a God. But I didn't believe God existed anymore. But Michelle . . .

Around and around, the wrestling in me circled till I drifted off to sleep.

CHAPTER 9

. . . *Makes You Stronger*

NOVEMBER 1996
MANHATTAN, KANSAS

I was fighting off homesickness by Thanksgiving and was glad to see my dad, who'd driven up to take me home for break. He would make the four-hour round-trip again in five days. This became a ritual of ours, going back and forth on Route 77, picking up fresh popcorn at a corner gas station along the way.

As we passed through the changing colors of the fields and prairies, we'd spot deer, wild turkeys, and red-tailed hawks. Dad would point out silos and barns and made retirement plans; he wanted to buy an old homestead tucked near the Cottonwood River. I reminded him he'd be alone because Mom wasn't going to be having any of that.

Dad often showed Mom and me an old barn near Florence. We had a running joke, calling it "Dad's retirement home." Dad knew Mom wouldn't ever live in a run-down place out in the boonies, and Mom believed he was kidding around.

Except, after he was arrested, Dad shared extensively about nefarious plans involving barns and silos, this one in particular. So Dad had more than one joke running all the times we passed it. Now he's spending his retirement in a maximum-security prison—he's still out in the country, though.

———

Over the fall, Grandpa Bill and Grandma Dorothea rode up one Saturday with my parents to visit the campus and have lunch at the downtown Applebee's. Grandpa was continuing to wear down but was in good spirits that day.

When they were preparing to leave, Grandpa hugged me tight and stepped back, putting his hands on my shoulders and looking into my eyes, making sure I was paying attention to what he wanted to say: "I'm proud of you, kid."

In November, Grandpa was well enough to escape the cancer wing. Frail and thin, he still greeted all of us on Thanksgiving Day with a smile, leaning on the black cast-iron railing on his porch. Grandma insisted on hosting dinner for a crowd and we cousins piled our plates high. We followed dinner with a game of Wahoo, yelling loudly, "Come on, sixes!"

We took the last pictures we would ever have with Grandpa that day, standing in front of his and Grandma's white-manteled fireplace. My grandparents sat in front of us, Grandma's hands clasped around Grandpa's. He'd been too weak to come downstairs to join us in Wahoo that day; I should have realized then how short our time with him would be.

Four weeks later, "Silent Night" was the last song we sang on Christmas Eve by candlelight in a darkened sanctuary, a sacred tradition in our old wooden church. Dad was an usher, wearing a gray suit and red tie, and he walked up the aisle, lighting the first person's candle in each wooden pew. That person turned to the next person, who then tilted their candle to the flame—one flame leading to a hundred as the sanctuary warmed with dancing light.

Standing between Grandma Eileen and Mom, sharing a green hymnal between us, I blended my voice with theirs, as I'd done for years. The light from the candles flickered off the stained-glass windows; my stomach was in knots from trying to hold back my sorrow, and my voice quavered as I sang. *Sleep in heavenly peace.*

I took a big gulp of air and gave myself over to the tears. At the end of the song, we blew on our lights to extinguish them, and the church sat in dark stillness.

As the lights came back on, a burned, acrid smell hung in the air. I nudged my grandma for some tissues, wiping hastily at my face. Mom and Grandma were dabbing at their eyes too. Folks were passing by us in the aisle, wishing us merry Christmas with looks of uncertain solemnity. Our congregation knew we had lost Michelle four months ago and were facing losing Grandpa soon.

This was the first year Grandpa Bill and Grandma Dorothea had not sat with us during the Christmas Eve service and the first year we would not be heading to their house afterward. On this night their home sat in darkness, while Grandma sat next to Grandpa in the ICU as he was succumbing to his battle, a *Do Not Resuscitate* bracelet looped on his arm.

Grandpa had been in and out of consciousness over the past week, trying to fight off an infection that was defeating his body.

The doctors had told us, "Days left, at best."

While standing in the emptying sanctuary I hugged Grandma Eileen and Granddad Palmer tight. They told me they would see me tomorrow for Christmas. Granddad, trying to get me to smile, joked, "You better get to bed early so Santa can come."

Out in the fellowship hall, I followed my mom as she visited with folks, some of whom asked me about college. Although I skipped some classes over the fall and hadn't studied as hard as I could have, I finished the semester with a solid 3.33. By most standards, I'd done well, but my GPA wasn't high enough to stay in the honors program. The Cs I received in two prerequisites for vet school didn't bode well either. Every time I thought about my grades, my guts twisted. *I could have tried harder—I'd made the choice not to do my best.*

Two days after Christmas, Mom and Dad thought it was best for Brian and me to stay home while they went to sit with Grandma next to Grandpa. His heart was still in the fight, but his body was giving up; he wasn't expected to make it through the day.

Sitting next to our Christmas tree, I spent the afternoon with the sniffles, curled up in our recliner, under our brown-and-white blanket Grandma Dorothea had crocheted. When the phone rang, I knew the news before I picked it up. Mom's voice broke as she said, "Grandpa has gone on home now."

Mom found comfort in the chime that went off in the hospital right after Grandpa died. It meant a baby had been born at almost the exact moment my grandpa passed.

Mom told me later that Dad had wept over his father's body. Wrecked with grief, he had walked hunched over down the hospital hallway. She said, "I don't think your dad had ever sat beside someone who died before."

When I heard these words, I was filled with sorrow, picturing Dad next to Grandpa's frail body. Dad was grieved over the loss of his father—he had loved him, very much. It's impossible for me to reckon that with Dad taking the lives of ten innocent people.

———

Our family gathered together a few days later at the cemetery. Huddling under umbrellas, we buried Grandpa, age seventy-four, on a rainy, wintry day.

Sitting around Grandma Dorothea's house that afternoon, I cheered up as stories filled the living room. Grandpa's three younger brothers spun tale after tale, much to the delight of the rest of us.

JANUARY 1997
MANHATTAN, KANSAS

I returned to college mid-January—the campus locked into frigid temperatures, the trees bare, the grass lying brown and dormant. I loathed winter, but I was relieved to be back in Manhattan because it was not Wichita, where we had to keep having funerals for people I loved.

It'd been gut wrenching to watch my grandpa waste away over the past two years; I knew he was at peace now, but I couldn't understand why he had to suffer. *Why didn't God help him?*

I was hurting, lashing out at God, then feeling guilty for my anger. God was holy, and I was supposed to be penitent.

But I wasn't feeling remorseful for my anger. I was peeved.

I'd been trying to walk away from God and I thought I'd done it, but now he kept wrestling with me.

Grandpa believed in him.

If anyone was in heaven, Grandpa would be—right there with Michelle.

Around and around, losing Grandpa on top of Michelle was compounding my grief.

I figured being back with my friends and having new classes would pull me out of the gray bleakness continuing to overtake me. But a shift began in my friendships and small rifts began to form. On top of everything, I had the lousy idea to take on an unforgiving, self-induced eighteen-hour course load with three weekly science labs.

What I didn't realize at the time was that I was going through my first bout of depression, and its sometimes companion, anxiety, was following right along, ganging up like a couple of mismatched brutes. It would be another ten years before I heard someone say the words "You have anxiety and depression" in regard to myself.

By the end of February, alternating between turning inward on myself, wanting to be alone, and lashing outward for feeling left out of our larger group of changing friends, I pushed Rita away. Deciding it was best to tiptoe around me, she would get ready in the early morning, gather her books and backpack, and quietly slip out the door. She wouldn't return till late at night, taking off her shoes before walking on our tile, afraid she would wake me up—trying to find peace for both of us.

I'd been a good student in high school, excelling even in the hardest classes offered. Now, midsemester, I floundered. I skipped classes, slept in till noon, crammed late into the night before tests, and frantically printed off term papers minutes before they were due.

I was killing my GPA—ruining my shot at veterinary school. I was even likely going to lose my scholarship that covered the cost of books and supplies each semester.

I was disappointed in myself but didn't know how to get out of the vicious cycle.

The smiling college students who'd visited our senior class the year before with brightly colored brochures neglected to mention losing your mind as an elective course curriculum.

This wasn't what college was supposed to be like. It wasn't what life was supposed to be like either. Days ended in tears, tossing and turning in my bed, silently screaming, raging inside at myself, at the ceiling, at a God who surely didn't exist.

One March evening, while standing in the middle of my dorm room, I reached an empty, gray nothing within myself.

Maybe I could end it. I could jump.

Walking with my shoulders hunched over, I reached my fourth-floor window in a few steps. I pressed my head against the cool glass pane fastened firmly in place.

I wasn't high enough. I'd likely just break my leg or somehow land in the nearby pine tree. I turned away from the window and walked slowly over to my hard desk chair, sadness descending throughout my body as I sat down, lowering my head.

I was in trouble.

I reached out to a long-distance friend whom I'd been emailing back and forth with since January. Although I didn't tell him I'd thought about jumping, he knew I was struggling and suggested I visit the mental health center on campus.

Me? See a shrink? I'm not in that bad a shape.

I hated the thought of having to tell a stranger I was hurting, that I couldn't handle things on my own. Raders dealt with their own crud in Kansas countryside tradition: head down, dug in, doing whatever life called for next. Dealing with it in your own way and time, you'd eventually get over it.

Or you wouldn't, but other folks wouldn't know you hadn't.

But I wasn't getting over it.

Resigned, I mustered enough courage to walk across campus to ask for help.

While sitting in the waiting room holding a clipboard, I hesitated before marking the little box next to "thoughts of suicide." My rear end landed on a couch in a little room, where I threw soggy, falling-apart tissues by the handful into my therapist's trash can over several weekly sessions.

The therapist had me recall the day of Michelle's death in detail, desensitizing myself to it. My therapist said replaying an accident was a common reaction to trauma. It was also common to think you're seeing your lost loved ones among the living.

Eight months after Michelle's funeral, I was finally beginning to face the loss. The therapist had me look at the hole I'd dug for myself, the one I wanted to crawl into and die—to honestly admit I was hurting. She didn't flinch when I told her I was angry with God.

There was no shame in the little room with the warm listener and helper.

In therapy, we worked on strategies to get through the remaining weeks of school and talked about what I was looking forward to—my upcoming Grand Canyon hiking trip.

PART II

Make Your Way Through the Wilderness

See, I am doing a new thing! Now it springs up;
do you not perceive it? I am making a way in
the wilderness and streams in the wasteland.

—Isaiah 43:19

CHAPTER 10

Know and Respect Your Limitations . . . Yeah, Right

Dad thought this hiking trip was "going to be great" and his daughter was doing "great!"

He didn't know his girl had splintered inside over the past months and was still fighting at times to hold herself together. Tucked behind a tough facade, flippantly trying to look and act as expected, I felt like I'd miserably failed everyone around me instead. *Failed myself.*

I'd scraped by with a bunch of Cs my second semester, dodging questions about my classes on our drive over Memorial Day weekend to the Grand Canyon, my face flaming red. I was relieved school was out—glad to be free for three months, glad to be back with my family, and glad to be back at this magnificent park.

Standing on the South Rim of the Grand Canyon was breathing life back into me. The canyon dazzled with color, setting the world ablaze in flaming reds, burnt oranges, and rusty browns. It mesmerized with sweeping vistas, towering buttes, narrow gorges, and sheer cliff faces. I loved it here, even if I questioned our sanity in backpacking below the rim.

"Are we really headed down there?" I said as I elbowed my

cousin A. D. "Whose idea was this again?" At five feet nine, I was usually one of the taller ones in a group, but the guys all had at least a few inches on me.

A. D. grinned. "It's his idea," he said, pointing to my dad, whose dark hair, cut military short, was beginning to salt and pepper. So was his mustache.

We were there "to have an experience," as Dad put it. I knew behind his dark lenses Dad's eyes were shining today; he was full of excitement that we had made it back here.

"It's going to be an adventure of a lifetime, guys," Dad said, spreading his arms wide over the view in front of us. "See that thin, brown line—way down below? That's Tonto Trail. We will be coming across it, around Battleship, and up Bright Angel a week from now." Dad pointed to a massive red-and-orange rock formation rising high from the plateau below.

"Not *we*. You and the kids." My mom stood next to Aunt Donna. "We're going to spend the week hiking in air-conditioned malls and sleeping in beds, not on rocks." Donna glanced between my parents and laughed.

"The girls," as my dad called them, were spending the afternoon sightseeing with us before heading to Phoenix to visit family. Reasonable sorts, they definitely didn't consider anything about what we had planned as vacation. But I was glad Dad had never considered me *a girl*. I much preferred going along with the guys instead of spending a week in malls, even though going along with Dad meant sleeping on rocks.

I felt bad for my brother who, on our drive in, threw up on the side of the road. Pale and nauseous, Brian was now sitting with his head down, facing away from the view. We grabbed a Sprite for my brother and sandwiches for us, and ate lunch overlooking the rim.

Day-trippers were walking up the popular, well-maintained Bright Angel Trail. Based on the flip-flops, I surmised they'd only gone down a short way. A few heavily laden backcountry hikers came up the trail, too, looking worn and unkempt, covered in red dirt.

I wondered if watching Grandpa decline over the past two years had driven my dad to embrace his long-held dream of hiking the canyon before he wasn't able to anymore. Dad let age dog him often—wound on an internal clock ticking down that the rest of us couldn't see. He'd joke that when it was his time to go, we should "just take him out to pasture."

I didn't get it—he still seemed capable of whatever he set out to do. I sometimes had a hard time keeping up with him; he could be so full of energy and excitement.

Dad had thrown himself into planning this trip, researching guides, shopping for the right supplies. Without fail, he followed the Boy Scout code: be prepared. I felt ready, with solid gear, decent know-how, and my dad along. I would follow him anywhere he wanted to go. He said we could handle a hike of this magnitude and I believed him. I trusted him with my life.

That afternoon, Dad gazed out over the canyon and Mom leaned in close to him, resting her chin against his back. She looked happy, content to be right where she was, but I knew she was going to miss us. I could tell she also was worried about what Dad had decided to undertake, especially with us kids along.

Aunt Donna took pictures of us standing on the ledge that day, a bunch of naive, grinning folks and one green-faced one, with no idea of what was waiting down the way for us. If anyone should have known, it would have been Dad. But that's impossible to say—then or now.

DAY ONE
SOUTH RIM

Our plan was to get up at the crack of dawn, as Dad said the night before, but none of us slept well in our small motel room near the rim. For me, it wasn't so much due to sleeping on the floor in a sleeping bag as it was my brother stepping over me to puke in the toilet. My cousin joined in the stepping over me and puking at least once too—in the toilet, not on me. My stomach wasn't feeling so great either, and I seriously contemplated it too—the puking, not the stepping over anyone.

We checked out of our room and ate breakfast in a cafeteria, mulling over what to do about my brother, who was in no shape to hike with us after throwing up for twenty-four hours.

He sat quietly next to us while I picked at my food, scooting watery eggs around on my plate. I wasn't sure if my stomach was off because breakfast was lousy, if I had the same bug my brother had, or because I was suffering from a growing case of nerves.

We didn't want Brian to miss out on the trip, but we didn't want to miss out either. Our backcountry permit was for specific nights and campsites—use it or lose it. Dad filed for those permits a year ago. It would be a long time, if ever, before we got back out here. I'm sure my brother was feeling bad about holding us up, but it wasn't his fault he was sick.

We settled on finding another room in the park for my brother; he would stay there till he was fit enough to join us. Dad outlined a plan so Brian could hike down and meet us later in the week; he showed Brian the route and checked to make sure my brother had enough gear and food. Dad told him to take a bus to the trailhead and join us at Granite Rapids on day two or three, or Monument Creek on day four. Dad emphasized he would need to reach us in one day, hiking up to ten miles, because we would be carrying the only water filter. Drinking unfiltered water can lead to a double-whammy-out-both-ends kind of sickness.

Dad was getting more uptight as the clock kept ticking, but it took time to find a room and get my brother moved. It was also an unexpected expense. Money could stress out my dad, but my folks carried an emergency credit card for these reasons.

I tried to keep Dad on an even keel, because without Mom

along, that job fell all on me. I was also the one who had to assure my brother he was going to be okay. I was on edge myself, trying to help my brother, managing my dad, and knowing we needed to get hiking.

Looking back, I'm not sure why we didn't call Mom and Aunt Donna and ask them to come back from Phoenix to pick up Brian. We should have never told him to come down on his own. I can blame my dad here, but he isn't solely at fault. My brother, an adult—albeit a young one—made decisions too. I was culpable also because I hadn't fought against my dad's ideas.

10:30 A.M.
HERMIT TRAILHEAD

My stomach continued to roll as we drove west, a straightforward seven-mile drive to the trailhead, away from the more populated part of the park. Coming back east, we would be meandering for thirty miles over the next six days: down Hermit, across Tonto, up Bright Angel.

I was feeling intimidated by the daunting task I was facing as I stared out our van window, catching glimpses of the canyon below. Fear—uncertainty—was continually trying to creep in. I wanted this "experience," but now I was questioning it.

Can we really do this? Is this insanity?

At the trailhead, I stepped out of the van onto chalky gravel and crouched down, tightening my hiking boots. I tugged on my army-green laces, looping them around their top metal fasteners, securing them with a double knot. Tucked inside my boots were two layers of socks: a thin liner and a thick summer-weight blend.

I was wearing cotton shorts and a cream-colored short-sleeved T-shirt. My hair was pulled back in a scrunchie and tucked under a cheap white ball cap. I pushed my sunglasses back up on my nose and secured my multicolored Croakies strap around the back of my neck. Dad handed me my fanny pack with my water bottle.

I turned to get my pack Dad had propped up against the van, heaving it on my back with a loud *oomph*. I teetered, about to fall backward from its weight.

"Whoa there," Dad said, as he reached out to steady me. Helping to hold up my pack, he asked, "Too heavy?"

"Nah, I've got it." I stood up straight. "Okay, you can let go."

The padded shoulder straps sat down fully on my shoulders. I anchored thin black straps across my chest and thick ones around my waist with firm, resounding clicks. Shifting my weight forward, I tightened the straps and attempted to recenter myself to offset the mass on my back. The weight of what was on me and what was awaiting me down the trail settled into my bones.

It was nearing eleven o'clock, a rather late start for an eight-mile hike. Dad kept checking his watch, and his mouth was set tight downward. I could tell he was anxious to get going. I was concerned, too, but I simply shrugged and uttered, *"Hrmph,"* as we passed by a large sign at the top of the trail, paraphrased as follows:

Warning—Heat Kills!

Don't hike midday in the heat; the Colorado River at the bottom of the canyon is the only reliable water source. This is a remote, unmaintained trail. Know and respect your limitations. Rescue requests by ill and injured people are frequent. Deaths have occurred. Hike at your own risk. The park seeks your voluntary compliance. However, individuals creating a hazardous condition for themselves or others through unsafe hiking practices are subject to citation and/or arrest.[1]

The first mile and a half of the Hermit Trail was familiar; we'd hiked this section two years ago. We headed down steep switchbacks that cut through creamy pink sandstone and passed by fossils and animal tracks left in ancient mud. Near the top of the trail, worn, paved cobblestones remained. In the early 1900s, the stones were laid down to promote tourism via burros.[2] Nowadays the burros stuck to Bright Angel and so did most of the tourists. Only the adventurous, capable, or possibly foolhardy were still willing to traverse Hermit's remote reaches into the canyon.

A. D. took the lead and behind him was Dad, whose hat for the canyon was a lightweight khaki boonie with a chin cord. It would keep the sun off his face and his growing bald spot. Dad's large navy-blue backpack, weighed down with about anything we possibly could need and likely things we didn't, was causing his broad shoulders to stoop over.

Dad held a metal walking stick in his right hand with a black loop that went around his wrist. Next to each set of footprints Dad was leaving in the dust was an animal paw print made from the rubber foot of his stick.

Small, colorful lizards darted across the trail with amazing speed right in front of my boots. Occasionally, one would stop in the middle of the path, attempting to stand its ground. Only a few inches long, it would puff its body out, bob its head up and down, laying claim to its tiny corner of desert. Another step by a boot would send it scurrying under rocks or cacti and bring forth a chuckle from one of us.

I'd never hiked with a pack this heavy, and the extra weight dug down into my boots—into my toes. I could feel my toenails press into the end of my toe box on the descents, even though I trimmed them back the night before. By my best guess, my pack weighed around forty pounds. I was feeling every bit of that weight on my 120-pound frame.

I was already analyzing the contents of my pack. I should have done another shakedown, a smart one—a really smart one, not the half-baked job I'd done. Now it was either carry all this crap on my back or chuck it.

NOON
HERMIT TRAIL

I was trying to find a balance between watching my foot placement on the narrow, rocky trail and remembering to look out at the overwhelmingly stunning, stark surroundings.

Looking down over the drop-offs made my stomach queasy; glancing up, to where we'd come from, was easier. I tried to settle my stomach, to ground myself back on the trail in front of me. I was trying to get my mind off the weight on my back, the sun bearing down, and the fruit punch Gatorade sloshing around in my stomach.

I called up ahead to Dad and A. D., "Hey, guys, I've got to stop for a few. I'm not feeling so well."

"It's too early to stop. We've only come a short way," Dad said as he pointed down the trail with his walking stick. "Let's keep going. We can stop in another mile, down in the basin where we can find shade to have lunch."

I unfastened my pack and dropped it on the trail, plopping down on the rocks next to it. "No, I need to eat something now. Stomach is empty." Digging around in the top of my pack, looking for food, I didn't care I was sitting under the blazing sun in stifling thick heat with no breeze.

"All right, we'll stop for a bit." Dad and A. D. set their packs down and joined me for an impromptu meal in the middle of a switchback. They seemed just as glad as I to have a break.

I laid out my gallon-size Ziploc bags full of portable lunches and snacks, settling on a package of warm tuna and bland wheat crackers that I washed down with more Gatorade.

I didn't want to eat much. I had no idea how much food I would need over the next several days, and my stomach wasn't cooperating anyhow. I wadded up my wrappers and tucked them in another gallon bag. *Whatever you carry in, you carry out.*

We ate quickly and helped each other get our packs back on.

Why the heck were we carrying so much dang crap?

I was afraid to look at my watch to calculate our rate of speed and the distance we still needed to cover. We made it down another switchback—then my lunch decided to make a return trip up. Things were not starting well.

CHAPTER 11

Miscalculations of the Ego Can Be Deadly

1:00 P.M.

WALDRON BASIN

I felt better after emptying my stomach's contents onto the trail. I swigged some water, sloshed it around in my mouth, and spat it out, saying, "Okay, let's go."

I got a raised eyebrow from my cousin and a look of concern from my dad.

"I'm fine, really, just nerves. I don't think it's what Brian has. Come on, this heat is something else—let's find some shade."

We kept hiking lower, passing by a century plant with a green stalk towering ten feet over us. It would soon bloom, erupting with white flowers all along its stalk.[1] They are known to flower once, sitting dormant as a small green plant for a decade or two before dazzling with their height and color.

We came upon the basin where we had eaten lunch two years ago; it was a rare shady spot, with rough scrub. Dad and A. D. stopped at an overlook to take pictures, but I found a gnarled pine to hide under. I sat squarely down, pack and all. It was a total pain to take the pack off and put it back on, and I was beginning to wear down. This was not going as planned.

"Come on, kid, we need to keep moving." Dad was coming down the trail toward me, motioning. He stopped and unfolded a topographical map. "Not far around that bend is Santa Maria Spring, where we can top off our bottles."

I took a deep breath, resigning myself with a sigh. "All right, let's keep going." I was trying to talk myself into it.

It would get better down the trail. It had just been a rough beginning. A bad morning.

As I began to get up from the rocks I was sitting on, my stomach took to sloshing around again. Closing my eyes for a second, I was able to settle my guts back down.

Steady. Steady now.

A. D. reached out to help pull me up, and Dad said with a small grin, "That's my girl."

I resettled my pack on my back and cinched the straps tighter.

"Okay, let's go." The words coming from my mouth sounded more confident than I felt.

3:00 P.M.
SANTA MARIA SPRING

It was the middle of the afternoon, and I'd about had it.

I'd never seen the canyon like this. I wasn't just looking down from the top or from the upper reaches of well-managed trails. I was smack-dab in it—on a remote, unmaintained, rockslide-prone, deserted, hairy-as-crud trail.

We hadn't seen anyone else in the last few hours, not since we'd passed through the basin where most day hikers turn around. I expected to see more people and found it eerie being by ourselves.

We kept passing by cairns—piles of stacked rocks that marked the way. I found growing comfort in them: we would question the path, it would fade into its surroundings, and then we would spot a deliberate pile of rocks. *Here's a cairn—here's the trail!*

We'd stopped at a natural spring a while ago, where the water came up through rock and out a pipe into a trough with brownish-green algae growing in it. We siphoned the water through our small hand pump with a microfilter and into our bottles. We were glad to have the water and the shade provided by the small stone hut next to the spring.

This wasn't like the hiking trip from two years ago; the warm daytime temperatures in the canyon had been welcoming compared to the cold on the rim. But now, two months later in the season, it felt like I'd stepped into a burning oven. The afternoon sun was unrelenting, continuing to bear down on top of us.

My gear in my pack was drenched from my own sweat, barely stopped by a bandana I'd twisted around my neck. My hair kept falling out of the scrunchie and I'd given up on my ball cap, which was making things worse, hotter. I'd risk the sunburn. At least my shades were keeping my eyes cool.

My T-shirt was soaked through—I wondered if anyone could see the sports bra underneath it. That was soaked, too, and so was my underwear underneath my shorts. My feet were drowning in their two sets of socks; I was sure my toes were on fire. My bare legs were covered in red dust, kicked up from my boots hitting the trail. The dust covered up long, thin red scratches where cacti had been catching my calves.

What had I got myself into? Why be sane and hike and camp on the maintained trails, with gobs of people, park rangers, bathrooms, and water flowing out of taps?

Against sanity—that could sometimes be Dad, and now it appeared I'd joined him. Doing things the stubborn, thick-headed way and taking my cousin right along with us.

In Dad's defense, the campsites for the sane trails were full by the time he filed for backcountry permits to stay overnight below the rim. He did try to request the more popular routes down to the river, the ones we hiked two years ago. Hermit was choice three, and choice three is what we were given.

We had found the top section of Hermit reasonable a few years ago, so we didn't have any reason to think it wouldn't continue to be that way. Dad had read up on these trails—I would have thought he knew what we were getting into.

The previous night, when we'd checked in at a ranger's station to let the park service know where we were headed, the ranger had gone over the roughness of this trail after the basin, the importance of hiking early and carrying plenty of water.

We seriously underestimated what we had been told and the warning sign we'd passed at the top hours ago. We'd only made it four miles, but I couldn't fathom turning back around and hiking up in defeat—the only direction I was willing to head was down.

5:OO P.M.
PIMA POINT

We were cutting back and forth, down sharp, short descents and taking long traverses that hugged massive orange-and-red walls rising high over steep drop-offs below. The path under our feet was rough, rocky in places, and narrow; it was only wide enough for one person at a time, and we proceeded cautiously, single file. Dad had me take the lead, letting the slowest one set the pace for the group.

Cairns littered the trail here and there, but they could have been marking an altogether different trail for all the good they were doing.

My guts were still rolling—my nerves now in full-on intimidation mode.

I've never been afraid of heights, yet I couldn't shake the fear of falling. I've never been claustrophobic, yet I felt as if I was becoming unhinged, seized by panic. Of course, I'd never been pressed up against a sheer cliffside thousands of feet below and above solid ground before either.

I was continually having to give myself a pep talk.

Don't look down. Don't look down.

Watch your feet. One boot at a time. One rock at a time.

Eyes in front of you, steady now.

You have this.

I reached out for the red wall I was up against. Heat radiated from it. My head was beginning to spin. Up was becoming down; down was becoming up.

I was staring into an abyss. A black hole. I wanted to quit. Give up. I wanted it over. All of it.

If I were to step a few feet more away from the wall and lean over the precarious drop-off, shifting the extra weight teetering upon my slight frame, I could go over. Landing a thousand feet below on jagged rocks.

I closed my eyes. I could feel my body beginning to lean . . . then warmth surrounded me. A strong presence pressed up against me, right alongside the edge. It was comforting. *Peaceful.* Felt like something I knew. Familiar. The same presence was in front of me too. It was only there for a moment, but it was enough.

Deep inside me, something I knew before but had forgotten shook awake. I uttered a prayer in my head. *Help me. I don't want to die.*

I snapped out of it, shifting my weight back to my center, planting my feet firmly. I took a deep breath, shaking my head, trying to clear it.

I looked down at the rocks below, where my broken body could be lying. I squeezed my eyes shut.

I shook my head again. *No. I wouldn't.*

"Whoa, careful now, kid. Why don't ya get closer to the wall as we keep going here," came Dad's warm, steady voice from a few feet behind me.

I stepped back closer to the rock wall, farther away from the drop-off, and kept hiking, one boot in front of the other. My stomach was in painful knots, my body tense, tight—I felt ashamed. I tucked my head low. Dejected, my shoulders hunched over, and not just from the physical weight on them.

I can't tell Dad and A. D.

But that presence, it felt like angels. Grandpa Bill? Michelle?

I thought for a second they were walking right beside me. Grandpa, warm, assured, with his big feet and his big heart, holding me up, pushed up right next to me. Michelle in front, a brilliant white light, leading me, showing me the way down the path.

But that's crazy, right?

A bit of hope buoyed my soul. My countenance lifted for the first time in hours.

7:00 P.M.

BREEZY POINT

We hiked another half mile down the trail, then the trail disappeared. Small boulders and a tree had crashed down at some point and piled up, blocking our way. *Come on!*

We came to a stop as we neared the pile, but it was too precarious and high to walk over. We decided to take off our packs and climb over.

A. D. went first, going slowly, hand over hand with his back to the drop-off. After he was over, Dad passed him one pack at a time. Dad helped me onto the red boulders and I worked my way over, trying not to look down. A. D. helped me down. Dad came last. *Whew.*

I gritted my teeth as I put my pack back on; my shoulders were about finished. A cairn marked the trail continuing on the other side of the pile. We weren't the first ones to cross the rockfall.

The sun was lowering, and soon it would drop behind the western reaches of the canyon. We'd been hiking for eight hours, covered five and a half miles, and descended two thousand feet. I was now teetering on empty. Yet it was still another two and a half miles to our campsite.

Disoriented, I hit my mental wall.

Hey, if you're up there, we're in a bit of a jam here. Can you help us?

Not long after I tossed out my plea, a rocky outcropping came into view, the first one in miles big enough and flat enough to sleep on. It had a cool breeze and a stunning view. I tossed my pack down and declared, "Done." I plopped down.

Dad had already gone about twenty feet past me down the trail, heading down a steep descent, trying to make out the trail with his small Maglite.

I stood up, hands on my hips, eyes blazing, hollering down to him with all the might I had left. "I'm staying here tonight!"

Dad turned and, with a quizzical look, walked back up to me. His face was ragged, tired, worn; his eyes small, darting side to side.

He dug in his pocket and brought out a folded piece of typed white paper, thrusting it at me. Tapping on it with his finger, his voice tight, he said, "We don't have permission to camp here. Only in the places listed on this permit."

"There are no rangers around, Dad. There is no one around! No one cares!" I waved my arms, pointing every which way to emphasize my point. "It's going to be pitch black soon. Someone is going to walk right off a cliff if we don't stop." I planted my feet. Lowering my arms to my sides, I dropped my voice. "My legs are toast. I'm spent. We can try again in the morning."

Dad turned to A. D. "What do you think?"

A. D. replied with a shrug, "This will be all right."

Using our flashlights, we put up a one-man tent for me, the one I'd lugged on my back all day, and a two-man for A. D. and Dad to share. The ground was too hard to drive stakes into, so we anchored our tents with rocks. Leaning through the tent flap, I unrolled my blue foam mat and purple sleeping bag.

We took stock of our diminishing water supply and decided it wasn't smart to use water to rehydrate a package of dried food. So for dinner, we settled on a hank of beef jerky the consistency of a leather shoe and a ration of a cup of water each, till morning.

I crashed for the night in my tent. My belly rumbling from hunger, my lips parched and cracked, my throat choked with thirst, I longed for the water at the river far below.

Worried about my brother, I wished there was a way to send him a note: *Don't come down, too dangerous, too far, especially by yourself. Stay on the rim!*

This had been one of the hardest, longest days of my life, and now I was stuck on a ledge, pushed up against rock walls. I blamed my dad, his bright ideas and overestimating conceit. I blamed myself too—a willing adventure buddy with him.

Mad at myself, sad I was willing to go over that cliff earlier today, sure I would never reach this much of a head-spinning, dizzying low point in my life again. At wits' end. Exhausted. Dang thirsty. Going to sleep in the middle of a rock-and-desert wasteland.

———

I trusted Dad—he said we could handle this trip. Instead he risked all our lives. Something in me grew up when I stood up to him. Dad could be scary when you pushed back, but he knew there was no reasoning with me. I knew he would cool off soon enough and be relieved to put his pack down and rest. After the arrest, he said he's like a pot, slowly heating and occasionally blowing its lid. The key to surviving life with Dad? Watch the pot cautiously, turn down the heat, and know when to get out of its way before it blows.

CHAPTER 12

The Milky Way Makes an Excellent Nightlight

DAY TWO

Hope had risen anew; light warmed my tent, bringing me back to life. I peeked my head out of the flap, finding myself greeted with a stunning sunrise, orange brilliance hitting pink expanses. The air was calm; the canyon was at peace. All was forgiven from the hard day before.

Tucked tight into rocks a thousand feet up in the air, I'd found some of the best sleep I'd ever had. Rested, I was ready to tackle the Cathedral Stairs.

While partaking of a breakfast of trail mix with melted chocolate pieces and a few sips of water, we contemplated the toll our feet were taking. We passed around a nail trimmer, cutting back our toenails even shorter than we had at the rim, hoping to minimize the pain we endured yesterday on the steep descents.

"Got any hotspots, kids?" Dad asked while inspecting his own feet carefully. "Take care of them now. You don't want flare-ups turning into full blisters."

I lifted each foot and worked slowly around my toes and sides of my feet, checking for any sores. Using tiny scissors that folded out of my small pink Swiss Army knife, I cut small squares from the soft moleskin Dad insisted I bring along. Peeling off the sticky backing, I stuck the patches on my red, unhappy skin. My feet protested as I put clean socks on. I slowly coaxed my feet into my boots with a slight groan.

Feet tended to, boots firmly tightened, camp packed and placed on our backs, we set out, navigating down the stairs with clear-headed minds and more confident footing than we'd found yesterday. Looking out on the immense red-walled world around me, I felt awake, more so than I had in a long time. I could hear the beats in my chest; I could feel the air filling my lungs—*I was alive.*

Descending a thousand feet and a mile and a half from last night's impromptu campsite, we reached the junction of Hermit and Tonto around midmorning. My head and shoulders were up, not hunched over. I was doing this. I'd accomplished something—I'd hiked miles down into a canyon. It felt insane, but I was doing it. It felt dang good after the failures and losses of the past year.

"Well, that wasn't too bad, right, guys?" my dad asked with a slight chuckle and shake of his head. "Good thing, though, we don't have to go back up that way, huh?"

I warily looked back up, where we had come from, bit my lower lip, and muttered, "Yeah, good thing."

A. D. shrugged. "Nah, it wasn't that bad." He pointed to a large cairn and a wooden sign marking a fork in the trails. A lone, lost sandal hung from the sign. "Now which way do we go?"

"Should we push on toward the Colorado River?" I asked as I swished around the remaining water left in my last bottle. I was wishing for cold, unending water, a beach, and my flip-flops.

Looking over his map, Dad took charge. "East is the river and Granite Rapids, where we camp today. It's four miles away, though."

He looked up, toward the other direction. "West is Hermit Creek, where we were supposed to camp last night. It's got water and should have shade. It's only a mile. We need to head there before we run dry. Before the canyon heats up any more today."

"So a mile to water and five more to camp?" I asked.

"Yes. We can't do another four without restocking our water supply. Got no choice." His face set firm, he turned west toward Hermit Creek. "Come on, let's go."

The trek to the creek gently curved up and down through the Tonto plain, only dropping three hundred feet in elevation over a mile. It was a nice break after the hard miles along the rock wall yesterday and the steep descent earlier that morning.

But Dad was right—the open plateau was heating up quick. My stomach was beginning to ache again, but I kept going, hoping with each downward crest of a hill we would arrive at the creek.

We finally reached our destination, setting our packs down next to a good stream of flowing water. Almost twenty-four hours had passed since we stopped at the spring far above. I crouched down anxiously next to Dad, waiting for him to carefully siphon from the creek into our awaiting bottles.

Water! I chugged half a Gatorade bottle's worth. Until these past two days, I'd never known what it was like to be without this basic necessity. To be thankful for simple water from a creek. And definitely not caring that it tasted faintly of iron and fruit punch.

We ate lunch with our boots off, tempted to stay and lounge, but we decided to head on. Topping off our water containers, we felt assured we could make the five miles to our second campsite before nightfall. If Brian was heading down today, he would expect us to be at the river.

We retraced our footsteps back near the junction.

Less than a mile later, I felt wiped out again by the relentless midday sun. It was straight above our heads, small, bright, intense. Heat rose from the ground, surrounding us, forming mirages.

I became lightheaded. There was no clear-headed thinking now. I looked back at my dad, who was pale and quiet. The weight in his pack seemed to be getting to him.

We should have stayed back at the creek for the rest of the day.

I stopped on the trail, leaning over, holding my stomach. "Hey, guys, should we turn around? Go back and try again in the morning?"

A. D. spoke up. "Over there is a huge boulder. I bet it has shade."

"Dad? What do you think?" I asked, hoping I could cease moving.

"That will do," Dad said, resigned. It was hard to watch him be discouraged. I wasn't used to seeing him like this, physically weary. He was one of the strongest guys I knew.

"Come on, guys, let's get out of this sun," I said, gesturing to a narrow, worn footpath that led to the boulder. We propped our packs up against it, took off our boots, stuffed our socks inside them, and lay down, side by side, under the shaded protection of the great rock.

5:00 P.M.

We were woken late in the afternoon by the sound of voices coming down the trail, the first people we had seen since lunchtime the day before. An older man and woman, fit, hiking lean with lightweight packs a quarter of the size of ours. They stopped and inquired with concern about us, three sleeping lizards under a rock. They tried to coax us back to Hermit Creek, but we stubbornly wanted to go on. We bid them a good trek and packed ourselves up, setting back out eastward.

Since leaving our napping spot two hours ago, we'd been hiking steadily but had only made it a mile. After passing the fork, we'd come over a ridge onto the broadening Tonto Platform. Cope Butte was looming over us as we headed east, crunching dark reddish-brown talus under our boots, surrounded by sparse vegetation.

The greenish-blue Colorado River was now only eight hundred tantalizing feet below us but still miles away. I could taste it in the slight breeze blowing up from the inner gorge we were hiking above. We couldn't make out the steep drop to Monument Creek, which we would have to traverse to turn toward the river. After the drop would be another mile to Granite Rapids.

God? Any ideas?

After ascending a never-ending darkening ridge that made me question my sanity, I stopped to catch my breath. Ready to stop, I said, "Sun is going down again, guys. We've got plenty of water. Could we bivouac again?"

Not long after I asked if we could stop, we came upon a jutting-out, large, flat area on a plateau. We parked it and dined with a view. Dad took stock of our water and determined we had enough to cook with—measuring out what was needed, careful to not let any spill. He poured it into a lightweight metal pot and mixed in a dark reddish-brown package of dehydrated BBQ meat.

Dad attached a small red cylinder of cooking fuel to the back-packing stove, which sprang to life with a hiss and hot blue-white flame. The pot went on the stove, and after a short time and some stirring, we had dinner—BBQ stuffed in pita pockets. It's still to this day one of the best meals I have ever had, in one of the finest locations ever to be found.

A. D. became the hit of the evening, pulling out of his pack a ginormous bag of sunflower seeds, cans of Welch's grape juice, and Sprite.

"Seriously? Where was that last night?" I fell over laughing with glee. Now life was getting good.

I was so happy to be right there, I yelled, "To heck with tents. I'm sleeping out tonight!" I laid down my plastic ground cloth, rolled out my mat, and tossed my sleeping bag down.

"You've got a first-rate idea there, kid," Dad said, laying his bed-roll out next to mine.

Not long after dinner, Dad and I scooted into our sleeping bags. We softly pointed out constellations to each other and the occasional shooting star. Some of the best moments of my life had been with him, outside, in quiet companionship, under the stars. I could hear his breath shallow and even out, and before long, he was gently snoring.

I lay awake awhile longer. I'd never seen the Milky Way this way—stretching across the sky. There was nowhere else in the world I'd rather be, although precisely where we were was hard to say.

Brian?

Was he high above us? Coming down Hermit? Maybe he'd wait for us on the rim. My stomach tightened and I sent a silent plea out into the canyon—*please, don't come down; stay where you are. God? Can you hear me?*

Drifting, my thoughts faded out into the canyon—out into wastelands.

DAY THREE

Dad woke A. D. and me up while the light was still low and murky, wanting to get moving before the sun hit. I was ready to get going, knowing we would have an endless supply of cold water hopefully before noon.

I checked over my feet; the moleskin had worked. I put on clean socks, laced up my boots, and packed up my gear, surprised at how I was adapting.

We set out on Tonto, continuing east, rounding massive buttes, and rising on stunning vistas overlooking dark cliffs that dropped straight down into the river. Nearing Monument Creek, we dropped down along a steep, narrow footpath, taking switchbacks into the inner canyon below. *This is not a place you would want to be stumbling around in the dark*, I thought.

Monument Spire towered above, greeting us at the fork where we turned north. We stepped off our last switchback and found ourselves in a dry inner wash. Smooth reddish-black rock loomed over us on both sides.

While covering the last winding mile, our boots got slowed down in large rounded gravel. There was no trail, just cairns. They marked the trails all the way down—a source of solace. On this day, I bent down in the creek bed and built my own. Stacking rock upon rock atop a boulder was life-affirming. *Hopeful.*

CHAPTER 13

Find a Stream in the Wasteland

DAY THREE

NOON

GRANITE RAPIDS

*E*uphoric might be the word that describes how we felt, finally reaching the mighty greenish-blue, ripsnorting, roaring, chilly-as-all-get-out Colorado River.

Water! All the water you'd ever want. I wanted to drink it, filtered or not, but Dad told me to wait as he pulled out the pump. Within a few minutes, we had cold, fresh water in our bottles. I chugged half of mine and asked for more.

"Slow down, you're going to get a belly ache."

Forty-eight hours ago I was bent over by my massive backpack, full of nerves on my shaky legs. So miserable I was contemplating flinging myself off a ledge. Now, after a 4,300-foot descent over thirteen miles, I posed for a picture a foot off the river's edge, in front of some wicked white-water rapids, standing tall, legs firm, grinning ear to ear. My backpack, flung off yards back, was forgotten.

After getting my water's fill, I went back and grabbed my pack, stepping over large river rocks to reach our sandy campsite where I had big plans to plant my rear for the remainder of the day. We passed by a few tents and were soon greeted by a handful of hikers.

One of the men, in his early twenties, said, "You must be the man hiking with his two young sons and the large winter-weight packs we heard about!"

How had they heard of us? It was like our legend (of stupidity) preceded us.

I took off my sunglasses and looked the guy hard in the eyes. "I'm a girl," I said with a smirk.

"Oh, that you are! Nice to meet you!"

"What do you mean, 'winter-weight packs'?" I asked, although I thought I already knew the answer.

The group of seasoned hikers explained. In the warm months in the canyon, you can manage well with lightweight clothing and basic necessities—you want to keep your pack weight down as much as possible so you can carry more water.

I ran through a mental list of unnecessary items I'd lugged around for two days and had yet to use, including jeans, my purple KSU jacket, and a large KSU plastic mug. And not enough water, not nearly enough.

Dad was still talking to the group, but I moved on, setting my pack up against a tamarisk, a small cedar tree set back in a long, narrow grove along the river. I tossed my mat down on the sand and took off my boots and socks. A. D. and Dad joined me; A. D. pulled his Chicago Bulls cap over his eyes and quickly fell asleep, and Dad soon followed. I picked up the red-and-black paperback, heavy on crime, that I'd thrown last minute into my pack but drifted off to sleep too.

A few hours later, we were woken by a party of a dozen or so loud, happy men and women in three rafts. They rammed their rubber boats on the sandy shore, and the guides were nimbly jumping out, grabbing ropes, tying the boats off to the trees. I was quite taken with these odd specimens, wearing bright-colored life vests, some in hard helmets, most scantily clad.

The guides inquired after us, and we told them about the last two grueling days. After looking over Dad, they mentioned he looked pale and offered him a salt pill to help stave off growing dehydration, then offered us cold pineapple juice in cans and some of the fish tacos they cooked for their dinner. We gladly accepted.

As the sun lowered for the third night, its remaining light falling on the massive brown-and-red walls surrounding us, I lay on the sand, happy, my belly full of water and food, thankful for this day.

My faith had been built with a firm foundation by my parents and my grandparents, Sunday after Sunday at church as a child. It had taken terrible hits over the past five years, but now it was beginning to show me some hope.

I'd been sure God had forsaken me. Yet my pleas in this canyon—for water, for shelter, for safety—had all been answered.

Had God *not* forsaken me? Was he hearing my prayers? Had he been with me this entire time?

Maybe, just maybe, there was something to this whole God thing.

With lots of living things scurrying around us due to the abundant water, I decided crashing in my tent sounded best for the night. I quickly set it up under the low-lying trees and snapped a glow stick so I could have some light to read by.

Huge mistake.

A gazillion bugs hit my tent in a flash. I heard Dad chuckling loudly outside, and I yelled to him through the flap I now refused to open. "What's so funny?"

"Your tent. It's glowin' like a gigantic lightnin' bug. And every insect for miles likes you a whole lot."

Oh heck. I quickly finished using the light and tucked it into my shoe, stewing at the man who was contently lying out on the sand in the cool air, watching the stars.

DAY FOUR

The next morning, Dad told me sleeping out on the sand was one of the more magical nights of his life, watching bats swoop above his head, catching bugs. I'd slept in fits, my tent too warm—but unwilling to sleep outside among the many river critters.

After breakfast, we walked down to the boulder-strewn beach to watch the rafters as they shot the rapids. They paddled hard as soon as they put in, and I held my breath as each boat hit the churning water and lifted with a good number of *yee-haws* coming from the boats. Each made it over with reasonable ease and was quickly sent downstream and soon out of sight. Dad and I determined right then we would take a rafting trip through the canyon before he got any older.

Dad wanted to make it up to Monument Creek before it got any warmer, concerned about the heat in the creek bed. A. D. and I wanted to stay at the river for the day and head up to our campsite at dusk. But Dad reminded us that if Brian were to come down, he would expect to find us there on day four.

It didn't seem worth the argument with Dad—or the likely fallout—so we packed up and trekked one and a half miles back through the same creek bed as yesterday.

You could make out the rim from this camp—thousands of feet above us, way off in the distance. There were likely people up there right now, sightseeing from the top of the Abyss.

It was hot on the platform, and I quickly sought shade. Dad told me before I wandered off that I needed to secure my pack. We had seen ground squirrels down at the river and here. Dad helped me rig up a rope over a tree branch, and we hung my pack high.

Dad was pale, uptight, and peeved; he seemed to want to spend the rest of his day in the awfully hot and smelly outhouse that was at camp. I'd stepped foot in it once but turned right back around and went back to using the desert with the lizards.

Trying to avoid colliding up against Dad, who was becoming more and more irritable, A. D. and I found refuge in a narrow slickrock canyon. I intended to spend hours reading and napping, with my feet in a cold stream, my back up against smooth rock. I was going to enjoy my day whether Dad wanted to or not.

When I got back to camp late in the afternoon, I found a two-inch hole in the side of my pack and the remains of my trail mix scattered on the ground. Dang rodents.

At dinner, A. D. and I were trying to help, and I accidentally spilled a small amount of cooking fuel. Dad snapped at us both, "Now look what you've done!"

"I'm sorry, I didn't mean to. It wasn't that much—"

"You need to be more careful!" Dad interrupted, overriding what I was trying to say, telling us how priceless the fuel was. It was common to have his mood switch on one of us kids, but I'd never seen him do that to any of my cousins.

Dad always fought hard to be in control. Not just his emotions or demeanor, but his whole body. He was careful about who got to see what side of him. He was almost always on excellent behavior in front of anyone who wasn't Mom, Brian, or me, but now he was losing a little bit of control and quickly boiling over.

———

We somehow managed dinner under tight conditions and a darkening sky. Not long after, Dad and I laid out plastic to sleep on; it was way too hot for a tent, even with rodents around. A. D. set up a spot near some young hikers who had come into camp that afternoon—I think he'd had enough of Dad and likely me too.

Not long after lying down, I saw a flashlight bouncing around off in the distance, up above the steep switchbacks that led down to Monument Creek.

My heart caught in my throat—*Brian!*

I sat up and nudged Dad, pointing out the light to him. "Look up there! Do you think it could be Brian? Can we go see? Help whoever it is?"

Dad looked out into the distance, but with his face and voice set firm, said, "No. It's not safe. It's farther than you think. It would be suicide to go up there in the dark. Stay put."

I got my small electric-blue Maglite out, stood up, and signaled S-O-S as best I could, three shorts, three longs, three shorts, twisting it to turn on, off, on, off. I didn't know how to signal anything else, and I thought it might catch the attention of whoever held the light. I thought maybe they were signaling back, but Dad said it was the person moving the light around.

It was Brian. I knew it. My whole body knew it.

I argued with my dad, almost in a panic.

He wouldn't budge. It was like coming up against a stone wall. And I hated him for it. He didn't need to be so cautious, so dang protective. That person might need help. But I knew it was Brian.

The light faded and Dad thought maybe the person had headed down toward the river.

I lay down and rolled over in a huff. Tears came forth and I wept as quietly as I could.

God? Brian needs your help. Please keep him safe, please deliver him to us!

With tears streaming down my face, I prayed for my brother or whomever the light belonged to. Broken inside, my hard, stubborn heart cracking in two, my soul splitting open. I rolled back over and looked up at the Milky Way laid out so perfectly, even better than it was two nights ago.

All is calm. All is bright.

God? You made this, didn't you? All of this—the stars, the rocks, the river—they belong to you, don't they? And I think they are as old as folks say. Because I think you're infinite—like this immense place but way, way beyond.

At Michelle's funeral, it was spoken of many rooms and Jesus going to prepare a place for us and coming back to take us to be with him. Where in the heavens above was his home? Was there still room for me? Were Michelle and Grandpa, who believed in him, who loved his Son, home?

They knew God as their Father.

God had promised to never leave me nor forsake me. And he hadn't forsaken me. I had forsaken him. That cut right through me, leaving gaping agony to the bottom of my being.

Would God want to talk to me after I'd walked away? Would God want anything to do with me after the way I had treated him?

God, forgive me for my doubts and all my wrong steps over the past years.

I looked up at the stars overhead and made a deal with him: if he could get us out of this mess my dad had gotten us into, I would come back to the faith I'd lost and accept his Son, Jesus Christ, as my savior. I loved him—loved God. I would make it right.

God, please help us get out of here. I will come back. I will do whatever it takes. Just get us out.

A peace like I'd never known washed over me.

I wiped my wet face on my sleeping bag and closed my eyes.

Hope—it was beginning to spring forth.

CHAPTER 14

If It's Good Enough
for Tadpoles, It's Good
Enough for You

DAY FIVE
MONUMENT CREEK

How much longer do you think we should wait?" I asked Dad, who was poking around last night's campsite.

"Don't know. Guess we better get moving. Have our longest hike of the trip ahead of us," he replied.

We were stalling, both hoping Brian was the person behind the flashlight the night before, both hoping he would come walking into camp any moment. Whatever odds Dad and I were at yesterday had been forgiven with a solid night of rest and a growing concern for my brother.

Maybe Brian would meet us back at the rim tomorrow.

A. D. left a while ago, asking if it would be okay for him to hike on with the small group he met yesterday. Dad agreed and said we'd meet him at Horn Creek, our campsite for the night, eight miles east.

Dad and I finally decided we couldn't wait any longer due to the rising heat and headed out after topping off our bottles. We needed to be careful with our water supply today; there was no reliable water till Indian Garden tomorrow. Dad's trail guide said not to count on water at Cedar Spring, and not to drink it at Salt Creek due to mineralization, or at Horn Creek due to radiation from an old mine above it. *Fantastic!*

The switchbacks out of Monument Creek were steep and taxing, but the trail soon leveled off. We would be broadly contouring around and through the three steep drainages today; other times we would be jutting up against thousand-foot drop-offs.

The trail cut between the river and massive red buttes rising off the distant South Rim, weaving through dense brown sagebrush and endless cacti. It was as if we had been dropped into an old western movie, and now all we needed were some proper hats and a pair of painted horses. *I'd even settle for a stubborn burro*, I thought.

My pack was no longer a burden; it had grown much lighter thanks to a chubby rodent and my own consumption. I felt like a different person from the one who'd begun this trip five days before. My legs held strong, and I was no longer fearful for myself. But I was growing more worried about Brian—if he was behind us, he would have an immense distance to cover. *We shouldn't have ever told him to come down on his own and meet us.*

There was no shade and the sun was already striking us hard by midmorning. The distance we needed to cover in the heat was going to be the battle today. Dad pointed out a large group of vultures riding the thermals and circling on the north side, joking maybe a hiker had fallen.

I didn't think it was funny.

About a mile down the trail, Dad said he needed a bathroom break and went back behind a ridge. He was gone for what felt like an eternity, and I was left stewing, stuck in the middle of the forsaken nowhere, waiting on what he could have taken care of back in our shaded camp.

When Dad finally came back, he sat down, pale and discouraged, his face turned down. "Just leave me here to die."

I'd never seen my dad so lost.

"You need to drink more water. Come on. We can't stop here—we'll roast. We need to find some shade. Cedar Spring? Can you make it there?"

Resigned, he stood up gingerly, looked me in the eye with more clarity, and said, "Yeah. I can do it."

I helped him put his pack on, feeling bad about what I was asking him to do.

We set out with a short third of a mile to go to get to a stopping point. We were both quiet; it felt like an immense shift had happened between us. He'd rallied me the first few days, kept me moving, kept me alive.

Now I was doing the same thing.

Dad never, ever showed weakness. He was the toughest person I knew, so it scared me to see him sink so low.

11:00 A.M.
CEDAR SPRING

We dropped down into a chalky, narrow drainage, hoping to find water to fill our bottles back up, but all we found was a tiny waterhole with black tadpoles swimming in it. I figured if life was able to live in the water, then it couldn't be *that* bad, so we set to work, filtering part of what was sustaining the spawn.

What doesn't kill you . . . makes you stronger?

Dad was wiped out and I was suddenly tired, feeling oddly weighed down, as if someone had placed a heavy, warm blanket on me. We decided to hole up there for a few hours, setting plastic and our mats down under small rock alcoves. We took off our boots and I settled in for a rest, with a bag of snacks and my book near me.

Around one o'clock, Dad woke me up to tell me, with a chuckle, that a raven had stolen my bag of snacks, scattering food all over the creek bed and was now munching happily.

In my bare feet, I went after the bird. It took off, flying low over a steep drop-off, landing far out of my reach. It looked mighty pleased with itself. I was able to salvage some unpecked, wrapped items the thief left behind—I wasn't going to waste anything down here if I could help it.

Dad thought we should pack up and head on, but something in me was telling me to wait. "Shouldn't we stay here through the worst of the heat and go on near dusk?"

"If we do that, we're going to get stuck with no campsite and too far to travel tomorrow."

"I really think we should stay a few more hours at least. It's so awfully hot on the trail."

Dad decided we could stay, and we went back to lounging, chatting off and on, our voices bouncing around the creek bed.

"Help! Help!" a man's voice shouted overhead.

I sat up and hastily put my boots on, not tying my laces.

"Where are you? Are you hurt?" I called.

"No, bring water!"

I knew that voice! "Brian?"

"Kerri? Dad?" His voice echoed. I couldn't tell which side of the creek bed he was on.

"It's us! Where are you? I'm coming—Dad and I are coming, keep talking. Tell me where you are!" I was seized with fear and adrenaline; I could tell from Brian's voice he was in bad shape. *Scared.*

I grabbed my first-aid kit and water bottles and ran, fast as I could, right past Dad, who was still working on his boots.

"Slow down! We don't need you getting hurt."

Brian was likely on the path we had come down and I raced up it, finding him quickly. He was sitting down with his pack on, planted directly above our heads. He was bent over like he had come to the end of all ability.

Thank you, God! Oh! Thank you, thank you!

He was exhausted, dehydrated, sunburned—but otherwise seemed okay.

I hugged him and handed him my water as Dad came up right behind me on the path.

Dad hugged him tightly, holding on for a while, and the three of us cried, so happy to be reunited.

"We need to get you into shade. Can you make it down the path? We've got water and food and a place to rest." I was speaking rapidly.

"Yeah, I can get down there, but something is wrong with my eyes. Can't see very well," my brother said.

We took off my brother's pack and Dad helped lift Brian up.

Dad reached out and held Brian's belt from behind as Brian took a few steps forward. I grabbed his green pack and almost threw it, it was so light.

"Where's your gear?"

"Chucked it, almost all of it. Too heavy, couldn't go on any farther. Tossed my tent, sleeping bag, clothes, back a ways. All I've got is some food and water, but my water is contaminated. I didn't want to drink it. Was afraid it would make me sick."

"That's okay! We've got plenty!"

Dad and I encouraged him down the trail and laid him on Dad's mat. I sat down close to him, making sure he was drinking, and we wet a bandana, putting it over his head. We also washed his eyes out with water. He didn't have any sunglasses, and he seemed to have sunburned his eyes, telling us his eyes felt gritty and painful.

Dad took Brian's water bottles that held the contaminated water from Monument Creek and filtered it into clean bottles. It wasn't the most sanitary way to go about it—but we needed water for three now.

Brian told us he rested for two days and hiked along the rim trail on the third day to build some strength. He'd taken a bus to the head of Hermit yesterday morning and hiked all day, knowing on day four we would be at Monument. He told us how hairy Hermit was and how worried he was about us. When he came across the sandal on the sign at the fork, he thought it was my shoe and was frightened, afraid something had happened to me.

Brian told us, "I kept going, as far as I could."

Nine miles. He hiked in one day what had taken us two and a half—with sleep and decent food.

He stopped last night above the drop to Monument Creek. He shone his flashlight around for a few minutes but couldn't make out the trail.

My heart caught in my chest. "We saw a light," I said it with my head down. Ashamed we didn't go to help.

"I decided to stay where I was. I propped myself up against a rock. Slept that way. At one point a small rattler came by. I killed it with a rock. And just in case, I cut it in two with my knife. I was terrified the entire night."

A sharp sting was filling my guts—Brian alone, all night, up there. Terrified. And we hadn't done anything.

"When I got to Monument this morning, I was so glad to see water, but then I wasn't sure if I should drink it. I took a wrong turn, went south for a while, toward the rim, up a drainage. Couldn't find the trail. Got turned around, lost. Everything looks the same. Finally found the way up and out and told myself to keep going. Got here. Heard voices. So I yelled."

"We're so glad you're okay." And we proceeded to tell him about the last four insane days.

CHAPTER 15

Coming Back from the Abyss Doesn't Have to Be So Dramatic

Late in the afternoon, we decided we should move on after letting Brian rest for a few hours. I was surprised he was able to go on, but he seemed stronger than we'd initially thought. By six o'clock, the three of us were descending along the pink-and-white streaked ridges of Salt Creek after passing by the Alligator and the Inferno, names for buttes that rose below the rim. We had hiked two miles since leaving Cedar Spring and were making good time considering the current state of our hiking party.

Having Brian back raised my spirits; I no longer noticed the heat or the distance. I was learning to make larger strides with my head up, to take in what was in front of me instead of fretting over my foot placement. I was learning to trust myself and the worn path under my boots. Even though it didn't look possible to go forward, the trail always led around the gaping expanses—it stayed steady, constant. The trail never fought against the terrain but went with it, alongside it, in tandem.

As our light began to fade, Brian told us again he couldn't see very well. We stayed as close as we could to him, Dad calling out what was coming next while I walked behind Brian to help with light. The three of us hiked for hours using our Maglites, continually checking on each other, encouraging each other to keep going.

Boot by boot, foot by foot, we crossed five more miles of the vast platform after leaving Salt. Through sure, stubborn willpower and internal strength, the three of us made it to camp.

What would have happened if Dad and I hadn't stopped at Cedar? Would Brian have been able to get down to shade? Would he have been able to cover this distance on his own?

Brian could have died if he hadn't made it to us.

I wasn't just tired at Cedar earlier; it was as if I had been burdened to stay longer—an internal feeling to stay put. *Was that you, God?*

10:00 P.M.
HORN CREEK

By the grace of God, we found our way into camp at Horn Creek in the pitch black sometime around ten o'clock, our lights bouncing around the barren campsite—no tents, no A. D. We hoped that meant he had gone on toward Indian Garden.

Even though the camp was bare, Dad sought out our assigned spot, marked with a letter and a number on a wooden sign.

Brian needed shelter, so I set up my one-man for him, and Dad cooked us a packet of food. Brian ate crossed-legged in the tent. Right after he ate, he conked out. Dad and I laid down our ground cloth again, covered in fine red dust, and slept outside under the stars for the last night.

DAY SIX

We set out early from Horn, facing seven and a half miles and an ascent of three thousand feet, hoping to reach the rim by nightfall.

As we meandered east, the early morning light was hitting the pink expanses of Battleship. Dad had said we would be coming up on it on this day and by dang—we were. Felt good, getting this far.

As we rounded an edge, my worn-down boot caught on a rock. "Ah—heck! Ankle went."

I sat down, hesitantly removed my boot with a grimace, and Dad looked over my foot. We decided the best course was to wrap it with a bandage and keep moving.

I put my boot back on and laced it up, standing up slowly. It held my weight.

11:00 A.M.
INDIAN GARDEN–BRIGHT ANGEL TRAIL

We made it into Indian Garden midmorning. My ankle was sore, but I was managing with a bit of a hobble.

A surreal scene greeted us after our week in the great empty beyond—water, huts, trees, and people. Gobs of them milling around, most looking much cleaner and put together than us, and some of them now staring at us.

I looked down at myself. My legs were caked in red, sandy dirt, and by the looks on people's faces, I might have been covered all the way to my head.

We made our way over to a water pump and a few folks stepped out of our way, letting us cut in front of them.

Do we look that bad?

After filling our bottles and chugging down a good amount of cool, fresh water, we set off for some shade.

A park ranger saw us, asked how we were, and wondered where we had come from. Dad dug out our permit, but the ranger didn't ask to see it.

I wanted to give this guy a piece of my mind: rockslides, cliffs, trails without water. But the three of us were polite—something about talking to someone in a uniform and official hat.

Dad settled in under some trees, deciding to make himself some ramen noodles for an early lunch. But we still had five miles and three thousand feet to go. I didn't want to stop.

"Since there are so many people here and Bright Angel looks like a highway—folks coming down and going up—could Brian and I go on ahead? Meet you at the top?"

Dad said okay and Brian and I set out, knowing even with my bum ankle and his exhaustion we could make quicker time than Dad, who was still weighted down with a substantial pack. *If you carry it in, you carry it out.*

From Indian Garden, you can see the rim but you can't make out the whole trail. I knew it was up there, though. Five miles and three thousand feet to a hot shower and decent food.

We've got this. No problem.

4:00 P.M.

MILE-AND-A-HALF REST HOUSE

Around five hours into our climb and with a good stop at the rest house, we had made it up two thousand feet of winding switchbacks. Even though we were ascending the whole time, red, smooth Bright Angel was a dream after rocky, scary Hermit and taxing Tonto. It was wide, which was good because people were often passing us coming down as we climbed up. I was surprised this late in the day to see day hikers still headed down, carrying little. I doubted they understood how long it could take to go back up.

Brian's vision had improved, and even with my bum ankle it was a good day, a quiet one, side by side with him, talking off and on, encouraging each other. Occasionally one of us would lag and the other one would stop and yell back down the trail, "Come on, it's only twenty more steps up to here!"

It wasn't far between stretches, and turn after turn, we had almost made it. Near a mile to go, we began to think of all the food we could eat back in the normal world. Taco Bell, McDonald's, Arby's: we were talking our way through menus as we climbed.

More and more, we passed signs of civilization: ice cream cones, flat pavement, indoor plumbing. A sturdy metal railing to keep you from going over the edge. *Where was that when I needed it six days ago?*

My tattered right boot hit the first blessed step of the man-made walkway.

A knock, straight down from the heavens, hit me on my head, and before my sturdy left boot set down, God said, *Hey, we had a deal. I have held up my end. Now it's your turn!*

Floored, I halted in my tracks. *Seriously? Right now? You're doing this right now?*

Yes.

Resigned, I accepted my fate: *Okay, all right, all right. You've got me.*

6:00 P.M.
SOUTH RIM—THIRTY MILES HIKED

We made it out of the beast and ran into A. D., who was waiting nearby. He had a big grin on his face, clean clothes on, and looked much better off than we did. He'd gone on from Horn last evening after realizing it was barren and the water wasn't safe, spending the night in Indian Garden. He climbed out earlier today, rode a bus down to the van, and checked into our room, which wasn't far.

A. D. said he would wait for Dad; Brian and I should go on to the hotel.

Inside our room, I called Mom in Phoenix and filled her in on one heck of a story, skirting around the worst of it. Then I got in the shower. I won't ever forget seeing red dirt and sand wash down my legs and pile near the drain while I stood under the water.

After putting on clean clothes, I headed back to the rim, and around 7:30 p.m., I got to watch Dad come up the last leg. He was tired but happy to see us and the end of the trail.

We ended up eating a late dinner that night at a fancy restaurant overlooking the rim. While waiting for our table, the bartender served us pineapple juice in chilled glasses and we all slugged them back like we were drinking the finest liquor to be found. When we got to our table, the waiter asked what he could do for us and we told him to keep the water coming.

The four of us sat around our table that night with huge grins on our faces, stuffing ourselves full. Dad didn't even look at the bill, just handed the waiter his credit card.

That night, I fell asleep on the floor, tucked into my sleeping bag, marveling at the carpet and air conditioning, already missing the Milky Way.

PART III

Love Will Never Fail You

*Love knows no limit to its endurance, no
end to its trust, no fading of its hope; it can
outlast anything. It is, in fact, the one thing
that still stands when all else has fallen.*

—1 CORINTHIANS 13:7-8 PHILLIPS

CHAPTER 16

Find a Hope and a Future

JUNE 1997
WICHITA

A month out of the canyon, I was sitting on my bed at my home in Wichita when I felt the prompting of God—a tugging on my spirit.

We had a deal. Go find your Bible.

I've often met God with a sigh, resignation, sometimes downright belligerence: *I don't wanna.*

Bible.

All right.

I looked around the wooden bookshelves in my room and didn't see it. After a search that included crawling under my bed, I found my red leather Bible, given to me at confirmation, my name inscribed in gold on the cover. I dusted it off and haphazardly flipped it open, falling on Job—*in spite of everyone and everything he lost, he remained faithful.*

In mid-August, I moved back to Boyd—this time to a single room on the third floor. We would move me and my carloads of stuff back and forth for the next four years to the same tiny, peaceful room, with its view of the tall pines and park across the circle drive.

On my first Sunday evening back, two girls knocked on my door. "Hey, we're from Campus Crusade. Would you like to go to a picnic?" I could smell the cookout from my window, and I was hungry. As I headed down the stairs, my spirit leaped a tiny bit—recognizing something it knew in them. *God? Is this your doing?*

They invited me to a Bible study that fall and patiently answered my questions, ranging from Genesis to Revelation. These women did "quiet times" with God, and I dutifully tried to do the same with my Bible, journal, and note cards for scripture memorization. But I quickly wanted to rebel against the Christian disciplines of being quiet, still, and getting up early.

I was also torn between these new people coming into my life while trying to hold on to my old group. After a final falling out, I finally laid down the past hard year—*here, God, take it. I can't anymore.* I called my folks, begging to quit school and come home. They told me I had to stay through the week and Dad would drive up on Friday. Dad drove up and a few days later drove me back to school, a little more able to face the rest of my fall semester.

My parents and brother began to visit Manhattan regularly. They often came up in the fall, decked out in purple to tailgate before football games. Dad called us the K-State faithful, and he embraced the games with gusto, yelling "K! S! U!" and trying to do the moves to "The Wabash Cannonball."

One game, after a touchdown, Dad and Brian lifted me high and passed me on to the waiting crowd behind us—surfing me to the top. Saturdays were magical, standing for hours next to the guys, yelling till we were hoarse.

I met Darian in August 1998. Darian says he remembers seeing me for the first time in a purple KSU T-shirt, my hair long and wavy, heading into the dining center. I remember meeting *him* while I was standing in the doorway of his dorm room, and I should have realized then—when I noticed his soft brown eyes tucked behind wire-rims, his gentle smile, and the way he wore his short light-brown hair—I was going to have a problem.

Or maybe he was going to be a problem when I noticed his black leather jacket hanging on the corner of his loft bed. I was curious about this eighteen-year-old freshman who had art supplies scattered across his desk, hockey sticks propped up in the corner of his room, and a black-and-white guitar plugged into an amp with punk rock stickers declaring their allegiance.

But my heart was wandering in other directions, and my feelings about Darian over the first fifteen months I knew him bounced between aggravation and pleasant surprise. I even spent a fair amount of time convincing a few friends he was irksome and they should not date him. They didn't.

I didn't date anyone else either. I tended to like guys who had only a vague interest in me, and then they'd hand me the dreaded I-like-you-like-a-Christian-sister card.

I read, more than once, Elisabeth Elliot's *Passion and Purity*, definitely in need of both, and would hand my worn copy to friends who came to my dorm room weepy and fretting. I'd been encouraged to pray for my future husband but found my mind wandering during these feeble attempts, far away from anything looking like prayer or patience.

I was trying to walk the walk but often fell flat on my face. I reckoned God likely got the raw end of that deal we made in the canyon, but I was also sure there were no take-backs. I was his daughter, whether I wanted to be or not.

Darian and I were part of a raucous group of friends who lived in the dorms next to each other; we'd push several tables together for meals. I'd miss out on dinner the evenings I was on dish duty— having begun a job for measly pay in the dining center. I usually scraped plates as they rotated around a carousel, stacked three high. Darian and a few other guys thought it was funny to leave me messages in their leftovers—I could hear their howls of laughter as the plates came around. It was not the way to get a girl's attention.

I didn't work Thursday nights so I could walk with this group to nearby Campus Crusade gatherings for praise and worship and a talk on faith. On the weekends, we might build bonfires at Pottawatomie Lake, make s'mores, and sing worship songs. We'd wrap up Saturday nights with a late-night, or early-morning, breakfast at Village Inn and try hard to get up in time for church a few hours later. Some of us were better at getting up on Sunday mornings than others.

Finishing up my third year, I was still struggling in some of my classes—not always putting in the effort, time, and work they required, falling into bad habits, scraping by semester after semester. I was passing but had long ago lost my scholarship and any shot at veterinary school. But it wasn't until the second semester of my junior year—the spring of 1999—that I finally worked up the courage to tell my parents the news over dinner.

I felt like God was redirecting me—changing my heart.

I told my parents that I had switched my major to life sciences and education with the intent of becoming a teacher. I was afraid it would crush my dad; he had dreamed right alongside me that I would become a vet. When I told him, his face fell and his eyes clouded, but he rebounded, saying, "That's okay. I know how hard college is; you're doing your best."

It was the hardest thing I ever had to tell him. Because I hadn't been trying my hardest or doing my best.

CHAPTER 17

Fall in Love at Least Once in Your Life

NOVEMBER 1999
KANSAS

Why did you swerve?" Darian questioned my driving ability as we headed to Wichita in my maroon Dodge Aries for Thanksgiving break. My parents bought my grandparents' old car for me so I could get back and forth to an elementary school in Manhattan where I was attending my first college practicum. I was happier now that I'd switched majors.

We were driving south on Route 77, in chunky drizzle. It was bouncing off the windshield and getting stuck in the wipers.

"Why did you swerve?" the boy with the kind eyes asked again.

"I was tryin' to avoid that chughole."

"A what?"

"Chughole. You know, a hole in the road."

"You mean a pothole?"

"Yeah."

He laughed uncontrollably. "You are *so* Kansan."

"Yeah? So are you."

"No. Dad's from Long Island, Mom is from Denver, and I've never, ever, heard anyone call a pothole a chughole before."

"Well, that's what my dad calls it."

Darian, soon to be twenty years old, needed a ride home, and my twenty-one-year-old self volunteered, or was roped into volunteering, I don't exactly recall which. Darian was trying to cheer me up as we tackled the bad weather and questionable roads, and I noticed—appreciated it. It was the first chance at a long conversation, and the drive was passing by quickly.

"What do you call that, Kansan?" Darian was pointing out the car window to a huge antenna sitting at the junction of Routes 77 and 50, near Florence.

"An-tanna." This was said in a hick Kansan drawl.

He laughed again. A lot.

As I rounded the corner to Route 50, I looked over at him and knew I was in big trouble. When we reached his home in west Wichita, I asked if he would like a ride back on Sunday.

Really, God? After fighting against it for so long, and trying to go every other way, is this who I am supposed to be with? This guy? Really?

A month later, over Christmas break, Darian picked me up for Sonic and a Thunder hockey game at the Kansas Coliseum. We had the chance to ice skate after the game. I was timid on the ice, but he took my hands in his, pulling me fast while he skated backward. My soul and heart were flying. I didn't want to stop, wanted to feel this way the rest of my days.

God? This guy.

A few weeks later, in early January 2000, Darian and I were driving out to Denver, Colorado, for a Campus Crusade conference. Friends were in a car ahead, and on a steep, icy overpass in Salina, Kansas, they slid into a skid. Their car hit ours as we passed, knocking us up against a guardrail on the right as we headed down. I was driving and pretty shaken up, but it seemed we would all be okay—until I looked in my rearview mirror and watched as my friends' tiny car was smashed from behind by an eighteen-wheeler that had come over the hill.

Darian was sitting next to me in the passenger seat as I began yelling, praying, and cursing: my crappy, low-tech cell phone wouldn't roam to call 911.

Our group pulled over at a truck stop while first responders tended to our friends. We made two of the hardest phone calls I've ever been a part of, notifying parents their daughters had been in an accident. Darian and I, along with three other guys from another car, stayed most of that day at the emergency room, speaking with the highway patrol and sitting beside our friends, waiting for their families to arrive. One of the girls was unconscious and later taken to surgery.

Late that winter afternoon, we finally headed toward Denver, taking turns driving. When it was my turn, Darian drew a funny picture on a sticky note and stuck it under the rearview mirror so I wouldn't focus so much on seeing the accident over and over in the mirror. We didn't arrive at our hotel until midnight, making the trip on the drifting snow and patchy ice of I-70, often passing by spinouts and cars in the ditch. That terrible day there was a good deal of praying, wondering why we still pressed on, and making phone calls from pay phones to update our worried parents.

My feelings were a mess and my heart felt like a rock. Originally Darian was supposed to be in the back seat of that two-door hatchback with another boy. While I was devastated for my injured friends, I was also relieved Darian and the other guy hadn't been in the car. Darian told me it had been a mistake to look at the car when he went to retrieve his bag from the police station; there were no more than inches left where he would have been sitting.

Realizing what I could have lost, my heart continued to shift. Late one evening, curled up in overstuffed hotel chairs, we didn't just decide to date—we settled on marriage. Darian told me, "I fell for you the first time I met you, and I've been praying since that you'd become my wife."

I wasn't sure if I should hit him for upending the past year and a half of my life with his prayers or to just go with it. I decided to go with it—it wasn't every day one heard "I've been praying for you to become my wife."

I'm guessing he was a little more focused in the prayer department than I'd been.

The next evening, walking in downtown Denver, when he took my hand in his, I knew. This was *it*. We would quickly become inseparable, and to this day, I have no idea what took so long for me to figure it out.

MARCH 2000

OKLAHOMA

"Is your dad always like this?" Darian was camping with Dad, Brian, and me for the first time. It was spring break, and we were in somewhere-nowhere, Oklahoma. It would be his first and last campout with us because my "idiosyncratic dad," as Darian would say later, was driving my sane boyfriend insane.

"Dad can be particular, likes things a certain way. It's better to just go with it. Otherwise, he's gonna get bent out of shape and tank our whole week." I said this while lying with my head on Darian's chest. We were hanging out in his tent, which was much roomier than my tiny one-man. "If ya go along with him, then he won't care so much if I spend an inordinate amount of time in your tent during the day."

"Oh, right. Go along with your dad. Got it." Darian wrapped an arm around me and chuckled. Darian was an Eagle Scout and more than capable of maintaining a camp. He hiked rugged miles for days at the Philmont Scout Ranch in New Mexico a few years before and had been quite a bit more successful at it than our own undertaking in the Grand Canyon.

But Dad, according to Darian, "had taken all the fun out of camping" by doing everything himself. I didn't care—I was used to Dad being in charge and fussing around camp, which left me more time to fish, read, be lazy, or make out with my boyfriend.

Dad hadn't made Eagle, but when he was young he hiked Philmont like Darian. And Dad was my brother's troop leader for years, helping Brian get to Eagle back in 1993. I figured Darian and my dad would bond and I'd gain another guy to fish with. But Darian wasn't into fishing, considering it too slow, and seemed to get Dad's ire up. Dad told me weeks before he thought Darian was a bit sketchy, with his wallet chain and leather jacket, and I shouldn't date a wannabe artist who wouldn't be able to provide for me.

My dad wore a similar leather jacket when he was younger—it still hung in our coat closet—and telling me I shouldn't date Darian pushed me all the more toward him.

We survived the week together, taking short hikes and clowning around on the park playground equipment together, Dad included. It was too early for decent fishing, but the March weather was a wee bit warmer in Oklahoma than in Kansas, and I considered it a good week. Afterward, Darian would question my dad's oddities, but Dad had gotten comfortable enough with Darian to never knock or question him again.

I'd argue that most fathers, if not all, give their daughters' boyfriends some grief. And, I'd reckon most boyfriends, at least quietly, hold opinions about their girlfriends' fathers.

It took time for Dad to adjust to someone new. My bringing a boyfriend along on a weeklong campout was likely challenging to my dad, but he grew to like Darian over that week. And at the time, Darian, a laid-back guy, simply was pointing out that my dad had eccentricities and could be particular—wanting things a certain way. It would be another five years before hindsight upended the lot of us.

CHAPTER 18

Make a Place of Your Own

MAY 2001
MANHATTAN

It took five years, a mess of lousy grades, and a good deal of fretting, but I did get to walk across the Bramlage Coliseum stage in a black cap and gown to pick up my bachelor's in life science. But I stayed in college another two years. I was on the seven-year plan for slackers who liked to pile up student loans and didn't want to leave nice guys with kind eyes they were falling in love with. I wanted to become an elementary schoolteacher.

I didn't want to be the oldest individual to ever live in the dorms, so I moved to a small apartment a few miles west of campus. I started summer classes and took a job at a college retail store. Darian stayed in Manhattan during the summer also, working on campus and living with a few guys in an old, run-down house.

Darian and I would spend as much time together as we could manage around work and classes. On weekends, we would go hike the trails at Konza Prairie or Tuttle Creek. I'd attempt to cook him dinner, and we'd curl up on my couch to watch movies.

I wasn't sure about renting that apartment since it was on the second floor and the sliding-glass door was my only way in and out. But I called Dad, asking if he thought it would be safe, and we talked over location, lighting, and an escape plan. He told me it sounded fine; it was on a busy, well-lit corner, and if I had to, I could crawl out my bedroom window and drop down to the ground. When Dad helped me move from the dorms, he rigged up a broom handle I could wedge into the metal track when I was home.

When I was in seventh grade, I'd stayed with a friend, and her mom told us that not far from their house, someone had thrown a cinder block through a lady's sliding-glass door. The lady had gone missing and was later found murdered. I remember eyeing my friend's door warily. From that time on, I didn't like glass doors.

Ten years later, I called Dad to ask what he thought about the little place I wanted to rent. Then, four years after that, I learned he was the one who threw the cinder block through the sliding-glass door I was told about in seventh grade, the door that belonged to Mrs. Davis.

———

Living alone still ended up getting to me. When I got home in the evenings, I checked my utility and bedroom closets plus the space behind open doors, and I even whipped the shower curtain back, making sure the apartment hadn't been inundated with bad guys. The night terrors I'd had since I was little grew into full-on haunting.

Usually less than an hour after falling asleep, I would jolt, jump, kick, sometimes scream. Only vaguely awake, I was seized with terror, barely aware of myself or my surroundings. Sitting in bed, I'd look around in the dark, convinced someone, or something, was standing in my bedroom doorway, near my bed, or at the worst, in my bed.

My body would go from dead sleep to fight, flight, or freeze.

Maybe if I fight with all my might, I will survive.

Maybe if I lie here real still, it will go away.

My heart racing out of my chest, I'd bolt up, soaked with sweat—fully convinced this was it, this was the end. It felt as if I was losing years from my life.

I slept with my bedroom door locked and would have to convince myself it was okay to leave my bedroom to go pee. Sometimes when I woke up startled, instead of freezing I would wander around my tiny place, thinking or muttering, "The Lord is my light and my salvation—whom shall I fear? The Lord is the stronghold of my life—of whom shall I be afraid?"[1]

I'd walk around with my gigantic black Maglite, which served a dual purpose as flashlight and weapon, compulsively checking the lock on the front door and the broom handle.

Still in place.

I'd even check the slightest spaces around my furniture and kitchen appliances—it was humanly impossible for someone to be in those spots, but I'd check.

Something kept scaring me, and I was trying to find it.

Climbing up on the couch my folks passed on to me, I'd peer down into the dark space between it and the wall. I'd look behind the fridge and the slight space behind the stove.

All clear. Back to bed.

My parents knew I could flip out at night, but I didn't tell them how bad it had gotten. I didn't tell any doctors I saw at the on-campus health center for the occasional sore throat or klutzy injury. I knew my behavior was reaching extreme levels, but I didn't tell anyone how wigged out I could get—not even Darian.

I'd also face thunderstorms, but at least those perceived threats had actual potential to cause harm. A few times in the predawn dark, I rode out blaring tornado warnings, listening to my battery-operated radio, pressed up against a dryer in the corner of the community laundry room. It was on the first floor, with sturdy interior walls. (Out of hundreds of residents, I was the only one who did this.)

In August 2001, I went back to my weekday job at the dining center, worked at the retail store, and sold loads of purple merchandise out of a tent near the stadium during football games. On Sundays, I worked in an embroidery shop, trying to make tight ends meet.

In September, I was on campus when the World Trade Center was attacked. My science-methods teacher notified us at Bluemont Hall, and by the time I reached my music-methods class at McCain Auditorium, I heard the Pentagon had been hit and the towers had fallen.

My class canceled, I drudged over to Putnam Hall in shock, tears falling. I found Darian in the basement, along with many others, watching the coverage. As I learned about Flight 93 crashing in Pennsylvania, trying to comprehend what I was seeing, I grabbed Darian's hand. I drove back to my apartment later that day listening to the news on the radio and didn't know what to make of a sky devoid of planes.

I drove home three days later, and Dad hugged me tight, his eyes wet with tears as he handed me a stack of the *Eagle*'s front sections, which I read through, then saved.

I fell into a hole of sadness, fear, and uncertainty after 9/11. Depressed, stressed, stretched too thin from work and school, I became sick. After struggling for several weeks, and a doctor telling me I was nearing pneumonia, I cut back on work and dropped several classes, setting myself back another semester. My parents helped me, bringing boxes of food to stretch my grocery budget and making sure I could cover rent.

In the spring of 2002, I retook the classes I had to drop in the fall and had only one more semester before starting student teaching full-time. In the summer, Darian went to Orlando for an internship with Campus Crusade and I fell into a crisis. I lost my retail job for failure to show up on time. To console myself I colored my hair, getting copper-red dye all over my white-tiled bathroom.

Not able to find another job, broke, I ended up staying with my parents part of the summer. To earn my keep and continue to pay rent on my place back in Manhattan, I offered to help with home improvement work. I turned Brian's old bedroom into a guest room, painting over the dark-blue walls with a cheerful lilac, painted the bathroom yellow, and helped my mom wallpaper the kitchen.

Darian helped me get through my lousy summer, calling long-distance and surprising me with a shipment of long-stem roses in soft pinks, whites, and purples.

In the fall of 2002, Darian and I were driving back from our good friend's wedding when I became peeved. While he was re-fueling his car, I inquired—by yelling—"When are *you* ever going to ask *me* to marry you?"

He said, "I'm working on that very thing—trying to save up money for a ring."

Oh.

We shopped for rings not long after at a family jewelry store on Poyntz Avenue near the mall in Manhattan. He proposed in November, getting on one knee in my apartment after dinner out at our favorite Thai place.

I was thrilled to be home with a princess-cut solitaire to show off at Thanksgiving. Over winter break, Mom and I hit up the after-Christmas sales at Hobby Lobby for decorations in my wedding colors, silver and burgundy. We also went wedding dress shopping, buying the second one I tried on: A-line, strapless, with embroidered butterflies zooming all over the bodice and skirt.

I spent the last semester of college off campus, student teaching fourth grade in Riley, a small town northwest of Manhattan. When my car finally shot the last of its life in February 2003, Darian loaned me his Chevy Corsica till my parents were able to bring up their Ford Tempo. It was a sacrifice on their part, shorting them a car, but much appreciated by their twenty-four-year-old daughter, who just needed to get through the last of her extremely long stay in college.

A month before I graduated, Dad drove up to Manhattan, picking me up for a weekend at Glen Elder. My brother met us at the lake too. I don't remember having much luck fishing that trip, but it felt good to be out under the blue sky. Dad drove me back on a warm Sunday afternoon, and we stopped at Sonic before heading back to my place.

He saw me in, hugged me goodbye, and with his hands on my shoulders encouraged me "to finish out strong." He told me he loved me and would see me soon. I stood on my wooden deck in front of my sliding-glass door and waved goodbye to him, watching as he drove off till I couldn't see him anymore.

CHAPTER 19

Head Down the Wedding Aisle, Even If You Have to Hobble

JULY 2003
WICHITA

O h, man. My glasses broke." It was the night before my wedding, near the end of July 2003, it was past midnight, and I was sitting at my parents' kitchen table, fretting.

"Let me see." Dad sat down next to me. I handed him the two pieces. "Hmm, we're not going to be able to fix these. The nose piece has broken in half."

"Darn. I still need to pack too."

"Well, kiddo, you better go do that, and we'll see about getting you a new pair of glasses in the morning before the wedding." Dad looked assured, although his eyes had been giving him away over the past month; his baby girl was getting married and moving sixteen hours away. I'm not sure he knew what to do about it.

Back in June, Darian called to tell me, "We're moving to Detroit."

It wasn't a question, asking if I wanted to move to Detroit. It was a statement.

We needed jobs, any jobs, anywhere in the country, and Detroit was it. Darian had been offered a graphic designer job, which he'd accepted and agreed to start a week after our wedding.

I hung up the phone. "Hey, Mom, we're moving to Detroit!"

She nearly spilled the spaghetti she was draining in the sink.

I had graduated (again) in May 2003 and moved back in with my parents for the few months before my wedding. I now had two degrees and no job.

In June, Darian flew to Detroit to meet his new company and find us an apartment in the western suburbs of the metro area. He called, saying, "I found a six-hundred-square-foot two-bedroom. It has a large picture window that looks out onto a small, green park. I picked it because of the view—for you."

I agreed it sounded perfect, and he put down our deposit.

A few weeks before the wedding, I was quickly rounding our kitchen corner, and I stepped into Dad's green toolbox he'd carelessly left open on the floor next to the stove. I fell, spraining ligaments in the same ankle I'd twisted in the canyon years before. Dad barked at me as if it was somehow my fault I'd gotten hurt.

The words stung, but I was used to it. He had been hard on Mom and me for our klutziness since I was little, repeatedly saying things like, "Watch where you're going! Be more careful! It's your fault you fell. Now you've done it. If you end up covered in scars, it'll make you ugly, and no one will want to marry you."

I spent the next few weeks hobbling around in a black lace-up brace, wondering how my fat, swollen ankle was going to fit into my petite cream heels. I rarely wore heels, but Mom insisted on them under my wedding dress. I would have preferred to get married barefoot, bum ankle or not.

Two days before our wedding, several members of our family helped us decorate Darian's church and reception space, which was larger than my parents' church. We wound twinkling white lights onto white canopies overlooking cake stands and hung silver and burgundy bows from wooden pews. In the sanctuary, I called out for help to Dave, my soon-to-be father-in-law, who gently replied, "You can call me Dad if you want."

"Okay. I like that."

Dave was a bit taller than Darian, with a head full of silvery-white hair. Darian's mom, Dona, petite with brown hair and a sparkle in her eyes, was busy scurrying from project to project. Warm and welcoming, his parents always made me feel included and often made me laugh—traits carried over in their son.

In the midst of decorating, I stepped outside onto a fire escape for some air; I was a stressed-out hot mess. Darian joined me, calmly handing me my engagement ring, already soldered to my wedding band. When I lifted it to the light, I was startled to read the inscription: *Love neve fails.*

The *r* was missing.

I lifted Darian's band. His was right: *Love never fails.*

Oh well.

We were moving to Michigan three days after our wedding, so I didn't get it fixed. To this day, it's still not fixed. *Love neve fails.*

On the morning of my wedding day, I woke up early, groggy-eyed, with broken glasses but my bag packed. By ten o'clock, I was waiting at the mall for the gate to be lifted at LensCrafters, my hair curled in ribbons, my nails freshly done in dark burgundy.

Peering into the closed store, I picked out my new wire-rims. I surprised the clerk when I said, "It's my wedding day. I get married in three hours, I need new glasses, and those right there—they will work just fine."

At noon, Dad, wearing his black suit and tie, picked up my glasses so I could see my own wedding and groom.

We gathered for photos before our wedding, huge smiles on our faces: Darian in a black tuxedo with a white vest and tie, me tall in my heels, desiring to spin like a princess with my fluttering butterflies and tulle veil set behind a sparkly headband.

Darian's groomsmen, including his brother, Eron, wore black suits and silver ties. My cousin Andrea and two of my friends were bridesmaids, wearing burgundy dresses with matching necklaces and earrings.

At one o'clock on Saturday, July 26, 2003, Dad looked at me as we waited in the vestibule. He was full of emotion, trying to hold back tears and nerves. He extended his arm and said, "You ready?"

Taking a deep breath, I took his arm, holding a bouquet of white roses ringed in burgundy daisies in my other hand, and we slowly set down the aisle to "Canon in D Major."

Near the front of the church, my foot slightly twisted and I bumped into a strand of flowers hanging from a pew, knocking them down with a thud. Red-faced, I gave Darian a half smile and a shrug, then turned toward Dad and hugged him tight.

Verses from 1 Corinthians were read: "Love does not delight in evil but rejoices with the truth. It always protects, always trusts, always hopes, always perseveres. Love never fails."[1]

We said our vows, sticking to a modern exchange; there was no plighting anyone's troth.

Darian's eyes were full of happiness, but I chattered nervously to him during our song "Come What May" from *Moulin Rouge*. I was immensely relieved when the pastor dismissed us as husband and wife, and we flew back down the aisle to Third Day's "I've Always Loved You."

After our receiving line, I stopped Darian on the stairs to our reception so I could remove my heels, thankful to be barefoot under my dress. At the reception, we tried to make it around to everyone to say goodbye. And it hit me: we would be leaving Kansas in three days. All of a sudden I felt homesick.

Outside, Darian's red Corsica awaited us, festively decorated, brimming full of balloons. After breaking through rolls of plastic wrap, we were greeted with a blast of bright-colored confetti from the air conditioner.

We honeymooned the next two nights in a suite in Old Town, and on Monday, we picked up a new mattress and jammed a moving truck full, with the help of our families. Monday night, wiped out and trying to save money, we settled for Darian's parents' basement.

He gave me the couch and slept on the floor with his blue heeler, Skipper.

Early Tuesday, Dad drove the moving van and Mom rode along. They took the Indiana route after Saint Louis, giving us newlyweds a few days to ourselves. We set out for Illinois in the Corsica, our AC breaking while crossing the sweltering Midwest the first day. We quickly blamed the confetti still occasionally spitting out at us.

Wednesday evening, after a detour to Chicago to shop at IKEA, we passed a large, blue Welcome to Michigan sign. I was mesmerized by the cooler air and majestic pine trees as we crossed I-94 to Detroit. We arrived late to our hotel and were surprised to hear my parents' voices directly across the hallway from our room. *So much for the honeymoon.*

The next morning, Darian and Dad unloaded the truck while Mom and I went to rent a car for their return trip home. That evening, surrounded by boxes and unwilling to search for our new bedsheets or anything else we needed—we splurged for one last night in a hotel.

On Friday morning, we said goodbye to my parents, Mom and I both in tears after butting heads the day before. I had tried to push them away because I didn't want them to leave, just as I had seven years before in college. Dad was more matter-of-fact as he hugged me tight, his daughter was grown up and married. Helping us move was his way of showing love.

It would be nine months before we would see them, or any other family, again.

CHAPTER 20

Some Carpet Cleaners Can Leave Unexpected Results

Your dad has been coming home late, playing catch-up with a pile of paperwork. He's stressed out—you know how he can get. Wanna talk to him?" Mom and I were chatting on the phone, just as we had every week for the past nine years.

I talked to Dad for about ten minutes, not about anything much—the tire tread on our old car, making sure to keep up with oil changes, and how the weather was (surprisingly nice for February in Wichita, cold and lousy in Michigan).

"All right, well, you stay warm, kiddo. Proud of you and Darian, making it there. Love you."

Making it there. It had been more like make it or break it, sink or swim. Whatever was said to young couples.

Darian's job started three days after we moved, but he wasn't paid for a month, so we lived off wedding money and a cashed-in life insurance policy from his folks our first weeks. While Darian was working, I alternated between unpacking, applying for teaching jobs, and wigging out, eating cheese puffs by the handfuls and watching *Days of Our Lives.*

I thought getting married and moving was going to be one big, fun adventure. But the reality of being far from home soon landed.

Not long after we moved in, the flimsy storage area in our apartment building's basement was broken into. We only had boxes in ours, but I grew fearful downstairs in the dark basement while doing laundry. I started waiting for Darian to come home before hauling the loads up and down the stairs. I didn't even want to park in the garage under our apartment, deciding instead to park near our building's front door when I was alone.

My night terrors also caught up with us after we were married. I'd wake up screaming in Darian's ear or landing a solid punch or kick. He'd jump while I fumbled for the light. "It's okay. You're okay. You're safe. Go back to sleep. It's okay."

"It's not—there's a man over in the corner."

"No. That's our pile of laundry."

Oh.

"But I was sure I saw—"

"No. Nothing there. It's okay. You're okay. You're safe. Try to sleep." He'd pull me close to his chest, blocking out the world with his body.

A few weeks after we moved in, our power went out late on a Thursday afternoon. I heard we were under another terrorist attack on my battery-operated radio, and when I couldn't reach Darian at work, in a panic I called his father, who was usually home from work by four o'clock.

Dave reassured me. It wasn't terrorism; it was a blackout in a good chunk of the northeastern and midwestern United States. Darian would be home as soon as he could be, Dave said. With the streetlights out, it took Darian two hours to drive the normal twenty minutes.

On Friday, I was hot and miserable with an earache and fever and asked if we could escape to Indiana where there was electricity. I pressed my head into the passenger-side window while Darian meandered far into the metro area, in search of an open gas station.

On fumes, we sat in a long line of cars, paying with rolled coins— our laundry money, the only cash we had on us. With enough fuel, we booked it south toward two nights of hot food, showers, and air-conditioning paid by credit card.

We arrived back home Sunday evening to a stinky apartment, a fridge full of groceries gone to waste, and more debt. I googled nearby doctors, was diagnosed with an ear infection and put on antibiotics. We got in more of a bind the next week when our bank misplaced our deposit, shorting us—blaming the blackout.

In October, after struggling for two months to find a teaching job, I gave up, deciding any job would do. I had a student loan to pay. I saw a poster for seasonal work at Target and was soon hired for second shift and weekends.

We only had the Corsica, so I'd drive Darian to work in the mornings; then I'd go to work in the afternoons. Darian would hitch a ride to my nearby store, pick up the car, and come back after my shift was over. We'd often run through Taco Bell for a fourth meal and crash, doing it all over the next day.

On evenings off, we sat in camp chairs that kept breaking, ate at a folding table, and watched *Hockey Night in Canada* through a foil-wrapped antenna connected to a flickering green-tinted television that had fallen during the move.

A few weeks after my job started, fed up with our lousy chairs, I declared to Darian, "That's it! We're buying a couch!"

Soon, a dark-eggplant couch and loveseat from Art Van were delivered. Propped up backward on the loveseat, I spent a lot of time staring out our picture window at the changing colors, missing the open air of Kansas.

I got darn homesick those first months; I wanted to click my heels and land back in the wheat fields, like Dorothy. We figured we would quickly find a church in Michigan, make new friends, and get settled. But we only visited a few churches before I started working Sundays.

During the fall, we had a few dinners out with some of Darian's coworkers and shared our first Thanksgiving with a couple who didn't have family in Michigan either. But most of the time, it was just the two of us.

I remember calling my mom in December in tears, letting her know we couldn't make it home for Christmas due to my job—I would be working Christmas Eve and the days following Christmas. Darian and I had a quiet Christmas Day, opening gifts that had been shipped to us, next to a simple tree we bought with my discount. I made Christmas dinner for two, and it was back to a busy store the next day.

It was just Darian and me against the world. Occasionally we'd get into it, but it was *still* just him and me.

One winter evening, we got into a silly fight about nothing I can remember, and I threw foot powder at him. I ran off to the bedroom but came back out when I heard the door slam, surprised to find a profanity sprinkled in the carpet.

Soon Darian came back home with carpet cleaner, and later I heard the vacuum.

That night, he broke in the couch after I tossed his pillow and a small blanket out in the hall. The next morning there was nothing to do but fall over and giggle when I saw a faint *swear word* stained permanently into the carpet.

He told me off with foot powder and made it worse with carpet cleaner.

In the new year, my temporary job became permanent, and we were able to buy a new TV and entertainment center, delivered in time for the Super Bowl. No more green-tinted sports for us. We also got word my folks would be visiting in May and his parents in June. Knowing family was coming in the spring helped pull me through our first long, dreary winter.

CHAPTER 21

Don't Say Goodbye— Say See Ya in a While

MAY 2004

The cherry trees were blooming when my family arrived in Michigan at the beginning of May. Dad, Mom, and Brian arrived on Mom's birthday, after driving two days in my parents' new minivan. I'd anxiously been fluttering around the apartment all day and was nearly dancing on my toes by the time they rang the buzzer.

"An authentic experience" is what Dad called Mom's birthday dinner at a favorite Italian restaurant that night, a family place nestled in a small downtown area a few miles east of where we lived.

The next day, we left for a short trip to the west coast of Michigan while Darian stayed behind, working. In Holland, we spent the afternoon walking up and down rows of brightly colored tulips at a farm, where Mom bought a blue-and-white pitcher for her collection. That evening, we walked out on the pier to the Big Red Lighthouse and watched the sun lower onto Lake Michigan from a sugar-soft beach.

Near Ludington, the next morning, Dad, Brian, and I hiked the steep, tree-covered dunes at P. J. Hoffmaster State Park, working our way down to Lake Michigan, whose chilly waves broke on my bare feet for the first time. We etched the sand with driftwood we trailed behind us and watched the water quickly erase our footprints.

Later that week we spent the day with Darian, meandering around the massive exhibit hall at the Henry Ford museum in Dearborn. That evening, we had dinner in Greektown and took a turn at the slot machines at the casino.

A Welcome Rader Family sign greeted us from a small motel in Frankenmuth later that week. We weren't sure we'd ever get Dad out of Bronner's, the world's largest Christmas store, after he spotted the miniature towns, festively decorated, with trains running in circles.

We dropped Mom off to shop the next morning while Dad, Brian, and I drove along the coast of Lake Huron, stopping at a wooden walkway along the Au Sable River to watch for bald eagles. I'd come to this spot with Darian the October before, catching a glimpse of an eagle fishing. That afternoon, I was thrilled to stand next to Dad as two eagles fought and tumbled in the sky for a few moments.

Dad let me choose where to go on the map that day and told me on our way back to pick up Mom that I'd chosen well. I thought it was the first of many family trips to Michigan, but I couldn't have been more wrong.

I had no idea we were just months away from the world crashing down on us. If anyone should have known, it would have been Dad. But that's impossible to say—then or now.

JULY 2004

During the summer of 2004, I read about the BTK serial killer who had resurfaced after decades of silence in Wichita. He had committed seven murders in the 1970s and sent taunting letters to the police and media, but then ceased communication in 1979. It had been assumed he was dead or in prison. But in the spring of 2004, he claimed an eighth murder from 1986 and started mailing letters and leaving drops, similar to his behavior in the 1970s. This led to an immense manhunt.

This was the first I'd heard of the murders or the infamous acronym. I was surprised and taken aback by the news that this was happening back home, but I don't recall following the local Wichita news closely in 2004.

I do remember two things: I mentioned the manhunt to Darian, who had read about it also. And sometime that summer or fall, I asked Mom on the phone about the murders in the 1970s. She told me that at the time a lot of women were fearful. She had been scared, since Dad would sometimes work late and was taking night classes at WSU—but Dad had reassured her, told her not to worry, she was safe.

In the late fall, I read about the new possible attributes of BTK. I remember puzzling over the list—coming back to it a few times because it was nagging at me.

BTK had written to the police that he had a cousin in Missouri and a grandfather who played the fiddle and died of lung disease. His father died in World War II. He was in the military in the 1960s, had a lifelong fascination with trains, and always lived near a railroad.[1]

I kept thinking of a hazy, dreamlike image of a white house with black trim and a train running right near it, close enough to rattle the windows. A house like my grandparents' house. But that didn't make any sense.

I determined the list was odd but couldn't make anything solid from it, and I dropped it when I heard in December there had been an arrest. It ended up being a false arrest, and I don't remember following the news after that.

Hindsight would come hurtling down soon enough, but I'm not alone in thinking my ordinary, normal, everyman dad was the last person on earth who could be BTK.

In September, I started substitute teaching in five districts. The farthest district was an hour away, so it was rough having to drive Darian to work and then out west to reach a classroom by nine at the latest. The pay was good, though, and I soon quit my job at Target, delighted to have evenings and weekends free to spend with Darian.

After being laid off from his avionics job in Wichita, my brother enlisted in the navy and commenced boot camp, located north of Chicago, in the fall. He invited us and my folks to his graduation ceremony in early November, after which he would be headed to the East Coast for submarine school and then out to sea for months at a time.

I was hopeful my folks could come to Chicago so we could spend a few days together, but Dad told us they couldn't make it, saying he was too busy to get away. I was unsure what to think; that was extremely uncharacteristic of my dad. But with Chicago only four hours away for us, Darian and I were able to drive over for a long weekend. On an early Friday morning, we cheered as Brian marched in with his shipmates.

After his ceremony, he gave us a hug, happy to see us and to get off base to spend a couple of days sightseeing. On our walk to the Shedd Aquarium that afternoon, stinging wind blasted us, and Brian had to grab his white sailor's cap so it wouldn't blow into Lake Michigan. The next day, we enjoyed the sun as we wandered around the Brookfield Zoo. Brian told us he might be able to fly home for Christmas; Darian and I already had our plane tickets and said we hoped to see him.

DECEMBER 2004

Several inches of snow fell the night before we were supposed to fly home in December, and the world was still a blur of bluish-gray when we left in the predawn darkness for the airport. Darian was calm as he cautiously made his way down the one cleared lane of the highway, but I was gripping the passenger armrest with white knuckles.

We reached the airport in time but found out at our gate that our plane was delayed and we were going to miss our connection at O'Hare. Between the snow, the delay, and having only flown twice in my life, I was an anxious mess, but Darian handed me a hazelnut latte and said we'd get home. He was used to flying and patiently talked me through the next several hours of holiday travel despondency while I wrapped my hands around my drink, trying to warm my entire body.

When we arrived in O'Hare hours later, we had to wait in a long line to rebook a flight for the next day and to secure a hotel. We stood in another long line to pick up our checked bags, only to learn they had continued to their destination. I only packed the bare minimum in my carry-on and froze in my thin hoodie outside; my winter coat, gloves, and hat were on a plane to Kansas.

We headed back to the airport on Christmas Eve and found out we were going to have to make a connection through Saint Louis to reach Wichita.

So much for Christmas Eve service with my family at church.

While sitting at the gate in Saint Louis, Darian's name was called to come to the desk—they wanted to bump him. I started crying, telling the attendant the story of the last two days.

"Oh, I didn't realize you were traveling together."

A man traveling alone overheard my tale of woe and offered to take the bump. I was so relieved, I could have hugged him; we were going to be home for Christmas just in time.

We crashed in my parents' guest room, the one I painted lilac two years before, and opened gifts the next morning. I will never forget my dad's face, aged overnight, his eyes oddly sad on Christmas morning, when he unwrapped a special frame for Brian's naval photograph.

A few evenings later, Darian and I went with Dad back to the airport to pick up Brian. He was wearing his US Navy blues and carrying a green duffel bag, which my dad hefted onto his shoulder after embracing Brian in a big hug. While Brian was home, we went to a movie at the Warren Old Town theater, a place Dad considered extra nifty because you could order food right at your seat. After having hotdogs and fries, Dad and I passed back and forth the largest tub of buttered popcorn you could get.

It's odd, the things one remembers, like looking to my left and watching my dad try to open a mustard packet with his teeth—just like I'd do.

But I can't recall what movie we saw.

What I can tell you is this—it was the last movie I'd ever see with him.

A few days later, we were up early to pack before our flight back to Michigan. I had stepped out of our bedroom and run into Dad in the hallway. He was dressed for work in his brown compliance officer uniform.

Before leaving, he added a stack of note cards to his right breast pocket, a dark-brown winter coat with a badge, a dark-brown hat, and an intimidating utility belt. The belt had a collapsible stick baton, mace, a Leatherman multitool, a knife, and Lord knows what else.

He was freshly shaven and smelled of Old Spice, and I embraced him in a long bear hug. He was warm, solid—comforting—and I didn't want to let go. "I'm not sure when we will get home again," I said.

"Yeah. We're going to try to come up to see you guys again soon, all right?"

"All right, love you. See ya in a while."

"Yeah, love you too. See ya in a while."

Just a girl telling her dad goodbye. I had no reason to think that was the last time I'd ever see him.

THURSDAY, FEBRUARY 24, 2005

"Yeah, love you too. Talk to you soon."

After the phone call with my folks, I pulled a chocolate Bundt cake out of the oven and set to work on the powdered sugar icing while it cooled. Darian and I ate a slice before going to bed, not knowing that by the same time tomorrow, our lives would be completely upended.

The last phone call.

When you lose someone, there are always lasts. The last hug, the last Christmas, the last vacation. The last chocolate milkshake, the last fishing trip, the last time you hiked side by side next to the person you loved.

As soon as you learn there is a last, you do your best to seal those memories tight.

Even in my case, in which the man I lost was still very much alive. Even in my case, where every memory I have of the man I love will be tainted with pitch black for years to come.

PART IV

When All Else Has Fallen Away

So do not fear, for I am with you; do not be dismayed, for I am your God. I will strengthen you and help you; I will uphold you with my righteous right hand.

—ISAIAH 41:10

BREAKING NEWS: WE INTERRUPT A REGULARLY SCHEDULED LIFE

12:15 P.M.
FEBRUARY 25, 2005
WICHITA

The suspected BTK killer, Dennis Lynn Rader, age fifty-nine, was pulled over and arrested while driving home from work in his white city truck at 12:15 p.m. today.

Rader, who has been on the lam for thirty-one years, was en route to have lunch with his wife of thirty-three years, Paula, age fifty-six. They had met for lunch every weekday for the past fourteen years at their three-bedroom ranch in the small suburban community of Park City.

Rader was arrested around the corner from his house, right near the crosswalk his kids used for years on their way to the nearby elementary school. Rader and his daughter, Kerri, age twenty-six, took long walks with their spaniels—Patches and, later, Dudley—around the school and nearby neighborhoods throughout her younger years.

With several guns pointed at him, including a shotgun and a submachine gun, Rader was detained without incident, handcuffed facedown on the pavement, right above the large drainage pipes his daughter liked to play in as a kid.

One of the first things Rader said after being arrested was, "Hey, would you please call my wife? She was expecting me for lunch. I assume you know where I live."[1]

CHAPTER 22

Offer the FBI Your DNA— It's Just Easier That Way

1:30 P.M.
FEBRUARY 25, 2005
DETROIT

Your dad is BTK."

I was spinning in the middle of our living room, trying to make the short distance to our dark-eggplant couch, trying to come back to life—trying to breathe. Trying to steady myself against the weight of the incomprehensible words the FBI agent had uttered.

Your dad is BTK.

Love never fails.

A moment ago, my hand had brushed against the brightly colored stained-glass picture hanging in our kitchen.

My left thumb twisted my wedding band with its inscription.

Love neve fails.

Darian—I needed Darian.

I grabbed on to the tall arm of the couch and turned toward the worried-looking man holding his yellow legal pad and pencil to his side. He was standing right near the worn cuss-word spot in the carpet. I was tempted to point out the faded words to him.

"Can I call my husband at work? He needs to come home."

"Yes. You can call him, but you can't tell him why I am here."

I sat down and called Darian's cell phone, shaking, my body blazing white-hot, my voice almost maniacal, with the oddest feeling of being on edge yet relieved the man in the car, in my home, with the badge, wasn't here to hurt me.

"Hello?"

"The FBI is here. It's okay. I'm safe."

"Where? What are you talking about?"

"The man? He's an FBI agent."

"What man?"

"The one in the car by the dumpster. He's in our home now. He's an FBI agent. You need to come home."

"I'm on my way already. What is going on? Why is he there?" Darian's voice was heightening with concern and confusion.

"I can't tell you on the phone. Can you come home?"

"I'm close. Be there shortly."

I hung up and looked at the agent again. "Can I call my grandma and granddad? They live near us—near my folks. I'm really worried about my mom, my family."

"You can call them, but you can't tell them about your dad."

I was already dialing. "Grandma, it's Kerri. Something has happened at Mom and Dad's. Mom is safe, she is with the police, but Dad has been arrested."

"Hold on, Kerri. I'm going to walk to the corner and I will call you back. Hold on."

When she called me back, she told me there was a swarm of police and other unmarked cars down the street at my house. Grandma was scared and worried. Soon, she and Granddad would be brought in for questioning too.

The agent sat down next to me, and that made me feel a bit better. I ran my hand through my hair and nervously redid my scrunchie, looking down at my mint-green PJs. "Uh, can I get dressed?"

"Yes. But the phone has to stay here."

I left my silver flip phone and somehow made it off the couch and down the hall to our bedroom. I tossed my pajamas to the floor (I'd never wear them again) and threw on a purple K-State T-shirt and jeans. I didn't even close the door when I changed.

As I came back out to the living room still in my bare feet, I heard keys rattling in the front door lock. The FBI agent looked at me, looked at the door, and stood up.

"It's okay. It's my husband, Darian."

Darian came in quickly and headed straight to the agent, his shoulders forward like a hockey defenseman, putting himself between me and the stranger. "What's going on? Who are you? Why are you here?"

The agent told him.

Darian was skeptical. "Can I see your badge?"

The agent showed it to him, and Darian excused himself to the bathroom, where he proceeded to call the Detroit FBI office, thinking someone must be playing a terrible joke on us.

They told him it was a real agent in our house.

Darian came back out and sat down by me, pressing his leg next to mine, taking my hand. I pressed up next to him. His body was tense, his shoulders down. I could tell from his eyes he was shocked and confused, scared like me.

The agent shifted his feet and cleared his throat. "I've been sent here by my office to notify you that your father has been arrested and to ask you some questions. I'm not used to this type of fieldwork. I'm more like an investigative accountant—white-collar crimes. I can see you're having a hard time. I'm a bit thrown myself."

I knew this guy wasn't like the FBI agents you see in the movies.

"I don't understand." I was stammering. "You think Dad—he's . . . he's . . . this . . . this guy the police have been looking for? The one from the seventies?"

"Yes, we have reason to believe so."

I stared off into nowhere for some seconds, then shook my head.

"That's not possible. In December, back in Wichita? The wrong guy was arrested. Maybe there is some kind of confusion again. Maybe Dad was trying to solve the crimes? Got himself tangled up in something somehow? You know, communicating with the police, maybe?" I was searching the agent's face, hopeful for something, *anything*, to make sense.

"I talked to Dad on the phone last night. He hasn't ever done anything wrong. He's a good guy." Rapidly I ran through my dad's credentials: military service, jobs, church president, Boy Scout leader, dutiful son. Darian spoke up when he could.

The agent said, "You could be describing me."

"Yes. He's a normal, regular guy. That's what I'm trying to say. That's him." I pointed to a photo of my dad and mom together hanging on the wall. They were dressed up and smiling; it had been taken for the church directory.

The agent looked at the picture, a bit puzzled, and down at his pad. "Your dad store things in your house? Containers?"

"He collects stamps. Those take up some space."

The agent scribbled on his notepad.

I stared off into nowhere again, then looked back at the agent. "What dates are we talking about? The crimes?"

"The years '74, '77, '86."

"Brian was born in '75."

He looked down at his notes. "Yes."

"And '86? What month?"

"September."

"We went to California, Disneyland, the month before—in August? Before third grade."

"Oh. Do you remember anything from September '86?"

"In '86? Third grade? I was eight. Dad worked at ADT, drove a white truck with a red ladder. The smaller one, not the big box van like he used to. Installed alarm systems in people's homes. Someone was murdered in '86, in Wichita?"

"Yes."

"That's not possible, I mean, Dad couldn't have . . . Dad's not . . . You guys got it wrong." I was off looking into space again.

Our neighbor was murdered down the street. Strangled. It was never solved.

Terror seized me. I closed my eyes tight, putting my head down. *Something is very wrong. BTK strangled women—and it was likely very true.*

Tears stung my eyes. I turned to Darian, my face wide with fear, my mouth open. I hadn't cried yet because I was too shocked. But now the tears began and wouldn't stop for a long time.

I turned toward the agent, dropping my eyes and wiping my face on my sleeve. I then wrapped my arms tightly around my chest and said quietly, "Our neighbor, Mrs. Hedge? She was murdered down our street. Lived between us and my grandparents. Her body was found out in the country, strangled. It was never solved, I don't think. Mom and Dad used to talk about a man who had taken her to dinner; she was a widow. But I don't think he was ever charged. I don't remember. I was young."

"When was this?" The agent's eyes stayed calm, his voice steady. He wasn't writing on his notepad anymore.

"Uh, '84? It was the end of first grade—I broke my arm at church around then. Before? After? I'm not sure." I counted on my fingers, thinking of years and school. "Oh, '85. Early May, I think. I was six—I turned seven in June."

I took a sharp breath.

"I lost my front tooth down at the river—Riverfest, we were at the bathtub races. I tripped walking back to the car with Mom and lost my tooth in a red snow cone. Then the next day, I broke my arm, bad. Was in the hospital for days after. Got pins and everything." I held up my scarred right elbow to the agent, like I always did when telling that story to someone.

Dad wasn't home that night.

My stomach sheared again. I squeezed my eyes shut tight, then slowly opened them and searched the agent's face. "Dad wasn't home the night she went missing. He was on a campout with my brother. Brian was nine, close to ten. Scouts, maybe?"

"How do you know your dad wasn't home?"

"It stormed that night. I was scared. Thunder rattles our home—sometimes the house shakes. I crawled into bed with Mom. I wouldn't have if Dad was home. Slept on his side of the bed. Did that sometimes when he was gone. I only remember that night because our neighbor lady went missing. Mom and Grandma Eileen were scared. My arm wasn't broken yet. I must have broken it after she went missing."

"You knew this Mrs. Hedge?"

"A little, yeah. Mom and I would talk to her when we walked past her house going to my grandparents' house. She'd be out in the yard. I remember her leaning on a rake, waving hello once. She was nice." I paused to think. "I was sad when I heard she had been killed. Scared too. Didn't want to walk by her house anymore. Would cross the street so I didn't have to be so close to it. Mom would have to coax me past."

More thinking. "A cop came by. I was bouncing on my pogo stick in my driveway. So . . . no broken arm yet. Asked my mom some questions, after she went missing. He was talking to all the neighbors."

"She went missing, you think, in early May 1985, and later that month you broke your arm?"

"Yeah."

"Do you remember anything else?"

"Dad didn't. I mean . . ." I stopped talking and was off looking into nowhere again.

"I need to make some phone calls," the agent said as he stood up.

We offered him our spare room we had turned into storage space and a small corner office for me.

When the agent came back he said, "Would it be okay to take a DNA swab from you? We need to match it to some samples we have."

The agent didn't have a kit, wasn't prepared. Standing in the living room, the three of us talked through this perplexity for a bit. My mind latched on to this solid problem—something tangible I could do and think about that wasn't Dad.

I finally said, "I can grab a couple of cotton swabs and resealable sandwich bags, and you can swab my mouth?"

Shaking, I went and got the items we needed while the agent called our local police department. He was thinking we might need to head down to their headquarters for collection.

We settled on taking the samples ourselves, standing in the kitchen in front of the Bundt cake. I swabbed the inside of my cheek with the cotton swab and dropped it into the bag. I repeated the process, at some point, joking, "This is how they do it on *CSI*."

All reality was lost.

The agent handed me his business card with his phone numbers. (I carried his card in my purse for years, but today, I can't remember his name.)

"The FBI recommends you don't talk to the media. It can make things worse."

Why would the media be trying to talk to us? Make what worse?

He picked the bags up from the counter, bid us farewell, and left. We never saw him again.

I walked down our hallway, gently lifted the picture of my dad and mom off the wall, and set it in my closet, facing the wall. That was the last picture of my dad I'd ever have. I'd never put his picture on display again. He'd soon be on the front of all the newspapers and on TV anyway.

CHAPTER 23

All Reality Can Sometimes Be Lost

2:30 P.M.
FEBRUARY 25, 2005

On the way home, I thought the FBI was at the apartment because I'd accidentally downloaded something I wasn't supposed to."

If only that was it.

Darian ran his hand through his hair, letting it rest there for a few moments, like he was stunned motionless.

There is a man . . . FBI . . . your dad is . . . Dad can't be.

"I need to call my parents, my brother . . ." Darian was pacing, occasionally walking over to his desk, jotting a note to himself. We had placed his computer desk in the corner of our living room so I could be near him, lounging on the couch, reading, or watching TV, while he sometimes worked late.

Dad can't be. Dad is. A man. FBI.

My mind wandered again; I hadn't heard him.

"Kerri? We need to go tell my boss. Okay? And Kerri, can you cancel any teaching assignments you have for the next few weeks?" Darian's voice was fading in and out, out and in.

Cancel work.

I stared for some seconds and came back to Darian talking.

He was looking at me, concerned, his eyes searching mine. "Kerri? Never mind. Don't move, stay on the couch. I'm going to pull down our family website. It might be a few weeks before the cache clears, though—and make a few phone calls, okay? Kerri, have you had lunch?"

Huh? Website? Cache?

"Lunch. No. Not hungry."

"You need to eat. We'll go pick something up. Let me call my dad first. Okay?"

Okay.

The neighbor lady had gone missing. She was murdered. Dad wasn't home.

I was wearing a sleeveless light-blue nightgown with tiny white flowers, I was sweaty—it got hot in the house when we lost power after a storm.

They found her in the country.

What if Dad . . . ? No. Dad had an alibi—he was camping . . .

I lay down on the couch and rolled up into the fetal position.

I broke my arm at church. I was six. Mom told me, twenty minutes before, "Get down out of those pine trees before you fall and break your arm."

My elbow came out of my skin. They called it a compound fracture.

Maybe if I lie here real still, I will stop shaking and the world will stop spinning and buzzing like it's white-hot on fire.

Dad slid a tray decorated with pink flowers under my deformed arm and wrapped it in dish towels.

Dad carried me out of church, placing me in the back of our silver Oldsmobile station wagon. Mom rode in the back with me, gently stroking my hair and face. Dad drove to Wesley, going over the train tracks as slowly as he could as I let out screams with each bump.

Maybe if I lie here real still . . .

I was put on a gurney out in the emergency drive-up.

They did X-rays. I got Cinderella stickers for cooperating.

They took me to surgery a few hours later.

I kept arguing with the nurses in the freezing room, as I was falling asleep, that my name was Nancy.

Maybe if I lie here real still . . .

I wasn't able to finish first grade.

We couldn't go to Padre Island in June.

Dad wasn't pleased our trip was canceled—all 'cause of me and my broken arm with the three metal pins sticking out that had to be wiped with stinky brown iodine every day.

I disappointed him. He wanted to go away on vacation.

Our neighbor lady had gone missing. Then I broke my arm at church.

I was six.

Maybe if I lie here real still . . .

I don't remember Darian coaxing me from the couch to our car that cold, empty afternoon. Although I can bet I was walking in a slow shuffle, holding on to walls and the porch railing. It wasn't just my body that was shaking; my brain was too. My mind was trying to fight off a total implosion. In self-preservation, it was trying to quiet down—to begin fixing itself—and my body was slowing, trying to follow.

I don't remember the drive-through at Arby's, but I do recall trying to choke down a roast beef and cheddar sandwich riding in the car to Darian's office. (It will be a long time before I have another one of those.)

I don't remember walking into the office, shaking, tears rolling down my face, but I do remember the kindness his boss showed us. His eyes looking into mine, concerned, saying he'd do anything to help us.

I do remember Darian standing up for his new boss, eighteen months ago, when my dad made some off-the-wall, sideways comment about the type of people who hired Darian. And I remember Darian saying, firmly and proudly, "My new boss, out of everyone in this country, has given me a job, taken a chance on me—on us," gesturing to me.

Dad's comment stung, and I was in awe of my new husband, but I'm sure I stayed silent like a coward, knowing it would cost me if I spoke up against Dad.

I don't remember driving home, except for trying to keep my lunch down as we rounded a couple of Michigan lefts. I don't remember the rest of that first awful afternoon after my dad was arrested, except for finally reaching my mom on the phone sometime long past when I should have been able to.

The FBI, the police back home—they should have let us talk to each other. We didn't know anything. It was cruel, and it scared me.

I don't remember who called whom.

Our voices echoed each other, overlapping, the same torn, distraught sounds, both overwhelmed with shock and grief, both falling into our own pit of hell, sixteen hours away from each other. "I kept telling the police they've made a terrible mistake. They won't listen to me."

"Me too, Mama. Me too."

"I've been worried sick about you, about Brian. Have you talked to him? I can't reach him." Mom was being kept in the dark like me.

Then she spoke in a rapid, frightened tone. "When I was leaving work to drive home for lunch, I saw a helicopter fly overhead toward Park City. I wondered, who were they going after now? I'd seen unmarked cars parked on our street this past week. I figured it had to do with a drug house.

"While I was sitting at the kitchen table eating lunch, waiting for your father to come home, I heard a knock on the door. Police said I had to leave right then, needed to go with them. I asked for my purse, I needed my medicine—my inhalers. They went back in and got them.

"I was taken downtown to be questioned. Soon I heard your grandma Dorothea's voice, and your uncles, then more family. They had all been picked up and brought in. We all told the police, 'You've got the wrong guy,' like they had in December. They aren't listening to me. They are in the house now. I don't know when they will leave. I'm staying with family . . ."

Mom was getting more upset, her voice fading in and out, stopping midsentence. I was having a hard time following. "Mom, I'm so sorry this is happening. I love you. Is Uncle Bob there, or someone else I can talk to?"

Dad was arrested, Mom was picked up, and my brother and I were notified halfway across the country all at the same time. A calculated coordination planned by the Wichita police, the FBI, and the Kansas Bureau of Investigation (KBI). The badges got their man, the world was breaking under my family's feet, and nothing would ever be the same again.

8:00 P.M.

"Your father is confessing."

"To what? What is he confessing to?"

"Murders. BTK's."

Oh.

"We also found evidence in your parents' house linking your dad to BTK, to the murders." An FBI agent was on the phone Friday evening. I don't remember if it was the agent who'd notified us of Dad's arrest or another one. I don't remember if I called them or they called me.

In my house?

"In my house? *What* was in my house?"

"Evidence from the murders, found under a false-bottom space in your parents' hallway, under a drawer. Your father told us where to look."

147

Oh. Evidence. Murders. He told them where to look.

We'd walked down that hallway umpteen times a day; it connected our three bedrooms. We kept linens in the top cabinet. A catch-all in the middle, a drawer with old towels and socks in the bottom—cleaning rags.

We rode out umpteen tornado warnings in that hallway, with all the bedroom doors shut, listening to KFDI over the battery-operated radio, hunkered down with blankets, pillows, and our emergency tornado box. Dad would stand watch on the front porch and get scolded by Mom for not being in the hallway with us.

I had hugged Dad goodbye in that hallway two months ago.

"The media is going to start showing up tomorrow or Sunday. Your family is going to need to be careful. Start making some decisions now—where you will be staying, with whom, if you are going to talk to anyone or not, what you're going to say."

"Uh . . . right now, we're having a very hard time believing it's true, that Dad could be . . ." My voice faded. I was getting upset again or was still upset. I didn't really know.

"Yes, we understand. You have our number—call us if anyone gives you problems."

I hung up. "Darian? Dad is confessing. The FBI says . . ."

Maybe if I say it out loud, it will make it true.

At some point that evening, Darian and I went to our nearby grocery store. I don't think that was our normal for a Friday night. Neither of us was hungry and I don't think we bought much. My brother called while I was standing in the frozen food aisle contemplating cardboard pizzas. We started debriefing, but Darian interrupted. "*Shh* . . . others will hear you."

I kept talking, wandering aimlessly around the tables piled with baked goods, sitting on a bench near the magazine section, waiting for Darian to finish shopping and check out. I kept talking while we drove home and went inside. I was back in our apartment, standing near our fancy folding table, when Brian choked up, his voice tearing apart.

"We're going to be okay." My voice ached in the same way as my brother's, and I didn't know how I was going to survive the night. But my brother needed encouragement, and maybe hearing it said out loud would make it true.

"Darian won't leave my side for nothing, and Mom is with family. We're going to be okay, all right?"

Dad was destroying us—his family. My family.

CHAPTER 24

Don't Google for an Alibi

10:00 P.M.
FEBRUARY 25, 2005

Late Friday evening—when I still thought Dad could be innocent, thought I could alibi him, thought I could help the man I
loved—I googled "BTK."

It was the worst mistake I've ever made.

With every click, scroll, and news article, I tumbled into an
abyss of despair and terror. I was assaulted by names and faces of
victims, graphic crime scene photos, horrific details of violent murders. I didn't know which were cases my dad was accused of, what
was internet myth, and what was fact.

I didn't know how many murders my dad had been accused
of committing. I searched for the national news articles I'd read
over the past summer after BTK began communicating with police
again, searched for articles on the *Eagle* website.

Eight.

He was wanted for eight murders, including two children.

Children.

I wanted to vomit.

Eight murders.

That didn't include our neighbor, Mrs. Hedge. Had I given the
FBI another murder of Dad's? Nine?

CHRISTMAS DAY 1981

JULY 1982

Fishing at a Kansas lake.

OCTOBER 1985

Visiting an ice cream shop at the Museum of Science and Industry in Chicago.

December 1988

May 1993

Dad and I in our
front yard.

March 1994

Canoeing at the
Strip Pits, near
Parsons, Kansas.

March 1995

Our first hike
in the Grand
Canyon.

March 1995

Dad in the
Grand Canyon.

March 1995

Camping on the rim.

March 1995

Making dinner at
our camp.

AUGUST 1995

Dad and I in
Yellowstone National Park.

MAY 1997, DAY 1

Hermit Trail,
Grand Canyon.

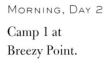

MORNING, DAY 2

Camp 1 at
Breezy Point.

DAY 3

Granite Rapids, Colorado River.

DAY 3

Building a cairn in a riverbed near the Granite Rapids.

DAY 3

Wading in the Colorado River.

DAY 4

A. D. and me at Monument Creek.

DAY 5

Dad on Tonto Trail.

DAY 5

Brian and me,
Cedar Spring.

May 1999

Durango to Silverton Train,
Colorado.

March 2002

Catching carp at a lake in
Oklahoma.

September 2002

Tailgating a KSU football game in
Manhattan, Kansas.

May 2003

My college graduation from
Kansas State University.

JULY 2003

My wedding reception.

MAY 2004

The Lake Michigan shore.

DECEMBER 2004

The last photo
I ever took with
my dad. Along
with my husband,
Darian, in the home
I grew up in.

I couldn't look away from the screen. I didn't tell Darian. I just sat there, continuing to expose myself to what would haunt me for a very long time to come.

I came across two suspect sketches from the 1974 cases. I don't think I'd ever seen the sketches before. I could vaguely make out my dad in the picture from April 1974—the recessed way the man's dark eyes sat in the sketch. I also came across an audio recording of a 911 call placed in December 1977 after a murder. I hadn't known of its existence even though it was released in 1979.

"You will find a homicide at 843 . . . That is correct."[1]

Through the static, in seizing fear, I recognized my dad's voice—younger, but him. I picked up on the clipped, curt, official way he could speak, especially if speaking to uniforms: police officers, park rangers, fish and game wardens. Dad could shift not just his voice but his posture; he could hold himself straighter, taller—tighten himself, hold back emotion, mimic them.

He's making a report. Calling in a homicide—like a badge.

Everything I'd ever known, loved, believed was falling down around me. My whole life was a lie—from before I was born.

I somehow made it out of my chair and staggered into the kitchen. Holding on to the kitchen cabinets to get to the refrigerator, I reached up and grabbed a bottle of vodka left over from Darian's office Christmas party. I poured myself a shot in a white coffee mug with red hearts on it and attempted to down it. I'd only ever drunk liquor mixed, and that had only been a few times.

"What are you doing?" Darian had come out to the kitchen to see what was happening with his falling-apart wife.

"Drinking. It's what they do in the movies. Ya know, when bad things happen."

"Is it helping?" he asked gently.

"No. It burns and tastes like fire."

He took the mug from me and poured the rest down the sink. "I think we better get you to bed."

"I don't wanna sleep. I'm going to have some cake." And I proceeded to cut myself a sizable chunk of chocolate Bundt cake, even though I wanted to heave. I'd regret that swig of fire and piece of cake—which sat in my stomach like a rock—for a long time.

MIDNIGHT

I don't know how I'm going to survive this. I think I am dead—feel dead.
Nothing. Feel nothing.
Am nothing. Dead.

The worst day of my life spilled over into the next. Numb yet shaking, sometimes uncontrollably, I was falling more and more apart—disintegrating.

Darian coaxed me to bed, but now I was too frightened to turn off my bedside lamp. I picked up my Bible from where it sat on a lower shelf on my nightstand. But I didn't have the strength to open it. I let it fall to the ground.

Where are you, God?

Michelle's photo in the light-blue frame caught my eye. The night we lost Michelle was terrible. I didn't know how any of us would ever recover. Her photo sat next to my wooden angel whose twisted wings had now rusted.

Growing up, my cousins had a brown lop-eared bunny I adored. I'd giggle when it twitched its little black nose. When I stood up with Andrea six years ago for her wedding, she had given me a ceramic topiary bunny that held dangly emerald earrings as a bridesmaid's gift. Now the bunny sat next to my picture of Michelle and my wooden angel.

We had changed, though we still missed Michelle acutely; we survived, even with gaping holes still scarring over. Falling in love, graduating from college, getting married.

Dad walked me down the aisle, nervous and proud, trying to hold back tears.

Love never fails.

Life had continued forward.

God was continuously bringing forth new life.

Psalm 23 began running through my head: *"Even though I walk through the valley of the shadow of death . . ."*

"I need the light on tonight." I curled up next to Darian, putting my head on his chest. Darian was solid, tangible, in a world gone mad.

"I will fear no evil . . ."

"That's okay. I'm not sure I can sleep." He wrapped his arms tight around me.

". . . for you are with me; your rod and your staff, they comfort me."

"Me either."

I felt like I was going on watch, waiting for more harm to arrive at our door. On alert. No one to tell us we can stand down.

I sat up, frustrated. Angry. Done. "To heck with it! I can't sleep here!"

"Wanna sleep on the couch? I can take the floor or something."

"Yeah." I grabbed our heavy brown comforter and my pillow, dragging them to the living room.

"The LORD is my shepherd; I shall not want. He makes me lie down in green pastures. He leads me beside still waters. He restores my soul . . ."

The rest of the night passed with the two of us taking shifts to sleep, one on the couch, one on the floor watching over the other one. I'd wake up in the night, foggy-hazy, and see Darian on the computer; he was standing watch over us there too.

"Surely goodness and mercy shall follow me all the days of my life, and I shall dwell in the house of the LORD forever."[2]

When early morning hit, I was on the floor anchored tight in the comforter, and Darian was on the couch, wrapped in a sea-green blanket that had been a wedding gift.

For a moment, I didn't remember what had happened.

I was on the floor in my living room.

Oh.

My brain stung.

There was a knock . . . FBI . . . your dad is . . . Dad isn't.

My hands were shaking again.

I sat up, looking around, trying to figure out what time it was.

My eyes hurt—almost swollen shut from crying so much the day before.

I lay back down, rolled up sideways into a ball, covering myself to my ears with my heavy comforter. Nothing on God's green earth that was covered in ice and snow was worth waking up for right now.

11:00 A.M.
SATURDAY

Midmorning, we were notified there would be a press conference in Wichita announcing my dad's arrest. Cable news would carry it live, but we didn't have cable.

Next thing I remember, our friends in Texas held their phone up to their TV so we could listen in. Darian put his cell phone between us on the couch and turned up his speaker. Surreal insanity brought to us by bouncing airwaves all over the country.

"BTK is arrested," Wichita police chief Norman Williams announced.[3]

This was met with a good deal of cheering and clapping.

Why are they cheering? They've just taken away my father.

My shaking was getting worse; so was the stinging in my brain.

A bunch of speeches followed—politicians. The national news cut away after about ten minutes; no one mentioned my dad.

Later I read that forty minutes into the press conference, the commander of the BTK task force, Wichita police lieutenant Ken Landwehr, was finally given the chance to speak:

Shortly after noon yesterday afternoon, agents from the KBI, agents from the FBI and members of the Wichita Police Department arrested Dennis Rader, fifty-nine, in Park City, Kansas, for the murders of: Joseph, Julie, Josephine, and Joseph Otero Jr., Kathryn Bright, Shirley Vian Relford, Nancy Fox, and Vicki Wegerle. He was arrested for the first-degree murder of all those victims.[4]

Not long after the press conference, he was also charged with the first-degree murders of Marine Hedge and Dolores Davis.

Ten.

Dad.

CHAPTER 25

Media Circuses Belong in Big Tops, Not Apartments

4:00 P.M.
SATURDAY, FEBRUARY 26, 2005

It's becoming a circus here. We're still trying to figure out if we should fly Mom to you or fly you here." Uncle Bob called and was briefing me on the latest in Wichita, which had been quickly invaded by the national media.

The street I grew up on was swarming with sightseers, and the Park City police were trying to keep folks from helping themselves to my parents' mailbox or whatever else they fancied from our yard.[1]

"Your mom is having a real hard time right now, so I'm calling to check on you guys. We're working on a lawyer for your dad."

"That's a good idea. I don't think this is going away."

"No, we don't either. It just doesn't seem possible. Not your dad. We're all very shaken; it just doesn't make sense. But I'm with you—we need to make some plans. Your mom isn't there yet. We need to be patient and take it slow."

"Okay, things are quiet here."

"We love you and Darian; we're praying."

Praying.

By Saturday evening, all the national news sites were having a heyday covering my dad's arrest and alleged crimes, using the nice picture of him in his coat and tie from the church directory that had hung on my wall till yesterday.

I'd gone back to the internet—it was our main source of information, but I was trying to be more careful and stick to credible news. Unable to solidly wrap my head around what Dad could have done, I'd begun to blank on the crimes. Not recalling them, I'd read it over and over, tumbling into a cycle of disconnection, dissociation, then remembering, reinforcing.

My mind was continually trying to narrow—like someone was coming along and tucking a thick, fuzzy blanket around the edges—trying to dampen the effects of the incoming information. But I kept fighting against it, thinking if I only knew everything and could grasp it, then I wouldn't feel so lost. Instead, I was piling harm upon harm, walking myself into a mental heap of trouble.

11:00 P.M.

Late Saturday evening, absurdity hit the internet and the news, mentioning a joke Darian made the year before on our family website, saying my night terrors "were gonna be the death" of him.

The cache had not cleared in near enough time.

I'd muttered half in my sleep about the pile of clothes in the corner of our bedroom looking like a little Mexican man. Now the internet thought I was a racist and assumed my mutterings had to do with the Otero family, who are of Puerto Rican descent.

Four members of a family, including two children, died, and this is what the internet comes up with?

Then I stumbled across this headline from CNN: "Report: Daughter of BTK Suspect Alerted Police." The story led with:

> The daughter of the man whom Wichita authorities arrested in the notorious BTK serial killings approached police with her suspicions

and voluntarily gave them a blood sample, Wichita television station KAKE-TV reported Saturday night. KAKE quoted sources as saying the blood of 26-year-old Kerri Rader, whose father, Dennis, was arrested Friday, came back as a 90-percent DNA match to the BTK killer . . . police began surveillance on Dennis Rader after the results were determined.[2]

The daughter of . . . Whaa? I alerted police?
Blood sample? What blood sample?

The national news was saying I turned in my dad. The national news based this on local Wichita TV news—unnamed sources, no confirmation. No comment from the police.

I gave them two cotton swabs from my mouth. No blood.

Surveillance? Before the arrest? Nothing was making any sense, but now I was getting angry. Angry at the media. Angry at the silence from the police.

The anger took away some of the numbness, helped me to remember I was still breathing.

CNN was blasting far and wide that I turned in my dad. I didn't.

Mrs. Hedge, I did.

I was six.

I need my bed.

SUNDAY

I slept in my bed the second night, but I woke up shaking again.

There was a knock . . . FBI . . . your dad is . . . Dad isn't.

A vivid, detailed loop circled from the first day. It lasted for minutes, and I stared off into nowhere as it flashed. As my mind replayed it, I felt fear again—physically, like it was happening over and over, my chest seizing each time. It would come and go of its own volition, as it already had several times since Friday. I couldn't seem to get rid of it any more than I could stop my body from shaking. I'd slept, at least to some degree, for two nights now, yet woke up still bamboozled.

Darian can see the shaking. I won't tell him or anyone else about the loop.

After willing myself out of bed, I headed to the living room and asked Darian what the latest was.

"You don't want to see the newspaper."

"Why?"

"We're on the front page."

"You mean Dad is, right?"

"No. I mean us." He gestured between him and me. "Us."

Darian pointed to the *Detroit Free Press* sitting on his desk. "We have kids. Did you know that?"

Whaa?

He handed me the paper. At the bottom was an article about the daughter of BTK and her husband, who had two children and lived in the Metro Detroit area.

"Darian, how does the newspaper know where we live?"

"Darian, why does it say we have children?"

"Why do folks keep calling me the daughter of BTK?"

"Darian, I'm going back to bed."

NOON

I convinced myself to get back out of bed. I don't know why. I shouldn't have.

Darian said, "A reporter tried to offer my dad a thick envelope stuffed with cash if he would give the goods on us."

Whaa?

"He shut the door on them."

"Also, a reporter offered money to my best friend in Wichita if he would videotape us somehow. He told them to hose off."

I'm getting the feeling I'm going to need my bed a lot today.

Midafternoon, I heard a knock at our door.

Darian looked through the peephole and saw two local TV reporters standing in our hallway with a cameraman. The camera light was already on. They were already recording—waiting for someone to open the door.

"Kerri, I'm from Fox News. Channel 4 is out here also. I doubt we will be the last."

I halted in the hallway and scrunched down like I was hiding. The world was buzzing white-hot again. My body felt like it was separating from my mind. My mind felt like it was separating from my body.

Father God? I'm not going to survive this.

Seized again with fear, I pressed up against the linen closet in the hallway, huddled up in a little ball, shaking. I wrapped my arms tight around my knees, trying to make myself as small as possible.

FBI questions, asking for my DNA, internet blowing up, cable news blasting out confusion, now cameras in our hallway—our locked hallway.

Shame washed over me like I'd done something wrong.

Our intercom buzzed. More reporters outside asking for BTK's daughter.

Guilty as charged. I'm BTK's daughter. No longer Kerri—she's gone.

Darian was standing by the door.

On watch again.

He looked down our hallway, saw me disintegrating in front of his eyes.

He marched to his toolbox, grabbed a screwdriver, and disabled our intercom.

He came over to me. "Come on, let's get you to the couch. We need to get you out of here—home—before this gets any worse."

Home. Kansas. Not here, where cameras were in apartment buildings.

BTK's daughter.

Darian called our local police and soon the police chief showed up at our apartment. The chief advised Darian as the FBI had: We shouldn't talk to the media. Whatever we said could end up harming my dad's case, harm my family.

Darian told him we wouldn't be talking to the media and that I was shaking in our apartment right now, terrified.

The chief told the reporters and the camera operators and the news trucks they couldn't be on private property or in private buildings, and then stationed a local police officer outside our building.

I was quickly developing a huge distaste for this circus and its clowns. But I began thinking the guys with the badges might not be so bad after all. Except the FBI—that was going to take some extra forgiveness and understanding.

3:00 P.M.

"We met with a lawyer. He told your mom, us, your dad is confessing. Told us how much your dad's defense could cost." Uncle Bob was on the phone again. "He recommended we let your dad rely on the public defenders."

"Yeah. We can't afford . . . I mean, whatever Mom thinks is best."

"She agreed with the lawyer. She's not doing well. We need to get you home, to be with her. She needs you, you need her."

Mom and my grandparents were headed out of Wichita soon, to stay with family. We decided to fly me to Kansas City where I could meet my family in safety—away from Wichita, which was oozing reporters. My family paid for my airfare, and I was set with a connection through O'Hare on Monday, to home.

Home.

I don't recall the rest of Sunday, except for two things. Our neighbors across the hall left a nice note on our door, offering to pick up groceries for us. And Darian told me twenty times or more I needed to pack.

Pack? Why? Oh, right. BTK's daughter was going home.

PART V

Seek Refuge

Whoever dwells in the shelter of the Most
High will rest in the shadow of the Almighty.
I will say of the LORD, "He is my refuge and
my fortress, my God, in whom I trust."

—PSALM 91:1–2

CHAPTER 26

Respite Can Be Found Thousands of Feet in the Air

MONDAY, FEBRUARY 28, 2005

In the early morning of the fourth day, Darian carried my bag down our apartment stairs, opened the door to our cold, dreary garage, and quietly placed it in the trunk of the car.

"What happened to our Powercat tag?"

"I removed it. The KSU frame on the back tag too. I didn't want it to give us away."

Oh.

"You ready? I checked outside a bit ago—I think we're in the clear."

"Ready, I guess."

"Once we get you home you will feel a bit better."

"Yeah. Okay. Let's go."

I held my breath as Darian slowly backed the car out of the garage and turned up the small, steep hill to the parking lot in front of our building.

Clear. No news trucks waiting for us.

We both let out an audible sigh of relief.

"See? We're okay."

As he turned out on the main road, I kept looking behind me—checking to see if anyone was tailing us.

"We're okay. No one back there." Darian turned and looked at me with a slight smile and a shrug, trying, trying, *trying* to cheer me up.

I reached over and patted his leg. "Okay. We're going to be okay."

Maybe if we said it enough to each other, we would eventually believe it.

I stared out the passenger window as we drove south on I-275 to the airport. The earth was frozen and bleak, but at least I was out under the sky and not stuck in the tiny apartment where we had ridden out the past few days. And we had a plan, were doing something, anything—finally.

Darian rolled my bag into the airport and waited with me while I checked in, going over last-minute instructions. "I know you flew two months ago, but this is your first trip on your own and . . ."

And . . .

He hugged me tight at TSA. "Love you."

"Love you."

He waited till I got through security and then with a wave he turned and left.

I was on my own, surrounded by hundreds of folks scurrying up and down the concourse, all of them unaware the daughter of a serial killer was among them.

Not long after sitting down at my gate, sipping a hazelnut latte, I heard a familiar voice. I looked up to the massive TV hanging down above my head to see a family friend from my parents' church giving an interview to CNN. He was standing in as the church's spokesman.

There was ticker running fast at the bottom: BTK . . . Wichita . . . Dennis Rader . . .

My God. Is this what it's been like for the past three days?

. . . church president . . . guy next door . . . father . . . I looked back up and stared with my mouth open at a photo of my dad from Sunday. He was in a neon-orange jumpsuit, tired, sullen, angry, disheveled. Scowling.

He's going to be peeved about that ugly mug shot.

I looked around the concourse; my dad was on every TV screen.
My hands started twitching.

Dear God. I'm not going to survive this.

My face blazing bright red, I scrunched up small in my hard
plastic chair, hanging my head in shame.

What if someone knows who I am? Who I belong to?

Then I heard his voice—Dad. A video of him "speaking cop,"
curt and official, in his dark-brown winter compliance officer coat
and ball cap.

My hands were now violently shaking.

It was a clip from an interview he gave four years ago for a local
Wichita TV station, KSN: "The dogs are somewhat territorial as
well as vicious, and we've been trying to round them up and corral
them as best we can."[1]

Like John Wayne—his boyhood hero.

*He sounds like he did when he called in the murder of a young
woman in '77.*

"You will find a homicide . . . Nancy Fox . . . That is correct."
Nancy was twenty-five years old.

I'm twenty-six years old.

Come, Lord Jesus. Come.

"*God is my rock . . .*"

Bits of Psalms were running in my head again.

I scrounged around in my carry-on, grabbed my black MP3
player and headphones, blasting *A Rush of Blood to the Head* by
Coldplay in my ears. And I ducked behind my thick book: *Harry
Potter and the Goblet of Fire*, a favorite to escape in. Survival.

"*. . . in whom I take refuge.*"[2]

I don't remember getting on the plane, but I do remember
scrunching up against the cold oval window and an off-duty attendant sitting a seat away from me, leaving a heaven-sent gap between
us. I do remember taking off, feeling freedom with the sweet *whoosh*
of the plane lifting, and tears rolling down my face as we rose above

the murky clouds, finding rare bright-blue sky as we turned toward Chicago.

BTK's daughter was going home.

Sharp, warm white beams bounced off the windows, warming my face.

"The LORD is my light . . ."

I don't know what's waiting for me at home. More CNN?

Dad.

Michigan is far away from whatever is coming.

". . . and my salvation—"

But Mom needs me.

And I need her.

I don't know if I can do this. If I'm strong enough.

I'm not.

". . . whom shall I fear?"[3]

God? Can't I stay up here forever?

As peace rushed by outside and tears splotched the dog-eared pages of my book, I twisted a soggy white tissue around my fingers.

A gentle voice interrupted my grief. "Would you like some chocolate? I picked it up over in Japan."

The attendant had a kind face to match the voice and handed me a chocolate bar.

"Thanks."

"Sure. You okay?"

I don't know how to answer that. Dad is . . . I'm going home 'cause . . . "Okay. Going home for a family emergency."

That works.

"Ah. Sorry. I hope everything works out."

Works out. Yeah. Not this time.

I turned my back more to him and leaned as close as I could into the window, putting "Worlds Apart" by Jars of Clay on repeat in my ears.

Let's never land.

It was a quick forty minutes to Chicago, and soon I was wandering O'Hare's unending concourses for lunch and my next gate. I remember grabbing orange chicken and noodles from Panda Express and texting Darian, "Got through my first flight, have a pounding headache."

I don't remember boarding the second plane or the flight. Maybe I slept.

4:00 P.M.

KANSAS CITY

My stomach was in knots as I walked down the jet bridge in Kansas City late in the afternoon.

I don't know what comes next.

Mom!

She was in her cheerful navy-blue raincoat with the yellow liner, but her shoulders were hunched and a pallor hung over her face. She was standing right on the other side of the security divider at my gate with Uncle Urban and Aunt Donna.

Family! Kansas!

I rushed into my mom's arms.

Tears flowed down our faces, both mirror images of exhaustion and devastation.

After I hugged my aunt and uncle, I walked, arm linked in arm, • with Mom as we went to the carousel to get my bag.

"I saw your father Friday morning. He stopped by Snacks for a cinnamon roll, gave me a kiss, told me he'd see me at lunch."

"I talked to him the night before. He reminded me to check the oil in the car."

Mom and I were debriefing each other, sitting in the back seat while headed westward.

I'd forgotten my phone charger in the frenzied packing, so we made a side trip to Circuit City. My uncle helped me pick the charger I needed and paid for it.

Granddad Palmer and Grandma Eileen were waiting for us that evening at my aunt and uncle's home, and A. D. and Jason joined us for dinner. We had Kentucky Fried Chicken with mashed potatoes and gravy, and nothing had ever tasted better.

I sat next to my mom as conversation fluttered in and out.

"It's like your dad has died," Mom said.

All of a sudden it was "your dad, your father," like he now belonged to me and not so much her.

Then with steeled eyes and determination, Mom said to all of us, "We've been through worse—we will get through this."

Worse referred to losing Michelle. I talked to Andrea that night on the phone, sobbing, rocking my body on the floor in the dining room.

"I can't stop shaking. I feel like I've been hit by a ten-ton truck."

"You're in shock," she said. "It's completely understandable. You're under a great weight of trauma still happening—ongoing."

Oh.

Shock.

I'd been physically and mentally in shock, to some degree, for four days. It took years for me to realize how badly I messed myself up those first days. I should have gotten help, gone to the hospital, had someone knock me out. I will regret it the rest of my life.

Later that night, my aunt was checking her answering machine and I heard that voice again. "Hello? Anyone there? Can you pick up?"

Dad.

I froze inside, but outside, I lost control of the shaking.

Your dad is BTK.

We listened to the message, but we didn't call him back.

At bedtime, I curled up next to my mom in her bed. Just like when I was a little girl—seeking solace. We cried together for some time, and I kept saying, "I'm so sorry, Mom. I'm so sorry."

A little later, I went downstairs to sleep in the bed my uncle had set up for me. Maybe I shouldn't have left her. But I couldn't take any more—not tonight.

CHAPTER 27

There Is Safety in Numbers

The shaking finally stopped on the fifth day.

I woke up early Tuesday morning on a mattress in my aunt and uncle's living room. Pale morning light was deepening in color, the house was still, and my body was at peace. I sat up and held my hands out in front of me—waiting for the shaking to return. They were still.

Maybe, just maybe, I will survive this.

Soon other folks were rising quietly. The smell of Folgers wafted from the kitchen, cereal bowls rattled, and newspapers rustled, pencils at the ready to fill in the day's crossword.

This was a home where I could stay barefoot in my pajamas for any length of time I desired. I could stretch out on the oversized leather couch, hide in Hogwarts for hours, and not be plied with questions I wasn't ready to contemplate answers to yet.

This was a quiet place, with gentle, kind voices that belonged to people with lives that would continue on as they had for the decades before my dad knocked a massive hole into all of it.

This was God-sent respite, and I never wanted to leave.

"Your uncle Paul was granted emergency leave from Iraq and is coming home," Mom told me. Dad's second-oldest brother had been called up to active duty from the reserves a few months before. I was glad he was coming home from the sand but not why.

"Uncle Jeff was in the newspaper yesterday," Grandma Eileen said, handing me the front section of yesterday's *Eagle*, pointing to a story at the bottom of the page.

On Sunday afternoon, my dad's youngest brother, fed up with reporters driving by Grandma Dorothea's home, stepped out on her porch to talk to two journalists from the *Eagle*. He told them Grandma was seventy-nine years old and frail. That he had to unplug the answering machine because folks were leaving harassing messages. "My mother still can't believe it," he said. "She's still very much in denial. And so am I. But maybe, with me, acceptance is starting to creep in. I don't think my brother is BTK. But if he is—if that is the truth—then let the truth be the truth."[1]

Let the truth be the truth. That's what Grandpa Bill would say if he were here to guide us. But his heart would be shattered.

Grandpa? Send aid—to us all.

My uncle went on to tell the journalists that errors and false speculation were flying around. No one turned in my dad. "Grandma is loving, Grandpa was tough but decent. Grandpa had served as a marine and was a God-fearing man, strict, but not unreasonable. There was no trouble in the family, no abuse."[2]

The FBI had asked him if he or any of the boys had been sexually abused by my grandparents.

Dear Jesus.

My uncle said, "I told them no. And that's the truth."[3]

That's the truth.

I read the article slowly, brushing my thumb over the newsprint, letting my tears fall where they would.

Grandma Eileen handed me a couple of tissues and patted me on the arm. "Your uncle Jeff did a good, brave thing."

"Yes, yes, he did. My grandparents never, wouldn't, didn't—"

"No. They were—are—very good people. You know strangers are making up stories."

My shoulders tightened, my jaw clenched, and anger flashed across my face. "This is all Dad's doing. His fault."

"Your father loved and cared a lot for your grandparents, his brothers, all his family—your mother, you, Brian."

Yeah, well. We all loved my dad very much too. Love, however much there was, hadn't been enough to stop him—to help him. And now he had left all of us to pick up the pieces.

I stood up, my shoulders slumping, and went to the patio door. The grass was brown but the sky was bright Kansas blue, laced with wispy clouds.

My eyes stung with tears again. Had someone abused my father when he was a boy? The thought seared right through me.

Who? When?

I racked my brain and couldn't come up with any answers, nothing but empty despair, confusion.

Then a flash of conviction, of knowing: Many people are abused as children and don't grow up to harm a soul. No matter what had happened to my father—it wasn't an excuse. There were no excuses for what my father had done. He was responsible for all of it. He chose this for himself—chose to harm others.

Why? Why those ten innocents? Children?

The headline on today's paper said yesterday Dad had been charged in court with ten first-degree murders. I was flying while he faced one of the worst days of his life—alone. I wasn't able to be with him. I wasn't sure if I'd ever be able to be with him again.

TUESDAY AFTERNOON

He's confessing.

Mom was scribbling in shorthand on a yellow legal pad, her pen alternating between flying and pausing in midair. She wrote, "He's confessing," underling it twice and tapping at it to get my attention.

Yeah, Mom. He's been confessing for days.

Let the truth be the truth.

Pastor Mike, who shepherded my folks' congregation, had called Mom after visiting my dad in jail. He was doing his best to try to relay a message to us from Dad—who had been trying to explain, grasp at what was wrong within him.

Mom was sitting on my aunt and uncle's bed, their homemade wedding quilt folded neatly at the foot. I was sitting cross-legged next to her, searching her face for signs of too much distress.

She wrote, "Has something wrong with him." Underlined, tapped again.

Yeah, Mom. He definitely, totally, has a whole heck of a lot wrong with him.

Mom wrote: "Monster. Hidden. Dark side. Black hat."

But Dad wasn't the black hat. He'd been the white hat—the good guy. The guy who saved the day. The hero—*my* hero.

Dad had grown up on cowboy lore: Gene Autry, Roy Rogers, the Lone Ranger. His love of the West had captured my childhood imagination. I'd watch him add oil and popcorn kernels to our red popper and wait for the *pop-pop-pop* while he poured us each a Pepsi over ice. Then after salt and butter was added to the crunchy white corn, we'd be on to John Wayne taking on the bad guys on a Saturday night.

I wasn't keen on being a damsel in distress. I wanted to be a cowgirl, wear jeans, ride horses, rustle up cattle, and pack a six-shooter. Cowgirls could rescue themselves. Mom would shoo my brother and me outside if we got too wild playing cowboys and Indians in her house. War cries, toy guns, and couches turned into forts led to exile till the supper bell rang.

Mom nudged me, holding the legal pad so I could read: "Sexual. Can't control. Bondage."

I winced at the words. My face blazing hot, I looked away.

We don't talk about religion, sex, or politics.

Mom's voice rose; it was direct but strained: "No, he never sexually abused me or the kids. He never hit us. The police asked the first day."

He never hit, but he still could be abusive physically. Brian. He tried to strangle Brian twice.

The second time was a few years after the first. Dad pushed Brian up against the kitchen closet, putting his hands around my brother's neck, like before. Dad told Brian, "My loyalty belongs to your mother; it's time for you to move out of my home."

Mom pushed Dad off Brian, who was pale as a sheet. She stood up to Dad. She was brave, all five foot seven of her.

Another time, Dad chased me down the hall when I was sixteen, threatening me within an inch of my life. I'd cussed at him in our living room, my eyes blazing fire. His face turned red with murderous rage, the angriest I've ever seen him. Mom stepped in, blocking him with her body—bought me a few seconds, kept me safe. He kicked a dent in my door, but I had it locked by then—I was safe.

Dark side. Black hat. Monster.

"The LORD is the stronghold of my life . . ."

"I know. It's right of you to ask, checking on us." Mom's tone softened. Her face was falling, turning pale. This was too much too soon for her.

The man we knew. The man we didn't. The man we thought we knew. The man who never really existed.

". . . of whom shall I be afraid?"[4]

The pen dropped, the legal pad now lying discarded by her side. She ended the call soon after.

"The police seem to think we were all abused. They asked; now the pastor is."

"I'm not sure they think it—they're just making sure we're okay. In these situations, often—"

Mom stopped me. "I took care of you and your brother, changed your diapers, gave you baths. I would have seen if he caused any harm to either of you when you were little."

Ah, heck. People think—assume—Dad sexually abused us.

Your Dad is BTK, you're BTK's daughter, he must . . .

Mom looked down at her notes, said, "Your father is confessing, says . . ."

I listened as she repeated the conversation from the phone. As she spoke, color slowly came back to her cheeks, and her eyes flashed with a spark I hadn't seen since I'd come home. Anger, I reckoned.

She repeated the conversation with the pastor to my aunt and my grandma. Each time growing stronger, gaining a bit more of herself. She knew the truth now—heard it directly. She was facing it, and it would eventually set her free.

THURSDAY

We fell into an easy, quiet routine at my aunt's, whom we coaxed to return to her teaching job because we were strong enough to take care of each other during the day. Mom and I were eating and sleeping, taking the first hard steps on our way to recovery.

We left the TV off, only turning it on to watch *The Amazing Race* or *Survivor* in the evenings. The only incoming news was from the day's newspaper, which each of us would choose to read on our own.

It was a safe place, far removed from the madness in Wichita and the camera-stalkers in Detroit. Earlier in the week, more news trucks were parked outside our apartment, and one followed Darian, who kept swinging Michigan lefts to shake it. Reporters showed up at his office, and his coworkers would answer the door for him. Reporters were calling him at his job and on his cell too: "I'm so-and-so, from so-and-so, and I would really like to speak with your wife. Do you know how we can contact her? Do you know where she is?"

Grandma had taken me to the bookstore, buying *Harry Potter and the Order of the Phoenix* for me because I wanted to keep going in the story. At the checkout lane, we nudged each other, seeing my dad's mug shot on the front of several magazines and national newspapers blaring BTK headlines.

"Don't tell your mother."

"No. I won't."

My grandparents were a steady, constant presence, a reminder my roots ran deep and strong. Granddad spent his days reading or working crosswords from a corner recliner. He would lift his head occasionally and give me a small smile or ask, "What does the paper say today about your dad?" I'd move near his chair and tell him while he listened and shook his head, his eyes pained.

Grandma flitted around the house, seeing to the dishes, taking care of everyone, making sure we were well fed. Mom and I often sat at the kitchen table, drifting in and out of conversation.

I said, "Do you remember on my birthday five years ago, Dad waking up after his stomach scope and freaking out? He was acting nervous, saying, 'Did I say anything crazy while I was out of it?'"

Mom asked, "Was that the day we had a tornado warning when we got home?"

"Yeah. That was a rough day—not birthday-like," I replied. "I remember wishing I'd thought to bring the cupcakes we had picked up at the store with me to the hallway."

"Do you think your dad was worried he was going to say something? In the operating room?"

I shrugged. *Who knows?*

Mom said, "Did you know I was teasing him this fall that he spelled like that guy—BTK?"

I grinned a bit at this, trying to stifle a laugh, as I checked Mom's face. She was trying to hide a smirk, too, and when our eyes met, we both started giggling. It felt good to laugh.

People died. I'm not supposed to be laughing ever again.

"I asked your dad once why would BTK use a cereal box to communicate with the police—like it was reported in the news. He said, 'Cereal—like a serial killer.'"

I didn't know whether to laugh or cry at that one.

"Where did he get those boxes? We don't eat that type of cereal."

And that's what my poor mom is wondering.

Mom continued: "When I got interviewed, they asked what was behind our hidden door. I asked, 'What door?' They said the one in the kitchen behind the table. I said, 'You mean the door the dryer is behind?'"

I snorted, tried to contain it, and gave up, laughing out loud. Mom and Grandma followed.

"The police asked me about safety-deposit boxes—I don't know why."

Later, we learned that Dad used secret ones to store BTK items.

Mom's face turned serious, her voice lower. "Early last year, there was a special about the thirtieth anniversary of the first murders, what happened to the Oteros. It was on TV. Your dad watched it."

Oh. I didn't know he had watched it.

"The paper ran a large piece about the murders around then too."

I leaned over onto the table, laying my head on it, crossing my body with my arms.

The first 2004 BTK communications showed up in March, on the twenty-seventh anniversary of Shirley Vian Relford's death. What I was learning about my dad's murders kept cutting in and out of my head, but I wouldn't say these things out loud, trying to protect my mom from the worst.

"I don't understand why strangers are saying that we knew what your father was doing, we were somehow involved, or we must have known." Her face was stretched and pained.

She needs rest. Her own books and stories to escape in.

As far back as I could remember, she had dozens of books with pretty covers depicting heroines full of hope stacked up against the wall next to her bed. They were quite the contrast to Dad's dark-colored true-crime books, propped up above his head on his half of the headboard.

"Mom, there is no way you would've stayed in that house with him, raised us kids with him. If we'd had the slightest inkling, we would've gone screaming out the front door and run straight to the police department."

Grandma said, "Your dad worked down the hall from a police department for fourteen years—they didn't know either."

No one knew but Dad.

SATURDAY

My uncle and A. D. drove to our home Saturday, picking up clothes, books, and other things my mom needed.

The thought of my house made my stomach tighten. It was the only home I'd ever known, and now I wasn't sure that I was even brave enough to ever set foot in it again. Mom already determined she would never sleep there again. Not one of us blamed her.

For now, she was planning on staying with her sisters and my grandparents, moving every few weeks, till we could figure out what to do about the house and find her a new place to live.

Dad had cost us our home. Thirty-four years. Gone like that.

I was anxious while my uncle and cousin were gone, worried about what they would encounter. But when they returned Saturday evening, they reported it hadn't been ransacked, which we'd been afraid of. It didn't even look as if someone had been in there, let alone a team of investigators, crime scene techs, and who knows who else. Mom's lunch plate that was left on the kitchen table when she was rushed out of the house was even sitting in the sink; someone had rinsed it for her.

My family talked me into looking at return flights to Michigan. "You need to get back to Darian, to teaching," my aunt said. "It will help—the kids will—having a routine."

I was worried about my mom, didn't want to leave her, but she said, "I'll be all right. I've got lots of help here; you should go on home."

Home. This was home—Kansas. Not Michigan.

I wanted to stay another week in the quiet, peaceful place where I was safe. And I didn't want to think about facing the coming months while I was sixteen hours away.

Darian said it was getting quieter—the news trucks were gone—so we booked a flight for me on Sunday.

I missed him—needed him. I had to go back sometime.

"The LORD is my light and my salvation—whom shall I fear?"[5]

CHAPTER 28

Maybe Love Is Enough

MARCH 2005
DETROIT

Pastor Mike thinks we should write your father. Try to get through to him—why we think he should plead guilty."

Guilty.

Let the truth be the truth.

A few days after I got home, I was on the phone with my mom. I wholeheartedly agreed with her: Dad should plead guilty. But I had no idea how one convinced my dad to do anything, let alone something so immense.

A guilty plea would spare all of us—this family and the seven families he'd devastated—months, if not years, of suffering through a long, drawn-out trial. We all knew what the inevitable outcome would be. Guilty.

But the man I didn't know wasn't into sparing anyone anything. He was a murderer. Of children. Women: daughters, mothers, grandmothers. A father. The man I didn't know, the narcissistic one, finally had the full spotlight on himself after thirty-one years. He wouldn't likely give it up for anything, not even his family.

Father God?

Love never fails. Love. I loved the dad I knew. Maybe love would be enough. Maybe he would plead guilty for us.

It was hard to think about writing to my dad; it hurt. I put it off that week.

On Saturday, March 12, I sat down to my corner computer and wrote to my father, two weeks after I'd fallen apart in the same chair. It was three days after his sixtieth birthday.

Happy birthday, Dad.

As the years have gone on, I've continued to find writing him painful and continued to drag my feet, the weight of it too much. But on rare days, it is enough to know it's the right thing to do—so I sit down to write. Tears fall every time. It guts me, but I do it for his sake and mine.

In the midst of Dad's arrest, arraignment, and plea, he and I wrote to each other monthly. My letters were typed, with colorful clip art added to cheer him up, then saved to my computer, printed, and mailed to the Sedgwick County Detention Facility in Wichita. His were handwritten and mailed in decorated envelopes to Michigan.[1]

Saturday, March 12

Dad,

Hello, I am physically doing okay. I am safe and home in Michigan. I was able to fly back to Kansas and be with Mom after all this happened. Brian is doing okay. The Navy has been supportive and helpful; we're glad he's safe on base where he can't be harassed.

The media was reporting I turned you in. That's not true. I didn't know anything (like everyone else) until the FBI knocked on my door. I tried to tell them what a great man you are, what a wonderful dad you are, how they totally had screwed up and arrested the wrong guy. I tried, we all did, but they didn't listen.

Pastor Mike relayed your message to Mom and me, and we passed it on to Brian. We're all so sorry you've been living with what you've been living with for so long. We still love you. We love the husband, father, and man we know with all our hearts. We don't know who that other man is. We understand there is something seriously and deeply wrong with that part of you. We want you to get help if you can.

We want you to be treated fairly, with compassion and respect. We're hoping there will not be a long, drawn-out trial, but we understand it is your choice and your right to have one. We'll stand by whatever you decide. We support you, the husband and father we know. I'm sorry you're alone and we're not able to be with you. I'm sorry I can't give you a hug and tell you everything is going to be okay.

No matter what you may have done or not done, you are my father and I love you. You raised me and Brian as well as any man could, you took care of us, protected us, taught us so much about life and the things in it. I am sorry I cannot be there to take care of you the way you took care of me the last 26 years.

I'm not ready to talk on the phone yet, but we can talk someday and someday we will come visit you. But right now, it is just too hard. Please try to understand, we haven't abandoned you, we haven't turned our backs, we just need some time to try to make sense of everything and get some firm ground under our feet.

I love you,
Kerri

MARCH

Prayers and support from all over the country, especially from other churches named Christ Lutheran, poured into my mom's church for our family and the whole church community. Several women at my mom's church put together care packages for my mom, my grandmas, and me. There were individually wrapped gifts to open a few at a time: lovely, thoughtful items to let us know we were cared for, including a hand-knitted teal-blue throw.

In the middle of madness, my family had been gifted humanity that shored up our spirits—reminding us we were not alone.

"The light shines in the darkness, and the darkness has not overcome it."[2]

Friends and distant family my mom hadn't heard from in years called and wrote. Rita, my roommate from college, sent me a note in a brightly colored card; I hadn't spoken to her in eight years. It meant an immense amount to me, tears of grace falling after years of separation.

Two other friends of ours from college sent a gift card to pick up dinner from Boston Market—I still remember how thoughtful and astounding I found that, and I still remember eating that meal.

Dad and my family continued to be an ongoing national news story, but a few trusted coworkers of Darian's were the only ones in Michigan who knew who Darian and I actually were. I was so infrequently in any one school to sub that I didn't bother telling anyone who I was. I wouldn't even know where to start, and maybe they wouldn't want me as a teacher if they knew.

My dad is BTK—I'm BTK's daughter.

The news trucks were gone, but the media would still try to contact us. I came home one day to find an envelope duct-taped to my door, with the words *National Enquirer* scribbled on the outside—the note inside written on a local hotel's stationery. A week before, standing in the checkout line at the grocery store, I'd been horrified to see on the cover of the *Enquirer* grainy pictures of Mom coming out of Snacks.

Our apartment building door was supposed to be locked. Was this reporter sending me a message that I was next to be stalked, photographed, and published?

Hearing our metal door knocker would send me jumping into the air. I'd answer the door, timidly, after looking through the peephole. Our mailman sheepishly handed me certified letters I didn't want but still had to sign for.

I received phone calls from area codes I didn't know, sometimes instantly regretting answering them instead of letting them go to voice mail.

Everyone from Oprah to Larry King was asking for an interview, and I told everyone no. So did Mom—a united front of solidarity.

We will fly you to New York City; you can come sit on our hot seat.
We will fly you to Chicago; you can come sit on our comfy couch.
No thanks—nothing to see here, folks. Move along.

March 26

Dear Kerri,

Happy Belated Easter Wish! Thank you so much for your letter. I was overjoyed with emotions and happiness. I was beginning to think no immediate family members was going to write to me. Your letter was very sincere and I can tell it came from a very loving and understanding daughter.

I just finish lunch and played a quick game of Solitaire, old "Sol" won. Although I did beat it last night. One of PD, (Pod deputy) show me how to play. Nothing going on the weekends and PD's and I are taking things easy. They don't have their supervisors and tend to be better at being at ease and not so hard on you.

Attorney visit every day, Pastor Mike visit. Doc had to visit to work on my in-grown toenails and I'm having problem with a right swollen foot, maybe my diet or poor shoe I have on. Also had another head doctor (Psychologist) visit me Friday. I have spent a lot of evenings working on past history good/dark for attorney.

So now, to keep my mind busy, I have the Daily Routine: old Sol to play, letters to read, letters to write, Bible Study, exercise, books to read, also started receiving the *Eagle*.

I also heard you turn me in, and I knew down deep, *you did not.* It was my own Follies playing Mouse and Cat with the FBI and Police, too long. They finally honed in on me like a missile. I do have some serious problems and I do need help on them. Need your prayers and thoughts on that.

I have been trying to steer my attorneys towards the concept of less family exposure. And that is what I really want to do, down deep in my heart. Arraignment is April 19—16 working days ahead. We talked about a plea for Insanity, but I don't know whether Larned (State Hospital) or El Dorado (Prison) will be the best in the long run.

I know there a lot of ugly-ness that will come out either way to the public. I just don't know what to do; I lost control of my life at this point and at the mercy of the Judicial System. Some people just think I can and at moments-notice, call the Judge and plea Guilty and everything will put in a box and locked away. Media exposure and possible ugly-ness brought to light before I'm sentenced. All the above is heavy on my mind and emotionally draining me downward into a pit.

Hearing from another source may help me decide for the good of the family.

I learn from the TV news I have been appointed a judge. My attorney said nothing about it, Friday AM, although they may have been a p.m. announcement to the media. I wonder if they have bit off more than they can chew!

I received a letter from Mom. Again, I was overjoyed and so happy. I will return letter to her this weekend. It will [be] fourth letter out. Hers is always the hardest to write. I'm concern about my letters reaching you, Mom, and Brian. I have mail three out, each week.

Tell Darian hi, for me. Be prepared as arraignment near, the media will be back, sorry for that.

Love,
Dad[3]

CHAPTER 29

Leave the Crime Solving to the Experts

MARCH 2005

Dad's letters showed up randomly, and I learned to steady myself before opening my mailbox. I would walk slowly back to my apartment, setting them on my desk till I summoned the strength to open them. They always had a faint odor of a place I didn't know: dank, musty, cigarette-like.

When I finally steeled myself to read, I fluctuated through a roil of emotions: sadness, anger, disbelief, disconnection. Darian braced himself, knowing a storm was about to hit: my pacing, cursing, shaking the yellow legal-size sheets at him.

Then the tears. Always the tears.

I had questions, I needed answers, and Dad's words were not nearly enough.

Dad wasn't telling us much, but answers were slowly coming out of Wichita. The police were releasing new revelations about Dad's crimes; their massive, decades-long search for him; and his arrest. The *Eagle* was covering these releases in-depth and the national news was spreading them wide.

Along with the rest of the world, I was learning the truth about my father. But unlike the rest of the world—who were merely following a story—I was also following my life. I struggled, trying to match what I was finding out with what I knew. Thought I'd known.

We found out that along with the much larger deceptions, Dad deceived Mom and my family in many smaller ways. He called Mom at times in the last year to say he had to stay late for work. He actually was working after hours on "BTK projects" at his office in the city building, placing incriminating items in his locked cabinet.

Dad normally left his office by six o'clock, and Mom almost always had supper ready by the time he was home—after she'd worked a full day. Thinking of him calling her and lying to her—and her sitting at the table, hungry, likely with a roll of Ritz crackers to tide herself over, waiting to eat with him—royally teed me off.

She'd wait in her chair, the one next to the stove, so it would be easy for her to get up and keep whatever she had fixed warm till he was home.

His chair was the one in front of the dryer so he could face the kitchen door and not have his back to it. You never sat in his chair if he was home—unless you wanted to push his buttons or find yourself in trouble.

While on a family vacation in Saint Louis in June 1993, Dad became paranoid that the housekeeping staff was stealing his Ritz crackers, and he started counting how many were left in a roll before we left in the mornings. When he got ridiculous, there was nothing left for Mom and me to do but laugh and poke fun at him.

On that trip, while eating at an "authentic" Italian place, Dad told me gangsters never liked to sit with their back to a door. He was big into mobster movies—*The Godfather, Goodfellas, Road to Perdition.*

I watched them all with him, and now he was on his own self-paved road to hell.

Dad also built his BTK projects while Mom was gone to church choir. But it hadn't been unusual when I was home, back into the early 1990s, to see Dad fiddling with stamps. He often had large albums, index cards, tweezers, and rubber gloves scattered on our kitchen table. His BTK letters and envelopes would've blended right in. And he hadn't started those back up till 2004.

Dad didn't just start back up as BTK in 2004 due to the thirtieth-anniversary documentary of the Otero murders being aired on TV. He likely partly did it because his kids were now grown, out of the house, out of state. We were safe, doing well; he had seen to raising us right.

Our leaving could have led to him going through a late-life crisis: the kids were gone and retirement was looming. He wanted to retire as BTK too. He had more time, but more time led to boredom, which often led Dad to bad things.

One of the letters my dad sent to a local Wichita TV station was mailed right before my family's trip to Michigan in May 2004. Knowing Dad, he could've casually dropped it in the mailbox in front of Leeker's, fueled up, and gotten ice for the cooler before heading out of town.

Dad had wandered off for an hour while we were window-shopping in Frankenmuth. Had he been trying to find news about BTK's latest mail drop, which had been discovered while he was conveniently on vacation? He came back with wine, saying he found a shop that offered tastings. It made sense at the time, but now I questioned his absence.

Dad's May 2004 communication, which contained a word search–type puzzle, was released after his arrest. I recognized it as something my dad might find fun. He preferred cryptograms—substitution codes—and my favorite kind of puzzles were logic problems. I printed it off, finding several familiar words, including names of our family, creatively scattered in it, as well as our address.

What had Dad intended? If that puzzle had been released to the public in the summer of 2004, would I have seen it in the news and tried to solve it?

I looked up other BTK communications. I knew we still had a typewriter, which he had used to type addresses on envelopes. I even recognized the old-fashioned train stamp on one.

In the fall of 2004, Dad didn't come to Brian's boot camp graduation. Was his odd "too busy to get away" excuse related to something criminal he was doing?

Dad wandered off at the airport the night we went to get Brian at Christmas. Why? Was he looking for a TV with news?

When Darian and I were home for Christmas, Dad set up the folding table in the living room and placed a stack of *Eagles* on it. While we all watched a movie, he methodically marked the top of each front page, tapping his house shoes as he did. Were the marks code for something?

Code. Substitute one thing for another.

Had I held the key to my dad—to who BTK was?

If I had been living in Wichita in 2004, I likely would have been up to my neck in trying to solve it. I could have—my family could have—been in deep trouble if one of us had stumbled onto something of his that was BTK's.

I realized why the list with the false leads that Dad had given the police had bothered me last fall:

Trains. Railroads.

Dad was in the military in the 1960s.

Did one of my great-grandpas play the fiddle?

Grandpa was from Missouri and fought in World War II.

Lung disease. Black lung was what coal miners died from, and there were strip pits around Columbus and Pittsburg where Dad lived as a young boy.

When I was young, we went to Dad's family reunions in Columbus and drove out to the rolling hills to visit Big Brutus, a massive, orange-and-black electric shovel that dug coal in the 1960s and '70s. We kids posed with Dad in the shovel to have our picture taken, grins on our faces.

Dad and I camped, fished, and canoed around the strip pits on spring break in 1994; my uncle Bill joined us. There was a fire ban because it was so dry, and it was terribly cold for March. Dad told me I was too old to sleep in a tent with him, so I got stuck freezing in an old leaky tent by myself. I'd stewed and cursed at Dad in the night but the next morning was thankful for his warm gear that he made me put on: his overalls, an extra coat, his gloves. I was also thankful that my dad and uncle were fine outdoor cooks, even with a limited fire.

I remember being scared of having to sleep by myself that trip, even though my dad and uncle were right there and would have let no harm befall me. I also think I might have frightened myself with whatever paperbacks I'd brought along.

I shared a tent with Dad the next year at the Grand Canyon, so I'm not sure why he was so opposed to it in the strip pits that spring break.

Trying to put together a massive, decades-wide puzzle with gaping holes, I was discovering slivers of truth, but I was also coming up hard against myself and my memories. These new pieces of truth cut like shards of glass as I learned them, and imbedded dangerously into my soul as I forgot them.

Coping mechanism. Dissociation. Survival. Self-preservation.

In the spring, the national media blurted that DNA taken from semen left on eleven-year-old Josie Otero's leg in January 1974 was matched on February 24 to my DNA taken from one of my Pap smears, leading to the arrest of my father the next day.

My DNA also matched semen left at Nancy Fox's apartment in December 1977, and scrapings taken from under Vicki Wegerle's fingernails from September 1986.[1]

Surreal doesn't even begin to describe it.

I remembered when Darian and I were home in December, Dad had asked him an odd question: "Can floppy disks be traced, like those folks on *CSI* do?"

Darian, not sure what Dad was asking and not wanting to go into technical details, brushed him off with a quick no, even though Darian knew disks could be traced.

Dad eventually ensnared himself with a computer disk he sent to the police in February. He had used the disk at the Park City Library and my parents' church, where he was listed online as the president. His first name and the locations where he had used it were in the file properties. The police found "Dennis," ran a search on "Christ Lutheran," and had their man.

After the police had my dad's name, they started staking out my parents' street. They were confident they had him but were waiting on DNA results to come back before they arrested him. In the spring, it was released to the media that the DNA they were waiting on was mine.

Detectives had collected BTK samples from crime scenes in 1974, 1977, and 1986. In 2004, the BTK task force asked over a thousand men in the Wichita area to take a DNA test—voluntarily—to rule them out as suspects. It was nicknamed the swab-a-thon.

From my understanding, I was the only woman swabbed to check against my dad. What I didn't know was before I was asked to give a swab voluntarily, my DNA had already been taken without my knowledge. After detectives determined my dad was likely BTK, they discovered he had two children and I had attended Kansas State and lived in the dorms while there.

They got a subpoena for my records at Lafene, the on-campus health center. When a detective arrived, he lucked out: I'd gotten annual Pap smears and had a biopsy done on a cervical polyp. He got another subpoena plus a court order for my tissue sample.

The slide was taken to the KBI lab in Topeka, and on February 24, I came back as a 10/10 allele match to BTK.

I was a college kid when I'd been told I would need tissue removed and biopsied. I was worried and scared till it came back benign. I was near the same age as Kathryn Bright, whom my dad murdered in 1974.

Twenty-five years after Dad murdered a twenty-one-year-old near Wichita State, he was moving his twenty-one-year-old daughter back and forth to Kansas State. Six years later, my DNA would help identify him. (I still don't know if that particular DNA came from a routine Pap smear or my biopsy.)

My dad invaded people's homes, bound and tortured them, murdered them, then caused even more violation after they were dead. I wasn't being told this gently by the detectives who worked my dad's case, who rummaged in my medical records. I was finding it out through the news along with the rest of the world.

My brother and I were kids when my dad committed his last three murders.

My dad was responsible for causing immense harm to his ten victims. He was also responsible for causing immense harm to my family.

He betrayed us.

Now I felt that the police had used me. They had accessed my private medical records without my permission.

The media was hounding my family, making us feel as if we had done something wrong. (In fact, we would have qualified for victim support services in the state of Kansas, but I wasn't aware of this until 2017.)

In a few months' time, I lost my faith in my father, I lost my faith in journalism, and now I was losing my faith in law enforcement. There wasn't going to be much of anything left once Dad was done with us.

CHAPTER 30

Light Will Overcome
the Darkness

APRIL 2005

Somewhere among the worst months of my life, my second major grief-filled descent into a pit of murky black began. Alongside the dull, thick walls that were trying to clamp down on my pain, came flashes of white-light panic, tinged with dark-red seething. My old bullies, depression and anxiety, were resurfacing and joining forces with a new brute—trauma. Which, in all truth, might have been an old tormenter of mine.

Dad.

Time began to fade in and out on me. My ability to keep it together came in spurts, and when I couldn't, I drew hazy-gray blanks.

Life divided. On the okay days, I taught, shopped for groceries, went to the Coney with Darian. We wandered around the Detroit Zoo, two of the rare few who visited in the semifrozen months. We looked like anyone else, but we were suffering.

Trying to stay anonymous, Darian often reminded me to lower my voice when I talked about Dad in public. Over and over, I told Darian the terrible things the world was claiming my father had done, and he patiently let me. Out at dinner, we looked around, wondering if anyone knew who we were. Both of us trying not to utter the name BTK.

Mainly for my sake. But maybe if I said it out loud it would become the truth: *My dad is BTK—I'm BTK's daughter.*

At one point we became stuck at the AMC, frozen in our seats after seeing *Hostage*, a movie with violent criminals, home invasion, and Bruce Willis trying to save the day.

Darian looked at me. "Are you okay? I'm feeling sorta dizzy."

"I want to throw up." I gripped the armrests while the credits rolled.

"Maybe we shouldn't have seen this one."

"Yeah. I don't think I can handle these types of movies for a while." I paused, looked down at the floor, then back at Darian, saying quietly, "I saw *Se7en* with Dad at the Palace in early 1996."

"Oh. Just you?"

"Yeah. Do you think he was trying to tell me something about himself? Taking me to that?"

"Dunno."

"I saw *Copycat* at North Rock. Dad was impressed I sat through that one alone. We talked all about it when I got home."

"Did you know *Red Dragon* is supposed to be loosely based on your dad?"

"No! Really? Heck. Saw that with him too. And *The Silence of the Lambs* and *Hannibal* and *8mm* . . . I could go on for a while."

"*8mm*? Wow. Well, come on, let's get going." He stood up, collected our discarded popcorn container and empty cups, then offered his hand and saw me out of the theater. We didn't go to the movies again for a while after that.

I kept rattling off serial killer and horror lore in the car, the same way a broken hydrant gushes water. "I read all those books too—the Hannibal Lector ones, *Kiss the Girls*, lots of Stephen King. Dad and I would swap paperbacks, suggest library books, talk about them."

"How old?"

"Middle school? High school? Mom didn't approve necessarily, but Dad let me read whatever I wanted to. I used to sneak-read her romance books under the covers with my flashlight. She finally gave up trying to stop me when I was about sixteen."

It always helped to talk to Darian. To say out loud what was running, endlessly running, through my head. Maybe, if I thought about it enough, it would feel like the truth.

On the broken days, which were many, I went unseen. I didn't teach. I slept till Darian called to ask, "What do you want for lunch? How about Taco Bell today?"

Love neve fails.

For better or worse, in sickness or in health.

I would eat what he brought me, do who-knows-what for a few hours, and crash on the couch, napping till he arrived home from work. We watched TV in the evenings, or I cross-stitched, a new-old hobby, while he worked at his computer. We'd stay up late—our attempt to fend off the darkness—then one of us would mumble about bedtime and the other would follow.

I'm not sure in what week of going through hell we found each other again as husband and wife, but early on, it became us against the world.

After the arrest, my night terrors came back with a vengeance. Now the thing trying to kill me in the dead of night looked an awful lot like my father. I'd sit up, silently, searching around the room with my eyes, looking for him. Or I'd startle and scream, tugging on a poor sleeping Darian. "Da . . . Da . . . Dad."

"It's not. Go back to sleep."

"How do you know?" I'd question Darian with accusation in my voice and knock things over on my nightstand reaching for my gigantic black Maglite or fumbling for the light switch on my lamp. "Oh. You're right. No one here."

Dad is in prison. He can't hurt anyone anymore.

My heart would beat almost out of my chest and I'd shake; then within a few minutes, I'd find my courage and will myself to turn the light back off.

Okay, nothing here, go back to sleep.

Sometimes I'd fight off the bad guy, inadvertently knocking into Darian, mistaking him for my foe. I'd usually wake up enough to realize my error. "Sorry. Night wig-outs again."

He'd grunt. "Mmph, it's all right. Sleep."

I'd always had night terrors. I didn't know which night they'd come back, but at least they were a beast I knew. What I didn't know was the loop. It was a new tormenter, and I had no idea how to shake it or when it would leave.

Home was no longer home. It had been permanently fixed into my bones as the place where I suffered immense life-threatening fear and pain on February 25. It created white-hot emotional toil, looping, looping, looping.

The FBI man knocked at my door . . . He asked for my DNA . . . He left . . . I never saw him again.

Over and over.

I was sure I was going crazy, though I continued to tell no one, not even Darian, who was trying to keep things together for both of us. I'm certain he also noticed his wife was continuing to fall apart in front of him.

I don't remember when, exactly, I landed back on a therapist's couch. I don't remember if I went because my mom talked me into it—she had started seeing someone in Wichita—if Darian coaxed me to get help, or if I waved the white flag of surrender myself.

I don't think I checked the suicidal-thoughts box this time, but I'm not sure about that either. I do remember taking in Dad's letters, folded inside their envelopes decorated from jail, and removing them in my therapy session—something tangible to point to, to say this was really happening.

Darian drove me. The office was in the community south of us, not far, but I wasn't able to muster enough strength to drive myself, plus my sessions were in the evenings. I'd become super jumpy in the dark again.

"The Lord is the stronghold of my life—of whom shall I be afraid?"[1]

Darian would sometimes go in with me, scrunching up next to me on the couch. Other times he would wait the forty-five minutes out in the lobby and then we would go eat a late meal at Steak 'n Shake.

My therapist pointed out I was grieving. I was allowed to grieve and needed to let myself do so, even though Dad was still alive and had caused an immense amount of harm. I was full of guilt and shame over what he had done and didn't always think I had the right to mourn his loss from my life.

Grieving the loss of the father I loved, grieving the loss of the man I never knew. Grieving for him, for my family. Grieving for the lives he took. Grieving for their families.

———

During these awful months, I realized I wasn't just running the details I was learning of Dad's murders and my own FBI trauma loop; I was also repeating the promises of God found in Scripture. I wasn't just stuck in the darkness; I was also clinging to the light.

"The Lord is my rock, my fortress and my deliverer; my God is my rock, in whom I take refuge, my shield and the horn of my salvation, my stronghold."[2]

"The Lord is my light and my salvation—whom shall I fear? The Lord is the stronghold of my life—of whom shall I be afraid?"[3]

Sometimes they would jumble out of order: *God is my rock and my salvation, whom shall I fear?*

The verses would cut through the darkness, and I had begun to teach myself not only to repeat them silently in my head but to utter them quietly under my breath when I was afraid. Especially in the dark.

"The light shines in the darkness, and the darkness has not over-come it."[4]

They brought me strength—defiance. Determination. The will to continue on. In the worst moments of my life, I was turning toward my faith in God, without even realizing at first that I had.

Sometime during these terrible months when I had nothing left—no ability to open my Bible—God gave me an image of *him*: Under me was his strength, a large, impregnable black rock he set me upon. Around me and in me was his Spirit, an impermeable shield of light. And over me, waving high, was his banner: *"Let his banner over me be love."*[5]

PART VI

Stand on Your Rock

He makes my feet like hinds' feet,
and sets me upon my high places.
He trains my hands for battle,
so that my arms can bend a bow of bronze.

—PSALM 18:33–34 NASB

CHAPTER 31

Long Distance Can Offer Sanity

April 17

Dear Kerri,

We start on pre-arraignment next week on April 19. The dog and pony show will start! Media and rest is a mess!

My attorney has planned on wavering the state. There will be a non-guilty plea enter at some point; that will give us time to review more evidence. At some point, we will make final plea. So much for all the legal.

I finally got to move into a Pod with 12 Inmates, I call them the "Dirty dozen gang." The system interviewed each for security risk and my high-profile status. They are a bunch of nuts and good guys. I learning their names and becoming Pod friends. One of them cutting hair this AM did a great job. I have my own chair-table (territorial) and everyone else does in the day-common-room. We share our meds, watch TV, play cards. I yet to play chess, although others play it every day. We also horse around, joke and carry on out here. As they say, "Do the time, and don't let the time do you."

The Dirty Dozen said, since I arrived, they have had special privileges. Although we have more cell shake down, enforcement of Detention Rules and the PD have been more official. I think because they know at some time I will speak out to the media, and they want to have their act covered or cleaned up.

We did get some fresh air last night. My first since arrest. Some guys hadn't been outside since September. Oh, it felt so good to breath fresh air and see the blue sky, half-moon. I had to be in chains but that, I am used to now. They chain me up as I move through the building. At arraignment, I will have leg chains and 50,000-volt shocker in case I get out control. I do get a lot of respect from the Dirty Dozen.

Mom said you haven't got any more mail from me? I don't understand? I have mailed out at least two or more letters. Could the FBI, be holding them? Grandma Dorothea fell and was in hospital? Can you or Mom let me know? So helpless!

I started envelope drawing. I hand draw some for Dirty Dozen. That is how we survive, help each other out. Trade. Hot chocolate, candy bar, Cheetos, tea, Tang, coffee, are basic need every day.

I'm amiss with news from family. I hope all is okay. I'm sure the media will be heavy again, sorry, forgive me.

Love,
Dad

APRIL 19

Dad's first court appearance, a pre-arraignment, only lasted minutes, which made me chuckle, imagining all the national media that had flown in for it. He wore his nice gray suit and a smart gray-and-yellow tie Mom and I had given him for Father's Day one year. My mom and I wanted my father to look appropriate for court, not to appear in an orange jumpsuit. Understanding it was important to us, Uncle Bob went to our house and selected suits, dress shirts, matching ties, and shoes for my dad.

My father was a criminal, but no matter what he had done, he still deserved to be treated with dignity and respect. He was called a monster, not human; it was said he should face the chair. It was brutal hearing folks knock my dad, calling him names, mocking him.

I understood this anger. He took ten lives, and there was absolutely no dignity or respect about what he had done. He should be in prison the rest of his life. But he was still my father, and while continuing to be torn apart inside, I quietly tried to support the man I knew through his arraignment and trial.

Let the truth be the truth.

I should've showed up at court and sat behind him, been there for him. But I was afraid. And I was ashamed I didn't have the strength or courage. I didn't want to be exposed by the media circus. I didn't trust the police, who I felt had used me.

And I couldn't imagine facing the families. They were one block of solidarity—they all lost someone they loved to him. They deserved justice.

My family was separate. We were his family. We would stay clear.

The best I could do, could handle, would be to follow Dad's court appearances online, checking news sites later that same day. I'd sob while reading through the details, carefully studying the photos of my dad, trying hard to hold on to what—and whom—I was losing. His suit hung looser, his belt was cinched an extra notch, his beard had grown out, his hair was a bit longer than I'm sure he preferred, and his face was haggard. He was aging overnight.

Jail was taking its toll.

And I was watching the disgrace and downfall of my hero, who was trying hard to keep it together. I could tell from the strain on his face.

"I need to write Dad before I fly home." I was on the phone with Mom after Dad's hearing.

"Don't tell your father about my foot." Mom had twisted her foot the month before and broken a bone. She was now hobbling around on crutches, wearing a boot.

What to tell my father and not tell him had become a matter of contention, not just with her but with his brothers too. There was an ever-changing and growing list of what I could and could not tell him. I also had little idea who was writing or visiting him and what they were telling him.

Word got to Dad anyway about Mom's injury, and he heard Grandma Dorothea was continuing to decline. My family was collectively trying to protect my grandma, but she wanted to write and visit him herself. She was diminishing, suffering from dementia and possibly Parkinson's. She was well taken care of by my uncles and their families, but it didn't seem to matter what Dad was told: he still begged for answers in his letters, worried about all of us.

When I wrote, I'd try to fill him in as best I could while attempting to dodge anything falling under the new "family privacy" label. I'd often say, "We're fine. Everyone's fine," figuring the more we could alleviate his concerns, the more likely he would be willing to plead guilty. (Survivor's tip: it's rather unlikely, two months after your father has been thrown in jail, that much of anything is "fine," let alone that you are "fine.")

April 23

Dear Dad,

Hi. I was happy to get your letters and hear how you're getting along—I worry about you being alone and in such a harsh environment. I'm glad you were able to go outside and can now talk to other inmates and have people to play cards with.

A part of one [of] your letters you wrote someone, maybe a stranger (fan mail?) is now on a website about the crimes. You might want to be careful who you write to, and who you give poems and drawings to. All that stuff could end up on the Internet or hurt your case in court.

Mom is planning to stay with Grandma and Granddad for a while. Dudley is staying with friends from church, he is doing well.

I'm coming to town this week, because our Corsica is struggling and Mom is going to give us the Tempo. I'm going to meet with your psychologist while I'm there. I've been in contact with your lawyers the last couple of weeks and Brian plans to help also.

We were glad you waived your hearing on Tuesday. Even though I am going to be in town, I'm still not ready to visit the jail. I promise I'll come see you sometime, though.

You were wondering about Grandma Dorothea. She stayed with family. Then she fell again and had to go to the hospital. She was there for a few days and then asked to be taken to a care home. She's doing better.

Brian is doing well; he is keeping busy with classes. Mom is doing okay and trying to adjust to her new life.

Darian and I are doing fine. I'm back to subbing. It finally warmed up here and the flowers and trees bloomed, but this weekend we are under a winter storm warning if you can believe that.

We know you are still deciding on your final plea, but the family feels if you are guilty, then you know you're guilty, so why do you have to look at the evidence? We don't really understand the legal issues involved but are trying to respect your decision. Things would be much easier on us, media-wise and court-wise, if you were able to plead guilty, but we know that's ultimately up to you.

I was wondering if something happened to you as a boy and if you wanted to open up and talk about it? I'm so sorry if something did happen to you. You should know it's not your fault if something happened when you were little. We've been told in cases like these, there is usually something that happened to the person committing the crimes that changed who they were.

Your psychologists and lawyers cannot tell me anything related to the case or anything you've told them. All I know is what you passed on through the pastor, in your letters, and the little the FBI told me on the first weekend. We know there's evidence but don't know exactly what that is.

Emotionally we all feel like it's still impossible you had anything to do with this—the man we know and love. Intellectually we know there is a whole other side to it and things that support that side. We're trying to come to an understanding—there could be two different people in you. Someday we would like answers, if you are able to give them or have them yourself.

Take care of yourself, watch your back, and try not to worry too much about the family. Some of them are having a hard time with things, and that might be why you are not getting as many letters or visits.

Try to stay strong and healthy. God is with you, he will never leave you nor forsake you. He has loved you even before you were created, he loves you no matter what, and will forgive all your sins if you ask for forgiveness.

> Sending you all my love and
> prayers,
> Kerri

Some letters were lost or held at the jail, possibly stolen by others somewhere along the way or misplaced in the early months. Brian wrote Dad, but the letter was returned because my brother kindly added a long-distance calling card and the jail didn't allow that. In this case, letters between Dad and I crossed in the mail. We sat down on the same day, sixteen hours apart, to write each other.

April 23

Dear Kerri,

Hi, how are you today? Are you and Darian doing okay and keeping busy???

I heard you maybe going to be in town to see Mom next

week. I would love to see you but know that would be hard and maybe too soon yet.

I can always write you, before the rest of the family. I don't know why, but you seem to understand me and these letters helps break the ice for other letters to follow.

A line or two would help me to overcome the sadness from not hearing from loved ones. And Kerri, it may be the mail is not getting through. I receive a lot of mail from others, pen-pals, but few from family. I did receive third letter from Mom and one from Grandma Dorothea.

Both you and Mom are welcome to visit me but like I said, the media may spot you or it may be too soon. It will be so hard to see any of you. I will be completely broken hearted, sad, but nice to see someone beside non-family.

By now you have heard the pre-hearing waiver on April 19. Mom was very happy I did the family wish. Arraignment is May 3, my attorney's want me to plea, Non-Guilty to buy some more time to decide our final plea. Bottom line, if I plea non-guilty, I'm not selling the family out at this time; I need time to make final decision.

Getting use to my new family, the Pod inmates—Dirty Dozen. Not only do I have respect now, the Pod is getting to be known and inmates are becoming Celebrities! Some Pod deputy won't guard us, due our rank now. Makes them too nervous. This week, we had a lock down for five inmates. No day room privileges. We took a pledge today all of us would face lockdown if the PD push us to hard. Some of the PD want to bust me so they can claim they lock me down for a day or two. I did 43 days of lock-down, big deal!

I busy my day with letters, pen pal (Christian and others) family, puzzles, *Eagle*, TV, games, cards, exercise, laugh, joke and war stories with other inmates. Also, some visitors, one pen pal and Pastor.

I keep track of those who wrote me and answered, keep me busy. I have received about 98 letters so far. A good portion I have returned. You may start to see some my letter, poem, showing up on Internet, I try not to write anything not already known or will be known, or hurt attorney-client relationship, or the family. But if this media event start to get out of hand, I shut it down quickly, with few pen-pal letters.

Take care, tell Darian hi, miss you!

Love,

Dad

CHAPTER 32

At Some Point You Have to
Face Your Fears Head-On

APRIL 2005
MICHIGAN

Early on a Sunday morning, Darian drove me an hour north to the Flint airport, in late-season, slowly falling snow. I found solace in the fluffy, white flakes dropping soundlessly, but flying home to Wichita felt like I was headed straight to the beasts with their cameras and microphones ready, mouths open to devour me.

God is my rock and my salvation, whom shall I fear?

I had planned to fly in the weekend before, but my father's two attorneys—kind, considerate public defenders—had suggested I delay my trip due to my dad's first court appearance. They figured a mass of media would be staking out Mid-Continent Airport awaiting my arrival. They even offered to pick me up and help get me to my family.

While sitting at my gate in Atlanta, waiting on my connection, I looked around to see if I recognized anyone. On alert. These people were headed to Wichita and would know about my dad.

On the plane, I scanned faces again while working my way back to my seat.

I don't recognize anyone, but maybe they recognized me? If they did, what must they think of me?

WICHITA

The airport was quiet when I landed: no media, no cameras, no beasts. I still felt self-conscious as I rolled my carry-on down the narrow concourse.

At the bottom of the ramp on the other side of TSA, Grandma Eileen and Mom were waiting for me. Mom looked stronger than she had in February. There was color and life in her face, but she was leaning on crutches, wearing a cumbersome orthopedic boot on her left foot.

I scanned the city as we drove to my grandparents' place, turning to look out the different car windows as if I were on patrol.

This place means me harm.

After exiting I-135, we slowly drove by my old house. It looked lonely with no brown-and-white springer spaniel waiting at the gate. And it didn't feel like my home anymore. It stung, and with tears I was trying to swallow back, I filed *home* into the list of things I'd lost.

I spent the next week around the corner from that house, at my grandparents' home, a peaceful, quiet place filled with memories. Looking out onto the park behind their house, standing where Grandma had stood for decades doing dishes by hand, it hit me how close Mrs. Hedge's old house was—and what insanity it was that my dad had murdered our neighbor when I was six.

I grew up playing in the narrow ditch that ran behind our three houses, coming home covered head to toe with mud. I played ball with my cousins down in the park on holidays, and we used to hit golf balls from my grandparents' yard over the low-slung chain separating it from the park. In winter, I'd trudge through new snow with my brother as he pulled our orange sled to my grandparents' tiny sledding hill.

On one blistering summer day when I was eight, Dad, Brian, and I took our sleek, aerodynamic neon-orange kite down to the park. Later I was goofing around, standing on a rusty red swing set directly behind Mrs. Hedge's old house. I slipped and fell, knocking myself hard between my legs on the metal pole.

Dad became edgy, irritated—like it was my fault I'd gotten hurt. In pain, and confused by his reaction, I asked to head back home. A few minutes later, walking along the ditch, Dad was swinging the kite haphazardly and one of the square plastic ends poked me in the eye, causing it to bleed.

Wincing, I quickly covered my eye with my hand and then winced again when I heard his booming voice: "Watch what you're doing!" There it was again—his irritation at my pain. Like my mishap had put him out. But something else was there, in his eyes and downcast posture. Shame.

I went inside and sat on the toilet with the lid down—our first-aid spot, where countless scraped knees had been patched up by Mom. I wanted Mom to stay near, as I always did when Dad was off.

She checked over my first injury, telling me she had done something similar falling on a bike when she was a girl. Then she drove me to Wesley—to the same emergency room I had been in a year before for my broken arm—to have my eye cared for. I had to wear a patch for a few days.

It was a lousy day, but my eight-year-old mind made it worse, tying it together as something bad that happened right behind the house where Mrs. Hedge had gone missing the year before. After that, I grew more fearful—not only afraid of that home but leery of the whole park.

Now I gripped my grandparents' kitchen counter, closing my eyes, nauseous. A long-forgotten memory, tinged in red static, attempted to sear through me.

Had Dad been "off" that day because we were playing behind Mrs. Hedge's house? Why did he get so mad when Mom and I got hurt? He didn't do that when Brian was injured.

Dad's in jail. He can't harm anyone else now. You're safe—stand down.

MONDAY

My dad and his public defenders asked if I was willing to speak to a psychologist who had been hired by the state as part of my dad's defense. Brian talked to her on the phone, and I agreed to meet with her while I was in Wichita at Aunt Sharon and Uncle Bob's home. The psychologist was friendly, and she quickly put me at ease. For the next few hours, sitting at my aunt's kitchen table, I shared what life was like with Dad growing up: camping, fishing, vacations.

All normal and fine. Nothing to see here, folks; put the DSM-IV *away.*

The psychologist's pen flew over a yellow legal pad. It helped me to talk openly about him, but it zapped me emotionally. And when she left, I still had no idea why my father needed a defense at all, seeing as he was guilty.

That evening, I had dinner with Darian's parents and his brother, Eron. It was my first time seeing Darian's family since the arrest, and I prattled on about everything that had happened over the past few months, talking myself hoarse. Dave and Dona were worried about me and tried to redirect the conversation for my sake. But I couldn't seem to stop.

Trauma.

That evening, Dave walked me out to my mom's car. Disheartened and wiped out, I said, "I don't know what Darian and I will tell our kids someday about my dad, their grandpa."

Dave replied, "That's several years off. Don't worry; we'll be old pros by then."

I hugged him and drove off with tears stinging my eyes—what he said had given me hope. I would hold on to those words and that hope for many years to come.

TUESDAY

Pastor Mike, wearing a black clerical shirt and white collar, visited my grandparents' house while I was there. Normally a laid-back, jovial man, I noticed a heaviness had come over him.

Mike was leading his flock through a terrible storm. He visited my father weekly, had taken Dad's confession, and now attempted to guide him as best he could. His eyes had pain in them I hadn't seen before, but his voice was as steady and warm as always.

I asked about the possibility of my dad pursuing an insanity plea.

Mike pointed out that the state hospital was likely a rougher, worse place to be than the maximum-security prison in nearby El Dorado where Dad would be sent after his trial.

"Your dad will likely be placed in solitary—for his protection and for the safety of the other prisoners and guards."

Solitary. I hadn't thought of that.

Alone.

"I don't think your father will last a year in a prison." Mom was looking at me pointedly.

"You mean 'cause the man loves his house shoes and your great cooking?" I grinned a bit, knowing those things were gone out of my dad's life forever. Mom smiled back.

"What does he call those things, Mom?"

"Creature comforts."

"Yeah."

We both were trying to contain our smirks; I was tucking my lower lip under my upper. Granddad scanned my face, his eyes twinkling, and I gave up, letting out a laugh, which he returned. It felt good to be home.

Mike turned to Mom. "He'll be fine," he said, pointing out how Dad would likely find "emotional comfort" in confinement. Dad would be contained, protected from himself. He could never harm another. Nor would he have to pretend—hide behind his facade.

Everyone now knew who and *what* he was. Dad might find some sort of relief in that.

"Dad might even enjoy prison. He won't have to deal with the stress of work, home projects, his to-do list." My sarcasm was evident. "He's gonna like that he doesn't have to deal with very many people—no more having to try to tolerate and work nicely with others."

"I agree." Mike spoke directly to me. "Your father is gritty and capable. He's excellent at dissociation. Got decades of time-honed skills. He's a survivor."

Survivor.

Dad was a survivor of a tough, tough sort. Tough physically, mentally, psychopathically. He would do fine in prison.

"Dad lied to us." I was looking at Mike again, searching his face for answers I so desperately longed for.

"He's not just a pathological liar; he outright betrayed all of you."

Betrayal.

Not just us, his family, but the whole city too: his friends, those who worked with him, the Boy Scouts, his community, his church. For decades.

I winced at the word *betrayal*, even though I'd come upon it myself a month ago. My brain shorted for a few seconds and my jaw went tight. I had to turn away from Mike and find something else to focus on for a moment.

Betrayal.

It was such a harsh word to hear out loud in regard to my father. But it was the truth. And the truth hurt like a real son of a gun.

CHAPTER 33

Most Folks Are Good and Intend You No Harm

Mom and her family had been busy working on our old home, preparing it for sale. I knew I needed to grab what I wanted before it was too late, but knowing I had to face the house made my chest seize.

On the drive down the block, I gripped the car door handle, searching the blue sky for a moment of peace. Grandma was with us and Aunt Sharon was meeting us, too, which alleviated some of my fear.

As I stepped through the back door into the kitchen, I was assaulted with memories—old smells, old sounds. This had been the only home I'd known for twenty-five years except when I lived in Manhattan. It didn't quite look like home anymore, though. It was still full of familiar items but had an air of loneliness and chaos. It was evident something had happened here; the feeling wasn't just of a family packing to move.

My mom, grandma, and aunt came in and set to work in the living room, settling into a routine they seemed to know well. The room was disordered: a half-full large black trash bag sat in the middle of the hardwood floor near a wooden filing cabinet from my parents' bedroom, a kitchen chair, and a shredder.

I should have been here weeks ago, helping.

Mom was going through a pile of financial records going back many years, shredding most of it. She didn't want to throw out anything with her or Dad's name or personal information on it, so she shredded them instead. Odd things of Dad's—like citations he'd written in Park City—kept appearing on eBay. We didn't doubt folks would dig through our trash either.

My aunt also said she thought the shredder was therapeutic: *Dennis . . . buzz . . . whirl . . . gone.*

I left them to it and walked around slowly, wandering into the bedroom I painted lilac three years ago. It was Mom's pretty guest room, the one Darian and I had stayed in at Christmas. Seeing her blue-and-white pitchers proudly displayed in a wooden china cabinet and the white bedspread with the delicate purple flowers made me want to bawl.

To heck with my father.

I stepped into my parents' bedroom but couldn't handle seeing my dad's odd assortment of knickknacks set on his dresser—like the little black stone figure with the tiny, piercing red eyes he'd gotten in Asia during his air force years. It had taken on a whole other dimension of weird. I wouldn't ever set foot in that room again.

I crossed the hall into the southwest corner bedroom—my old room—noticing the crushed wood at the bottom of the door where Dad had kicked it in a decade ago. My old bed and dresser were still there, but Dad had mainly been using the room for storage. In the middle of the room sat a folding table with *Eagles* still stacked on it.

I adored my bedroom growing up—it was a sanctuary where I'd passed countless happy hours by myself—but it had never fully belonged to just me. Mom used the fold-down desk for her typewriter when I was little, and my parents kept books on the top built-in bookshelf until I was tall enough to stand on a chair and snoop in their grown-up paperbacks. They both had always used my closets for storage; Dad even kept his handful of shotguns and hunting rifles, in their light-brown leather cases, in my back closet at times.

Dad's guns.

Used mainly for target practice, the guns were not loaded when they were in the house, or that was the assumption, anyway. It was also assumed they had not been used in the commission of a crime, but now there was no way to know for sure.

Dad had usually kept his long guns in the heater closet, which was harder to reach because it often had a cabinet pushed in front of it. I never knew where he kept his bullets, though, or his large handgun in the black case with red padded lining.

He had gotten into gigantic trouble with Mom when I was around twelve. She had come across a green fanny pack under the desk in our living room that held a small snub-nosed revolver. It looked like one that could be stuck down a sock in an ankle holster.

Loaded? Not loaded? No idea.

She rightly flipped out on him, yelling, and he actually looked abashed, muttering some nonsensical explanation while he took the pack away from her.

I'd gone target shooting with my dad once when I was in middle school, on a Rader family campout in the fall. We fired his shotgun and rifle at yellow clay targets we set in cornstalks and tossed high into the air. With his heavy handgun, we shot across a small ravine into hay bales.

I liked the long guns better but wasn't fond of the bruise the shotgun kicked into my shoulder. I only fired the handgun a few times because I disliked its purpose—I knew it wasn't for hunting.

On this day my eyes darted to my closets. I knew the guns had been removed by the police, but now I questioned my father, my memories—my life. What kind of man kept guns in his kid's closet?

Can't we go back to how things were?

They weren't really ever that way, kid.

I wasn't doing a very good job of choosing keepsakes; I kept getting lost in myself. I wandered back out to the living room, where I'd stacked two large tote boxes near the door. They were full of stamps, mainly unused unique ones my dad had been collecting the past several years. There was also a large stack of many first-day issues, hand-canceled, sealed in plastic, addressed to my dad. Those were expensive compared to the price of a stamp, but they weren't usable, nor could we sell them due to his name on them.

I bet he had done that on purpose, thinking they would be valuable *because* his name was on them.

"Hey, Mom, do you want me to leave a pile of unused stamps with you and Grandma? You won't have to buy stamps for years!" Dad wouldn't like us using his precious stamps to mail the utility bills, but that was exactly what we were going to do.

How had he afforded all these stamps? My folks hardly had money to spare. They had even remortgaged the house at one point. The house was barely worth more than the mortgage owed on it. I had no idea how Mom was going to make ends meet on her small salary. Another betrayal.

I grabbed a few empty tote boxes and carried them to my bedroom, sorting through my old stuff from high school and college.

Keep. Keep. Trash. Trash.

I rifled through my bookshelves and noticed a black-and-red paperback set at an angle on a lower shelf. It looked like it had been set there absentmindedly.

Dad.

I picked it up and turned it over; it was true crime.

Of course.

It wasn't mine. I had never seen it before.

A gray business card he'd been using for a bookmark fell out— one of my dad's old cards from his census days.

I turned over the business card; it had odd shorthand scribbles on it in his small, boxy handwriting.

In January 1991, Dad murdered Mrs. Davis. Dad's business

card from 1990 had CliffsNotes for a murder he was planning—when? In 1990? 2005?

I'm not going to survive this.

The room started spinning, turning electric, bright red. Hazy, like I was going to pass out.

Not this again.

I reached for the bookshelf.

God is my rock and my salvation, whom shall I fear?

My now oft-repeated jumbled verse saved me. I straightened back up. This was actually happening. Dad really was a murderer. Seeing his chicken-scratch on the back of that card had done it for me—it was true.

You're BTK's daughter—BTK's your father.

I put the card back in the book and slowly walked with the book down the hallway, past the place where we had been told Dad stored his trophies under the floor. I stopped in the living room, looking around with wary eyes. What in the heck else was *still* in this house?

I told my family about the book but didn't show them what was on the back of the card. I asked for the phone book and looked up the number for the Wichita Police Department. I hoped to reach someone from what had been called the BTK task force before Dad was arrested.

"Hello? I found some BTK evidence." I paced in the kitchen.

The male voice on the other end seemed bored when he replied to me. I wasn't the first caller, obviously.

"What and where did I find it? Well, you see, I'm his daughter. I'm home from Michigan, helping clean out our house and I came across—"

Now I had his attention. "Hold on, miss."

I spoke briefly to a detective.

"Hey, Mom? Landwehr and Otis are on their way."

Within ten minutes, there was a knock at our front door. I

looked through our small glass window—like Dad taught me. Ken Landwehr and Kelly Otis were standing there.

I unlocked the deadbolt, undid the screen door latch.

"Hi. I'm Kerri Rawson, Dennis's daughter. Come on in." I looked them both in the eyes and stuck my hand out. They both grinned a bit at me. And I gave them a slight smile.

You're going to be okay.

Ken was the homicide unit commander and the leader of the BTK task force. He had been out front in press conferences when BTK was in the news the previous summer. Ken was wearing a soft gray suit, with his badge and cell phone attached at his waist. He didn't strike me as just a badge; his dark eyes were surprisingly kind—sad, even. I wondered what he had to be sad about.

Kelly Otis, a detective who had worked tirelessly on the BTK case, wore his light-brown hair in a short buzz and struck me as grizzly bear–like in the best ways possible.

I instantly took a liking to these two. They both looked intently at me, truly seeing me. They were kind, respectful, and stood in our living room politely listening while my mouth ran a mile a minute. I handed them the book and card, they both looked it over, and Ken casually tucked it next to his side.

No careful handling, no crime-scene bags—he didn't need it as evidence. I think they had just wanted to come see us and the house. (For the record, it looked as if a tornado had passed through the living room.)

We didn't talk for long, but I think I attempted to thank them for Dad. I might have even worded it like that—"Thanks for Dad—catching him, and all . . ."

They got out their own business cards and scribbled their cell phone numbers on the back. "Call us anytime, day or night, if you or your family need anything."

They left not long after that.

I never got a chance to see or speak to Ken again before he

passed away in 2014. I carried his and Otis's cards next to the one from the FBI in my purse for many years to come, and I later programmed Otis's number into my cell on speed dial—just in case.

These weren't bad guys. They were genuinely concerned for me and my family. They had been aiding and assisting us for years, trying to catch my father. To stop him from hurting anyone else, including us. They were defending us now, saying publicly in interviews they were sure my family—including my mom—had not known what my dad was doing.[1]

They were also trying to protect us from the local media. They said we didn't want to be bothered, didn't want to talk. They said, "Leave them be."

I called, asked for help, and they came flying.

These guys are heroes.

I felt terrible at how mad I'd been at them: the entire Wichita police force, the KBI, and FBI for taking my dad away, for using my DNA.

I need to let my anger go.

I didn't like being mad at the police, but it was easier than being mad at my dad. It was too much to put on just him, so I'd spread my anger around.

Forgive.

I needed to forgive them for taking away my father; it was their job and they had done it well. He deserved to go away—forever. That was on him, not them.

Maybe I could still be mad at the FBI for botching how I was notified back in February? And the media. Definitely still them. Yeah.

CHAPTER 34

Fight for Those You Love

APRIL 2005

After Landwehr and Otis left, Mom said, "Well, I think that's enough for the day." She was a seasoned pro at the understatement.

It had been shocking to come across Dad's book with his murder notes, but in light of what had already been removed from our house and his office at work, it seemed way down on the scale of insanity. I didn't think the police missed anything else, but if they had, I wasn't about to go play detective.

On the night of my dad's arrest, worried the police might ransack our home, Dad drew a map to incriminating items he had hidden. What was found included old detective magazines up in the attic and down in the crawl space, magazine clippings of women and children stored in a tote box in a closet, and a hit kit.

The question still comes up over and over: How could we not have known who my dad was and what he was doing? Skepticism from strangers—and their insistence on vocalizing it publicly—was one of the most infuriating parts of this whole disaster. They'd say, "He kept evidence in their house, for Pete's sake."

The thing is, you didn't go rifling around in Dad's belongings. He could cause enough grief without any of us needing to deliberately seek it out. You could even get snapped at for being in his corner of the bedroom, for "messing with things that don't belong to you."

Mom and I would open Dad's bedroom closet to hang up his work and church clothes after getting them out of the dryer, but all I ever saw were some suitcases and a couple of filing tote boxes, nothing out of the ordinary. Mom's much-less-tidy closet, with shoes of many colors piled up, was more interesting—and the one that held the Christmas gifts, anyway.

Dad was the one who ventured up in the attic and down in the crawl space—both of them dingy, tight areas.

He kept the Christmas decorations up in the attic, standing the small wooden ladder in the kitchen closet and climbing halfway up into the dark hole in the ceiling with the cold draft, passing down odd-smelling boxes to us kids. When I was tall enough, I went up the ladder, curious what an attic looked like, but all I saw were white boxes marked "Xmas Deco" and a stack of dusty old magazines I glanced at, then dismissed.

I remember Dad clearing the hole and lifting the cover above the crawl space in the kitchen closet only one time. That was the day an F-5 hit southeast Wichita and Andover in April 1991, killing seventeen people. We were riding out the warning in the hallway like always, but Dad had actually been scared that day, moving hurriedly through the house, repeating, "This one is really bad, and if it shifts tracks, we will crawl down under the house." Mom replied, "There is no way I'm getting down there with all those spiders." She meant it too.

As for the tote box with the magazine clippings, I don't know where it was found. But I would simply have to revert back to the basic rule of the house: "If it's Dad's, you leave it alone."

I scoffed when I heard that Dad had left a hit kit lying around. It sounded quite a bit like our tornado preparation box: plastic, rope, duct tape, tools. Not knowing for sure whether it was a tornado box or hit kit, or maybe both, bothered me for years, though.

I also wondered what would have happened if any of us had stumbled across Dad's criminal paraphernalia. If Dad had been discovered by one of us, if he felt cornered, would he have hurt us to protect himself? Would we still be alive now?

It hasn't escaped me that the fact my family was still alive seemed to disappoint a few of the most vocal strangers.

Dad also kept severely incriminating items at his office—which was down the hall from a police force. I'm sure people called foul on that too. And I'm sure Dad found it funny—he had been right there under their noses. Mocking them.

Dad was keeping items he took from his victims in his locked cabinet at work, just like he had under our floorboards. He also had binders full of original copies of his BTK communications, crime and bondage drawings and photos, and meticulous logs.

There was no reason for any of his colleagues to question a locked cabinet though. He was a good employee, a hard worker who went the extra mile.

He was also a con man who had snowed all of us for three decades. Mocked us.

———

Best I can recall, I only came back to the house one more time to pick up what I wanted to take to Michigan. Along with my dad's stamps, I packed his state quarter collection, his Boy Scout manual, and his guides to birds, astronomy, and hiking.

I was fighting hard to hold on to the man I loved—how had it only been eight years since the Grand Canyon? I wanted some of his camping gear, too, but that meant having to go outside and open the small attached shed. I wasn't sure I could muster the courage.

The shed was where we stored gardening tools and fishing and camping gear and where we hung Patches's and Dudley's leashes. I often went to the shed for those things. But now the newspaper said

Dad had stored some of his BTK logbooks in there. From what I understand, he built a false back into the shed, which is maybe why the FBI asked Mom about the dryer in our kitchen; it vented out from the side of the shed. I remembered the miniature plants that were perched high on a platform covered in bright-white insulation with pink fiberglass sticking out.

Were Dad's logbooks—where he had written down graphic details of his seven murders from the 1970s—in that shed? Next to where I'd stood when I was tiny, learning about life from him? Concentrating really hard, I can vaguely remember three-ring binders with the ADT logo on them—red, blue, and white. I couldn't tell you, though, if I'm recalling them from my dad's office downtown or on the upper shelf of the desk that sat in the living room, or if I'm picturing them somewhere else—someplace odd—like the shed.

Concentrating that hard is gonna be the death of you, kid. Go get the things you want. It's okay. You don't need to be afraid.

The LORD is my light and my salvation. Whom shall I fear?[1]

Mustering my courage, I walked outside. I instantly recognized the familiar metal clink as I closed the gate behind me.

Oh. No dog here. You don't need to latch the gate anymore.

I walked a few more steps to the shed, took a deep breath, and pulled on the door; it had been sticking for years. The door opened with a slight pop of air.

Nothing scary in here. Just Dad's tools and fishing poles.

I grabbed the camping gear I wanted and closed the door with a shove of my hip. I took a quick glimpse of the backyard, then turned and carried my dad's gear to the car.

It would be ten more years before I would step foot in that backyard again, and if I'd known, I would have taken my time.

I would have walked to each of the four towering trees I'd always loved so that I could say goodbye, especially the one whose large branches shaded the porch swing that sat on the red-brick patio my dad had laid. It was the best tree for climbing and I had spent hours lounging in it, reading.

I would have visited the treehouse and might have even been brave enough to climb the rickety, gray wooden ladder, still propped up to reach its door, and look out the windows toward the ditch. That treehouse was magical to me as a child and big enough to sleep Dad and us kids on overnight adventures.

It didn't hit me that day, as I packed Dad's things to prepare for the upcoming sale of the house, that I would be losing something else—a place I loved. As can happen with the things we lose, it would only hit me later, after it was gone.

CHAPTER 35

Refuse to Let the Bad Stuff Win

MAY 2005
MISSOURI

Mom and I left a few days later for Michigan in the teal-green Tempo; she wanted to be out of town for Dad's arraignment and didn't want me driving the long trip alone. Due to Mom's broken foot, I did most of the driving. While I was getting fuel at a travel stop along I-70 between Kansas City and Saint Louis, it struck me how much our family had changed in such a short time.

Mom, Dad, and Brian had driven this same route a year ago, coming to visit. Now it was just Mom and me, and I was the one driving long distances and refueling the car.

Dad was always the one who drove. Dad was the one who pumped the fuel. Dad was the one who knew the best route around the big cities. Dad was the one who packed and unpacked the car. Dad was the one who carried the heavy bags into the hotel.

Dad.

The weight of the absence of this man in our lives settled into my bones. Everything had changed, and nothing was ever going to be right again.

Dad was gone.

MAY

DETROIT

At my dad's arraignment in early May, a not-guilty plea was entered by the judge as my dad stood silent. We had been told this might happen, to buy his legal team more time. We didn't understand the wait if Dad was going to plead guilty eventually, but we trusted his lawyers and hoped Dad would do the right thing.

Trying to gauge the state of my father, I sought out pictures of his court appearance online, studying them closely. He had trimmed his beard and his hair looked neater, but he continued to grow thinner, his dark-blue suit coat now a size too big.

At the end of the hearing, my dad looked upset as he was escorted out. I could tell from the pain across his face that he was trying to keep it together, fighting back tears. Was he sad?

He looked the same as the night we lost Michelle, his face darkened, his countenance broken. He also appeared similar to how he'd looked at my wedding, welled up with emotion, trying to hold it back.

The first time I saw my dad cry was in May 1993, the day we had to euthanize thirteen-year-old Patches. Dad had come across her in the backyard, unable to move her back legs. Dad came bounding into the house and I quickly followed him back outside. We tucked an old sheet under her and gently lifted her onto the faded orange sled, pulling her to our old Chevrolet.

Our vet told us there wasn't anything that could be done. Her back end was wasting away, likely due to a stroke. As he gave her the medicine to sleep, I heard an odd utterance from my dad and was shocked to see tears escape his eyes. He looked at me with a slight lift of his face and, with a shrug, attempted to wipe his face with his sleeve.

On the day Patches died, my dad dug a grave for her under a tree and marked it with a paving stone. A month later, he arrived home with a wiggly springer spaniel that had hitched a ride in the cab of his work truck. The puppy had been running loose, and after no one claimed it at the animal shelter, it became our new dog—Dudley.

May 2

Dear Kerri,

As you read this, the big day will be in the past and hopefully the team made the right decision.

Received your wonderful newsy letter from April. Oh, I was so happy to get your mail. I read it over and over again. The good and sad of it.

I really liked the colorful print on the paper. You are so thoughtful.

Things are going okay, although I am so tired of "Boot Camp 101." I'm ready for closure, Kerri.

Mail that goes to the "net," I'm trying to be careful on what's said. My poems will show up soon, that okay. But any letter could be used as a "spin."

Tonight, on TV-3, my poem show up. Last night, they show a letter on the news, speaking of family wishes for closure. It was type and out of focus, so you could not tell. I think it was a fake, or maybe one your letters that didn't get here. What a mess for us.

I hope the Tempo drove okay. Oil that it uses should be in the glove compartment. I assume you kids had some monetary problems, in not obtaining a new-used car a[s] planned. I pray it was not me!

Glad to hear you and Darian are working and going about life as you should, and the bible study (verses) you sent me was the most hopeful. I'm finding peace in the bible more than ever nowadays; it and other Christians are my new friends. And communications to family bring peace and the unknown—known. I miss Dudley, but it does sound he has adjusted.

Attorney said you did talk to Dr.'s, while here. I met them; I believe more confused about me.

I have kept busy, writing letters, day room activities and heavy thinking. Learning more card game, but boredom is slowly creeping in and I'm starting to get aggressive or attitude-ly towards this whole mess.

I design Mother's Day Card, Birthday Card for Mom. Also need to do a wedding anniversary one. I feel like a school kid doing this, but that is only way we (inmates can express our self.) Jail art, drawing, poems, and letters.

Love to you, family. Keep Mom in heart on her birthday, Mother's Day, and our anniversary, she will need extra support and love those days.

Love,

Dad

MAY

Dad had written: "Keep Mom close and help her. Her heart will mend someday, but I broke it; I'm sure it will never mend completely."

My heart is broken, too, Dad. I'm sure it will never mend completely.

"I'm so proud of you and how you turn out. Both you and Brian. A Dad could never ask for anything more."

I fought hard for two and a half decades to hear you say these rare, valuable words: "I'm proud of you."

"Did you know they took your medical DNA from records when I was a suspect before arrest?"

Yes, Dad. I'm quite aware.

He also wrote: "Sad about the house, all this loving years there. I know it the best. Did the police ever go through storage shed? Don't forget the book in the SW room up high. What time frame do we have: anything weird needs to be removed and thrown away from property."

Found the book. My room, Dad—that was my room.

Dad's blatant criminality and narcissism just reared its ugly, dark head. Like he flipped on the light switch and let himself really be seen by those he left living for one of the first times.

Thirty-one years. Ten murdered.

Anything weird about that? Yes.

Cursing commenced. And didn't stop for a good long while.

May 17

Dear Dad,

Hi, sorry it's been awhile since I last wrote. Included are pages from a puzzle book I had—I sent all the cryptograms.

We thought it might not be a good idea to send you family photos right now; we were afraid they would be stolen and end up in the media. Your lawyers agreed with us. None of our pictures have been in the media yet and we'd like to keep it that way.

Brian is doing well and keeping busy with classes and duty.

Mom has a lot of help from family getting things boxed up. She's getting help with the yard also. The tulips you planted are beautiful!

I saw Dudley, he has a permanent home now with our friends. He wanted to stay near me the whole time. He seemed okay when we left; he watched us through the glass door but wasn't too upset.

Mom and I had a good trip back here to Michigan and the Tempo ran fine. We did the trip in two days and I did most of the driving. Mom did about an hour each day so I could rest. She stayed for a week here and we had a good time. We went shopping and out to eat a lot. We went to Greenfield Village at the Henry Ford. We flew her home from Michigan on a nonstop flight and she got along fine.

We put new tires on the Tempo and had the brakes checked. The car is running good now and should last a few more years at least, fingers crossed! We didn't feel like we could make car payments right now.

Mom and I went to see Grandma Dorothea while I was home. She likes the care home and is getting along okay. She was doing all right when I saw her, but I guess she isn't eating well and has fallen down a few times since.

Darian and I are going to drive to New York and Connecticut at the end of this month to visit his grandma and Brian. We are looking forward to a vacation, I am always ready to see something different. I get that from you—wanting to travel, explore, get outdoors, be on the open road. I miss that drive between Wichita and Manhattan. We don't have anything like the Flint Hills around here—the open space and beautiful sky.

The police removed everything from the house they needed, they also searched the cars, sheds, and the rented storage unit. I don't think you have to worry about us running into anything else.

We weren't very thrilled to see your written interview with the local TV station. We also didn't like seeing your poems and letters on TV. We know you can and will do what you want to do, but we would really appreciate it if you could control that stuff better.

Any publicity is bad for the family, especially for the ones that live in Kansas. Brian and I have the grace of living in areas where we're not known; and that's been a blessing these last three months. Mom and everyone else doesn't have that grace. We're asking you to stop this type of communication on behalf of us. I have shared this view with your lawyers, and they were going to talk to you about it.

Mom is having the hardest time with everything that has happened. Brian and I share a different kind of bond with you than she does. It is easier for children to love their parents unconditionally (and vice versa) than it is for spouses. For her own sake, she might need to start distancing herself from you, and you're going to have to try to understand that.

She's stronger than we all thought and she's going to get through this, just as the rest of us are. We refuse to let the bad stuff win. Mom shared 34 good years with you, Brian 29 years, and me 26 years. We're trying to hold on to that—not let the other things define you or us. You should not let that define you either. You're stronger and better than that.

I love you and I know you're trying to do the right things. I'm truly sorry your life has turned out this way. I want you to know you're loved and cared for. You're loved by your children, family, and most importantly God, whose love and forgiveness is much more powerful and greater than any on earth could be. I'll write again soon.

Love,
Kerri

CHAPTER 36

Try to Hold On to
the Good Times

May 21

Dear Kerri,

Hello today and how RU? I know you are really busy and time does fly for those outside the 4 walls.

It's quiet this Sat AM. Out in the day room, a rare moment anymore due to "original" Dirty Dozen changing to different inmates. Some are noisy and younger and not very serious type people. I tend to use this quiet time outside my room to do correspondence and more serious matters before the noisy start. My own room is cold and not very comfortable.

I receive letter from Brian. I was excited, any mail from family is heart-felt and warming. It sounds like he's doing good and enjoying his Navy career.

Since I was without so much at first after my arrest, I tend to take new inmates under my wing until they have commissary funds. I have been bless with pen-pals helping me out. This week I bought some approved Health shoe for my feet. $42, but I really like them. Before I had sandals, made of cheap plastic and little support. Any way I share coffee, oatmeal, paper, pen, envelopes, and Jolly Ranchers. My mission of grace work!

They see me study the Bible at time and strike up a conversation. I explained I'm middle of the road, find a peaceful mood within the book and verse.

Had a quick haircut for Snicker-bar, a safety razor cut. Our hair clipper broke and we only get one set-3 month. So, my hair will be getting longer. A good hair cut cost me 2–3 Snickers bars.

AM exercise: 30 laps in the day room, 30 wall-push-ups and 9 pull-ups on stairway bar.

Received letter from Grandma Dorothea. Mention your visit. She was hoping I would write her more often. I have, but I think brother is sitting on letters. I might need to mail her directly. I hope there isn't a problem with my brothers, between them and me now. No love or do you think it's like lots of relatives feeling at this time. They have not wish to communicate or even think about me. Not very Christian.

I glad [you] kids are [at] least open to me. I understand you do not have to accept the problems I created but have open up to me as a human being.

I have many people write me, accept me, don't condone what happened but are friends. This is the way I treat people here. Accept but don't condone them!

I'm starting to enter a phase in life that Mom may not accept me and her loyalty is beginning to weaken. I sent her a birthday card, Mother's Day card and no letter or thanks. Her last letter was a month ago. I realize I broke her heart and the wound is deep. Do you think I should still write, it hurt to write and not get any reflection? Can you talk to her and find out her feeling? Or will you talk? Or will you write?

I'm enclosing a picture of the flower tulip bulbs we bought last year in Holland, MI. I so enjoyed that trip's time. I have a print on my desk. Neighbor took the picture.

By the way, there are things the police took that are family items and they need to be returned. I want my journal, my old guns, computer, return. They may have Mom's jewelry. I have a list of items they took from house, work, and storage shed.

If I go to prison, it will be just like it is here, at first. Lonely at first, months of no contact, except visitors. No monetary funds unless someone step forward. I will need book, magazines, hobby supplies, mailing item, pads, pen, pencil, health items and snacks. I now average about $25 per week on items. 25 x 52 week = 1150 per year x 10 year = $11,500

There is the chance I may be able to work, but at my age I don't know. I'm so close to retirement, the prison jobs may not pay well or none. Bottom line either the family support me, visit, letters, monetary, or I will have to create another support system!

There will be a plea from me, please keep this quiet. That will be part of closure for me and Sedgwick County.

All is going okay. I have a schedule, keep to myself a lot but socialize some and befriend all who crossing my path or attempt to. The guards like me and now I don't wear belly chains, except to court or outside the main area. I sit at Table A, the higher pecking order table, and better seat now, better control of my back and good view of others. My art is improving and everybody want some poem, from me. My friends endless or people that talk to me. Tell Darian Hi.

Love,
Dad

JUNE

Jewelry? Why would the police have Mom's jewelry? Had Dad given Mom stolen necklaces from homes he had broken into? Oh, dear Lord—had he given her jewelry from one of the women he murdered? Had he given me anything that belonged to someone else?

My stomach churning, I dropped the letter and went to my jewelry box, rummaging through my necklaces and earrings.

This isn't ever going to end, is it?

June 7

Dear Dad,

Just received your letter dated May 21. Darian and I've been on vacation and picked up the mail today. If you haven't received that last letter from me, the lawyers might be holding them, they were upset about the media leaks.

Darian and I just got back from traveling to see his grandma and Brian.

We drove to Groton, Connecticut, to spend the weekend with Brian. We walked around Mystic with Brian looking at the ships and eating mussels at dinner while overlooking the river.

We drove to Boston the next day and saw the USS *Constitution* (Old Ironsides) and a naval destroyer from WWII. We walked around downtown Boston on the Freedom Trail, stopping at the church Paul Revere hung lanterns in and touring his home.

Brian had duty on Memorial Day, so Darian and I walked around Groton and New London and we went to the *Nautilus* museum. We saw the Long Island Sound, visited a fort from the 1800s and walked along a pier. I finally got to put my feet in the Atlantic, accidentally falling off a rock into the bay.

Darian and I then drove to New York. We stayed at his grandma's until Saturday. She's in a care home, but Uncle John was at the house and we hung out with him and Dave, who flew in to spend the week with us.

Saturday, we drove back to Niagara Falls and stayed in a hotel near the falls on the Canadian side. We saw the falls lit up at night. On Sunday, we took the *Maid of the Mist* right up to them. We got soaked, even with ponchos on.

We took the Tempo, we had to add a quart of oil on that first Saturday and Dave checked and added other fluids that were low at Grandma's, but it did well.

I am glad you were able to buy some better shoes, they sound like they will be more comfortable on your feet.

Please be careful around the other inmates, what you tell them or give them. Under no circumstances should our personal information be given to other inmates or the media.

About the items the police took, your lawyers or the detectives can contact me when they are ready to turn it over if they legally can.

Your younger brothers are having a difficult time with everything. They are handling this by trying not to think about it, not talk about it—acting like it didn't happen. If a person starts communicating with you and visiting you, then it makes it real or more real, at least. People handle grief and stress differently. Paul, your mom, your uncle, along with Pastor Mike, have been willing to come see you, but don't hold it against the rest of our family for not coming.

Your family is not condemning you; we're trying to cope with our own thoughts and feelings. Strangers can write and visit or hang out with you in jail, because they are not emotionally attached. Your family is—and it's too hard sometimes.

In one way, it's as if you died on 2-25. You're no longer around to share our lives, and that is something we have to deal with. We're going through a grief process, like if you had died, because we are grieving the loss of you as a husband, father, brother, and son.

There will be no more: camping trips, fishing trips, vacations, Christmas mornings, Christmas get-togethers, walks around the school, fireworks—with you. That list could go on and on and on. You've lost so much, but so have we, and we need time to come to terms with that.

You've had these secrets, this double life, for 31 years; we've only had knowledge of it for three months. Give us some time and try to be patient with us. This family is not "being un-Christian," we are trying to cope and survive. This is the only way we know how.

You're still a husband, father, brother, son, and friend. However, you lied to us, deceived us—we have been hurt more than I ever could have imagined—and you need to realize that. Life isn't the same for you, but it's not the same for us either.

Our lives changed forever also on 2-25, and by no choice of our own. You separated those two lives you led, never let them intersect. You seemed fine with this, and you seem to not understand why we're all not fine with it also.

Mom, Brian, and I are trying to hold on to all the good times—all the years we shared, but even that is somewhat tainted right now, because after 12 p.m. on 2-25, that all changed.

You did things in your life that were not true to your character—unthinkable things to have been done by someone as good, trusting, moral, and loving as you are—as we knew you. You don't seem to get what it's like to have to try to reconcile the man we know and love, the man we looked up to, the husband, father, brother, son—with this other man.

I don't even think it is mentally possible to do it.

I've tried not to get upset or angry with you in my other letters, but you seem confused about the family, seem confused about our feelings. Maybe it's part of your mental illness, if you have one, you can't understand why we're not acting the same, why we are not as loving, understanding, caring as we were before 2-25.

I'm sorry if I've upset you but you needed to hear it from someone. Life is not hunky-dory, everything is not okay, but this family is trying to make things okay again in the only way we know how.

Things will never totally be okay again—ask Andrea and her folks about losing Michelle. Mom is trying to start her life over, Brian and I are trying to make the best of it, and everyone else is coping in the only ways they know how, but you're going to have to be a little understanding of us also.

Maybe Pastor Mike or the psychologists can help you make sense of some of this, but it needed to be said. I'm sorry if I've upset you. Thank you for writing and letting me know how you're doing.

Love,

Kerri

BREAKING NEWS: GUILTY TEN TIMES OVER

MONDAY, JUNE 27, 2005
WICHITA

The BTK suspect, Dennis Rader, arrived at court this morning in Wichita, Kansas, wearing a cream-colored sports coat and a black tie. He quickly pleaded guilty to ten counts of first-degree murder, and then, in the presence of the victims' families, proceeded to describe in horrifying detail his crimes that terrorized the Wichita community for decades.

Under direction and questioning by the judge, Rader's statement went on for over an hour. Rader's testimony was broadcast live on TV and was reported with frequent updates on the internet. Some say Rader's tone was flat, monotone, and showed no emotion. At times, Rader was confused, mixing up addresses of crime scenes and even the names of victims.

Rader's family was not in attendance, nor were they available for comment afterward. Rader's next appearance in court is scheduled for mid-August, when he will be sentenced.[1]

CHAPTER 37

Truth and Justice Can Hurt

After my dad's arrest, Wichita police detective Tim Relph questioned him. Relph said, "People will think ninety percent of him is Dennis Rader and ten percent is BTK, but it's the other way around."[1]

I've always argued he's 95 percent my dad and 5 percent, I don't know—don't know that man. Never met him. My father himself has said, "I was a good man, who just did bad things."[2]

Wherever my father falls, I've still not reckoned fully with who my father really is.

JUNE 27, 2005
DETROIT

We knew the guilty plea was coming. But we didn't know my dad would be asked by the judge to describe the murders to the court. I don't think my dad knew either.

I didn't watch it live. Instead, I watched a few short clips of my dad speaking and read through the court transcript posted online. That's all I could handle.

Along with the rest of the world, on the day my dad pleaded guilty, I learned many horrific details of his crimes. Unlike the rest of the world, I was able to tie many of my dad's details to my own life. His words wreaked devastation in my life for years, though I lost some of those memories.

Self-preservation. Survival. Dissociation. Denial. Call it what you want.

There are things I knew in 2005, knew deep in my broken soul, knew in minute detail, that I forgot and wouldn't be able to recall until I faced them again. It took the next ten years to piece together what I know now.

DECEMBER 1973

While driving Mom to work one winter morning in late 1973, Dad spotted Julie and Josie Otero leaving their home. Mom had been skittish about ice and snow-packed roads since her accident, and Dad, who had been laid off from work, would have naturally offered to drive her.

Dad stalked the Otero family for the next month and committed his first four murders while Mom was at work a few miles away. Dad also stole Joseph's silver wristwatch and Joey's black transistor radio.

It wasn't until 2015 that I realized the Otero home—a sharp white bungalow with black trim and shutters and a black cast-iron railing on the porch—appeared strikingly similar to my grandparents' home. The Otero home was near Edgemoor Park, inside of which sits the Rockwell branch of the public library, a place I sometimes visited with my dad. I can recall driving along their street but couldn't tell you if Dad ever slowed down as we passed.

I know that when I was young, a transistor radio sat beside my dad's bed. I still don't know if it belonged to Joey or not.

APRIL 1974

In April 1974, after murdering Kathryn Bright and almost killing her brother, Kevin, Dad hid his bloody clothes and murder weapons in my grandparents' white tool shed and chicken coop. He disposed of them later. I played hide-and-seek with my cousins in that shed ten years later.

Kevin gave a good description of my dad to the police, including that he was wearing an air force parka, green with fur around the hood, and a silver wristwatch with an extendable band on his left arm. I didn't know about Kevin's description till 2015.

I wore one of Dad's air force shirts for Halloween when I was in high school. It was green, short-sleeved, and said Rader on the pocket, but I don't recall seeing the parka when I was younger. Dad always wore a silver wristwatch when I was growing up, though I still don't know if the watch I so closely associated with my dad was Joseph's watch, nor do I know which one Kevin saw.

In 1974, a sketch based on Kevin's description to the police ran in the *Eagle*. In the drawing, the suspect had a round face, small dark eyes, and a dark mustache. Dad said later he thought the drawing printed in his newspaper was "uncomfortably close to me, but no one will come for me."[3] I didn't see the sketch till the night of my dad's arrest.

MARCH 1977

In March 1977, Dad, carrying a briefcase and posing as a detective, showed a picture of my mom and my one-year-old brother to a little boy, asking if he had seen the boy in the picture, then followed him home. Dad knocked on the little boy's door, spoke to his mother, Shirley Vian Relford, then forced his way into their house and murdered her after locking her three screaming children in the bathroom.

I don't know which picture my dad showed the little boy that day.

DECEMBER 1977

In December 1977, Dad spotted Nancy Fox working at a jewelry store in the Wichita Mall. He stalked her and strangled her with his belt in her home.

I occasionally shopped or saw movies at the same mall with Dad. I remember waiting at that mall for the Oldsmobile to get new tires at Montgomery Ward when I was around ten. We walked through the parking lot over to Taco Bell for lunch, and I can recall watching Dad fill out a pile of job applications while we shared a bag of churros. He had been laid off from ADT not long before.

It wasn't until 2015 that I shook out a memory of Dad taking off his belt and snapping it at me when I was around the age of four. I can still see him, framed by the dim light in our hallway, looming, menacing, threatening to hit me. When I remembered that, I understood what sometimes felt sinister in our home.

Not long after I recalled the memory of the belt, I spilled a jar of nails in my home. As I picked up the nails, my PTSD monster reared its ugly head. I remembered visiting the hardware store with my dad when I was little. Did Dad buy items he used for murders when I was along?

Dad had stolen some of Nancy's jewelry, and years after his arrest, he said about that time, "I thought, no, I'm not going to give it to my wife, that's too cruel. I thought about giving it to my daughter once. And I maybe did give it to my daughter."[4]

APRIL 1985

Dad told the court on the day of his plea he left a "commitment" on Friday evening, April 27, 1985, to break into the home of our neighbor Mrs. Hedge. My dad was a Scout leader for years, and Mrs. Hedge attended the church in Park City where my brother's pack met.

I told the FBI agent in February my father wasn't home the night Mrs. Hedge had gone missing—he was on a Cub Scout campout with my nine-year-old brother. That was the night we had a thunderstorm and I curled up with Mom in her bed.

Dad hadn't wanted to say openly in court he had used my

brother's campout as an alibi. But that night, Dad left the Scouts, drove to a bowling alley, sloshed some liquor in his mouth, pretended he was drunk, and took a cab to our neighborhood. He carried with him a bowling bag as a hit kit. He walked through the park behind my grandparents' house, cut Mrs. Hedge's phone line, and broke into her home. A home with a floor plan identical to ours.

He waited in a closet for her to come home and then strangled her. I still don't know which closet he waited in. Which room was hers? Mine? I don't know.

I vaguely remember seeing an old maroon bowling bag with a white stripe when I was young. I don't know if that's what Dad used. I also bowled at the same alley in middle school.

At my dad's plea hearing, he told the court he wrapped Mrs. Hedge's body in a blanket and used her car to drive her to our church. He carried her body in, dressed her up, and took Polaroids. He then drove east and discarded her body out in the country. Dad went back to the bowling alley, left her car, and drove back to the campout in his car.

I likely attended church that Sunday with my mom and likely played among the tall swaying pines after the service let out.

Mrs. Hedge's body was found a week later, with odd, out-of-place pine needles lying nearby. From my understanding, they had inadvertently been picked up when Dad laid her body down on the ground at church.

A few weeks later, Mom scolded me for climbing the tall pines at church, and minutes after, I broke my arm running around inside. Dad carried me out of the church and placed me in the back of our silver Oldsmobile.

I realized after finally learning the truth at the plea hearing that Dad was likely upset about missing our Padre Island trip because it meant he had to stay in town while the police were looking for Mrs. Hedge's murderer.

I learned about my dad, Mrs. Hedge, and the photos at the

church at his plea hearing. Sometime during the next ten years, I suppressed that knowledge. It only came back to me after I read about it in 2015, and at the age of thirty-six, when I read about the odd pine needles found by her body, I found myself racked with grief—sobbing.

SEPTEMBER 1986

A month after my family's vacation to Disneyland, while I was sitting in my third-grade classroom, Dad took a lunch break from ADT, disguised himself as a telephone repairman, and forced himself into Vicki Wegerle's home. Dad murdered her while her two-year-old son cried and her older daughter was at elementary school. Dad dumped evidence in a trash can at a nearby Braum's before returning to work.

In 2015, I found out Mrs. Wegerle volunteered as a babysitter at Saint Andrews Lutheran Church, the same place Mom and I had watched children during aerobic classes before I was old enough to attend school. I have no idea if we ever met Mrs. Wegerle or if my dad was aware of the possible connection.

JANUARY 1991

Dad said again in his plea hearing that he left a "commitment" the night he murdered Mrs. Davis in January 1991. He actually was at Trappers Rendezvous, a winter Boy Scout gathering north of Wichita with my fifteen-year-old brother. He left, parked at the church in Park City where the Scouts met, and walked a mile and a half in the cold to her home. He threw a cinder block through her sliding-glass door, murdered Mrs. Davis, used her car to move her to a fishing lake, hid items of hers under the old white shed at church, and then moved her body again using our silver Oldsmobile. After that, he returned to the Scouts.

We fished a few times at that lake tucked along I-135, and as a kid I played back by the white shed at church, where I petted horses over the barbed wire.

He used our car. The one he used to teach me how to drive. The car I accidentally hit the brakes too hard on at a yellow, sending Dad and me on a 180-degree wheel-screeching spin. The car I drove to high school with a K-State Wildcat bumper sticker that poked fun at rival University of Kansas, declaring, "Jayhawk in trunk." I was mortified when I found out about the car and Mrs. Davis.

When Dad mentioned throwing the cinder block through Mrs. Davis's sliding-glass door at the plea hearing, I remembered the conversation I had on the phone with Dad in 2001 about renting an apartment with a sliding-glass door. He told me it was safe.

JUNE 2005

I'd been fighting hard the past four months to not completely split apart, fighting to hold my tattered remains together. On the day of my father's plea hearing, the weight of what he had done, the enormity of it, crushed me once more.

Dad had taunted and mocked the community of Wichita and the police with his BTK communications, but he also mocked my family's church and my grandparents—using these beloved places as cover for his crimes.

Stalking, then breaking and entering. Torturing and violently killing ten people. Almost killing an eleventh person. Desecrating their bodies. Part of a family: a father, mother, two children. Orphaning three children. Terrorizing children in homes where their mothers were murdered. Daughters, sisters, wives, mothers, grandmothers.

Seven families were destroyed by my father, never to be the same again. Eight: his family—my family—too. *My* family—not his, no longer his.

No longer his.

CHAPTER 38

175 Years Is a Long Time

On July 11, my old home was auctioned off in a circus. The police barricaded the street and folks stood around watching the show. The local and national media, potential home buyers, and curious folks trampled through my house and backyard, now emptied of everything but the appliances.

I'd been home that week, staying with my grandparents and Mom down the street. I flew out the day the satellite trucks arrived, chuckling loudly as I glanced down the street to the gathering clown show trying to score a big scoop. The national media seemed to be unaware that the interviews they so urgently sought were sitting a block away. I was relieved to take off for Michigan a few hours later, though.

At the auction, a woman purchased our home for $30,000 more than it was worth, saying she wanted to help my mom. Later the sale stalled when lawsuits were filed, one by three of the victims' families and one by the state of Kansas. While dealing with the lawsuits, Mom kept making payments on the old house to avoid defaulting with the bank. She also began renting a new place. None of this was her fault, of course, yet she was stuck with Dad's costs and consequences.

On July 26, Mom was granted an emergency divorce from my father. She actually apologized to me for her divorce finalizing on my wedding anniversary. I don't remember if I laughed or cried when she told me.

Thirty-four years, one marriage. Gone like that. Two years, one marriage, fighting and holding on against immense odds. It felt like many lifetimes had passed between my wedding day and July 26, 2005.

I wrote my dad later that day.

July 26

Dear Dad,

Hi—sorry it has been a while since I wrote.

Even though I knew what was coming the day of the plea, I was still thrown for a bit of a loop—along with most everyone else. We were told you were guilty from the first weekend, because the FBI told us you were confessing. And we had also talked to some of the Wichita Police later on, who confirmed what the FBI told us.

There was no way to refute the evidence they had, so intellectually we were able to start accepting the truth. Knowing you would be in prison the rest of your life, we were able to start dealing with this new reality early on.

Even though we understand the truth intellectually, emotionally, it's much more difficult and confusing. I'm not sure we will ever be able to accept it on that level.

Mom's doing good and starting to move on. Brian's school is going well, it will not be too much longer, the fall, when he will be ready to go to fleet.

Love,
Kerri

At the end of July, I received a letter from Dad after I wrote and mailed mine.

July 27

Dear Kerri,

Forgive me for missing your wedding anniversary on July 26. I had it marked down and meant well, but didn't get it done. So, this card (made by another inmate) cost me a Snickers bar, will be the wish.

This Sunday PM, after supper, I'm in my room with fresh cup of coffee and finishing letters and correspondence. Wrote Brian last week to wish him his birthday wish. Well, I'm glad you, Brian and Darian had a good time back east. Brian last letter spoke of positive time. He is always so positive and upbeat.

The lien on the house has caused a wedge between me and defense. They mention nothing of this early as we try to make decisions on a non-guilty or plea. I wanted Mom out of harm from the onset. I cooperated with the police, I cooperated with the court, to save tax payers millions and family wishes on plea. And then they screw me with a lien. It's out of my hand. I'm still very upset. And trust no one in the legal world anymore.

I understand Mom has moved. Her letters are brief and she may not see me for a long time. I can write, but will be writing to a brick wall? Kerri, will that be the same for you? I hope not!

Just a few lines, to let me know what going on helps. Maybe after sentencing and the dust settle, Mom and the rest of the family will write.

The crime did sell you and the rest out, but I'm still family and need a little letter support if nothing else.

I be shutting down here each day. Cleaning up room, etc. Soon, El Dorado, "old soldier's home!"

I always hope for open letter from Mom, but afraid that is gone, she was open until the plea, then it dropped.

Please write, if nothing but thanks.

Love to you!

Dad

JULY

DETROIT

Dad had written: "By the way, you should contact a lawyer and sue Wichita-KBI-FBI, for obtaining your DNA without your permission. I don't hold that aspect of the crime/evidence against you."

No words would come close to describing how angry that made me: He didn't hold my DNA against me? Well, how mighty big of him.

"That aspect of the crime/evidence."

Uh, his crimes. His evidence.

"Please write, if nothing but thanks."

No. Not going to thank you for pleading guilty to what you were guilty of. Taking ten lives.

I tucked away his letters from this time period for ten years. I didn't even know these words still existed till I accidentally came across them in the summer of 2015:

Want you to know I do not hate you or don't love you. The problems I have are far away from family love. I know they hurt and hopefully, someday your heart will mend and you can forgive me. You will always be my baby girl I raised right-proud-independent and now is a grown adult with many years of love to give . . . I'm so glad we had that family vacation in May 2004. So many memories! Life before the arrest was a good time, and the dark side took me away.

AUGUST

I accepted a full-time job as a coffee barista at a nearby Borders bookstore in August. It wasn't ideal, but it was a paycheck.

I didn't bother to tell anyone I was the daughter of the serial killer featured in the newspapers and magazines stacked by the front counter.

I did come home smelling of espresso beans, though.

AUGUST 17

My dad's two-day sentencing hearing in August was almost the death of me. I figured it would be a simple declaration from the judge of how many years my dad had been sentenced to.

I was woefully unprepared.

At his plea hearing in June, my dad's account of his crimes was horrifying, but he glossed over aspects of the murders, minimizing his torture of victims. It was a one-sided, narcissistic view.

Considering my dad's narrow telling, the public's need to hear the full truth, and the victims' families' rights to closure, the prosecutors decided to go forward with a full disclosure of my dad's reign of terror. They checked with the victims' families before proceeding, making sure they were okay with a full release of the evidence. None of them objected.[1]

But the prosecution didn't check in with this family. The eighth family.

I found out later that others had come to the defense of our innocent family, asking if there was an actual need to do this. Wouldn't it embarrass my family further?[2] Shame us? Hurt us?

No one asked or warned us it was coming.

Over a two-day period, the detectives who had worked the cases went into gut-wrenching descriptions of each murder from the witness stand. They showed actual murder weapons, crime scene photos, and brought to light photos of my dad in self-bondage.

I couldn't stomach watching this horror live, but I read through the court transcripts later in the *Eagle* and caught video clips online. A national TV audience tuned in out of morbid curiosity.

But I wasn't the public. I am his daughter. I know his tube socks. I know his legs.

And I know where some of the pictures were taken. For example, my grandparents' basement, where I ran around with cousins and where we celebrated holiday after holiday.

I continue to wonder: After Brian and I conked out in our three-man tent set up on a sandbar at Lake Cheney, had Dad possibly dug a hole and tied himself up?

I don't have any solid answers to that horrible thought. Nor do I have answers to what still terrorizes me awake at night.

In hindsight, I understand why the prosecution—the detectives— did what they did. My father degraded ten people, including two children, beyond comprehension. But he was still my father, and I loved him—no matter what he had done.

AUGUST 18

The families were given the opportunity to give statements after the prosecution finished. (I still have not read those transcripts. I tried once, ten years later; I made it a few lines in and almost threw up.)

After the families made their statements, my father was given a chance to make a final statement—to show remorse. Instead, he selfishly rambled on for twenty minutes, in a speech nicknamed "the Golden Globes" in Wichita. I listened to some of it and read a transcript of the rest.

Dad stood up in court and called us—my mom, my brother, and I—social contacts, pawns in his game.

Dad taught me and my brother chess, using the beautifully

carved stone set he brought back from Asia while he was in the air force. He patiently showed us how each piece moved, and I can still recall the earthy smell of the brown-and-white checkered board. When you opened the box, you were met with knights, bishops, rooks, kings, and queens, and, yes, pawns, resting in soft red-felt lining.

My family lived with—and loved—this man for decades. We fed him, did his laundry, and took care of him when he was sick and injured. I adored him. Even though he could be a brute.

And now he called us "social contacts."

How dare he.

He could rot in hell.

———

That speech of his was the last time I would ever hear his voice.

I cut off all communication with him and tried to distance myself from the news.

They were saying BTK—my serial killer father—was a sexual, sadistic psychopath.

But I was in no condition to begin to understand what any of it really meant. What I did understand was Dad had lied to us, betrayed us, every day since my brother and I were born.

Every day since my mom met him—he knew what he was capable of, what he was.

He should have never gotten married or had children.

I shouldn't be alive.

He should have checked himself into a mental hospital and never left.

He should have turned himself in before he took the lives of the Otero family.

After he murdered, he should have turned himself in to the police.

He should have been in jail the past thirty-one years.

People should still be alive.

But my brother and I wouldn't be.

I was okay with that—I'd trade my life for theirs.

AUGUST 19

WICHITA

The morning after my father was sentenced, he was driven by the sheriff's department to the El Dorado Correctional Facility thirty minutes east of Wichita.

It was a route my father knew well, and the last time he'd ever get to take it.

The Kansas prairie was an unexpected green for so late in the summer, the sky was blue, and my father's life, as anything he had ever known or wanted, was over.

Dad arrived at his final homestead wearing a red jumpsuit, cheap sandals, and chains around his waist, wrists, and ankles. It was a far cry from the nice suit he'd worn to court the day before. Looking weary, thin, and as if he was continuing to age overnight, he shuffled toward the barbed wire–topped walls.

Dad had been sentenced to 175 years in prison. Ten consecutive life sentences. Twenty-three hours a day, alone in a concrete cell in the maximum-security wing, next to death-row inmates. It sure wasn't the retirement he dreamed of.

In the coming years, well-meaning folks would ask, "How long will your dad be in prison?" I would answer, "For the rest of his lifetime and the one after that."

PART VII

Binding Up a Broken Heart

He heals the brokenhearted and
binds up their wounds.

—Psalm 147:3

CHAPTER 39

Keep Faith in the Good

AUGUST 2005
DETROIT

It was over. Dad had been locked away.

And I was done.

After my dad's sentencing, the past six brutal months of my life slammed down on my soul. A dense, dark gate barred my memories.

Time, and the way I spoke about it, forever divided: before my dad's arrest—after my dad's arrest.

Before Dad. After Dad.

There was the before, but it now had a gray, murky tinge: nothing was really ever the way it had seemed. Dad had never *really* been just Dad.

And now there was the after, waiting on the other side of my dad's sentencing: a hope, a future, a life. But how could I continue forward with my own life, knowing so many lives had been destroyed by someone I loved?

I had the rest of my life in front of me—they had theirs taken away. It wasn't fair. I didn't know how to reckon with the shame I felt over what my dad had done—what he had taken. Guilt-ridden, any choice I made to try to find normalcy felt fake, hollow.

I didn't have any answers, but I longed for space and time to recover: to mend my wounds, to heal. Tired of grieving, tired of hurting so badly, I couldn't breathe.

Determined to not deal with any of it anymore, I attempted to gather all that had transpired over the past six months and haphazardly shove it to one side of my mind, one side of my life. I figured if I bandaged the immense ache within me tightly enough, it would eventually heal in time. And I assumed the loop from the day of my dad's arrest would go away once our lease was up and we could move away from where I had suffered so much.

But hiding the pain away only caused it to fester. And the loop followed me to our new place, where the sliding-glass door to our patio multiplied my fears.

SEPTEMBER

By Labor Day, we were reasonably settled into our new apartment. It came with a washer and dryer, and an address my dad and the media didn't have, thanks to a post office box.

If you had come across us, you would've seen a young couple trying to make their way. Even if you stopped to talk to us, or worked with us, you likely wouldn't have noticed anything amiss. You wouldn't have known you were standing next to the daughter of a serial killer.

Yet I knew it, and it continued to traumatize me internally, even if I only showed outward signs occasionally.

God?

A quiet, peaceful little life.

I prayed it over and over.

A week after my dad's sentencing, I had an interview at a struggling charter school for a first-grade teaching position, for a classroom where the teacher had already quit after two days.

They asked me to teach an off-the-top-of-my-head math lesson. I winged it well enough, was hired on the spot, and stayed the rest of the day as the new teacher. The same day, I quit the coffee job.

I was so happy to finally have my own classroom and a decent paycheck that I didn't realize what a difficult external challenge I had piled on top of my massive internal ones. I should have heeded my own prayer. And possibly stuck to espresso beans.

There was nothing peaceful about teaching first graders, even in a well-run school. And this was not a well-run school. In hindsight, I have no idea what I was thinking—flinging myself into a teaching environment even seasoned veterans around me struggled in.

The room was bare, so I bought a heap of colorful posters, but the room still looked bleak even after Darian helped me decorate. I bought most of the classroom supplies I needed; my kiddos quickly broke most of the crayons. I scrambled around searching for teaching manuals and begged for two more copies of the daily math sheet. I'd be gone twelve hours, bust my rear scraping together enough curriculum to hold the class together for the next day, and fall into bed at 2:00 a.m.

This insanity wasn't sustainable, but I didn't want to quit on my kids—life was already unstable for so many of them. I was so busy during the day and so exhausted at night, Dad and the heartbreak of the past six months took a faraway back seat.

Dad kept sending letters, but I didn't reply.

September 22

Dear Kerri,

Hope this letter find you and Darian in good spirit and health. The sentencing was too much on my mind and trying to shut down there.

At my level, I can't order too many stamps. There is talk of garnishment of commissary here, for lawsuits, restitution, and court costs. If so, letters to family will be far and few in-between. I only get four envelopes and stamps per month.

So, I have to write, maybe, every three months or so. You

can write often, and if you do, please understand why I don't write back.

Lawsuit, divorce, house sale—ongoing mess, has caused a strain on Mom, I'm sure. I wish she would write me, if nothing but let me know, if she's okay and the family. If you write, please let me know what going on.

No TV, radio, or newspaper at level one—that I'm at now. Cannot accept visitors, but on TV screen, weekends, by appointment only.

Please both you and Darian be extra careful due to all my crimes. I would wish no harm to you but some crazy individual might try something. Are you ready for winter? Is the Tempo still running okay? Has Brian gone to fleet yet?

I have a routine now, that helps, and we get to shower and shave 3X a week. Can go outside, for an hour 5x a week, but haven't yet. There is like a dog run, chain-in area, you can exercise or pull up bar. I read a lot and think of past good memories. Right now, I'm reading *Centennial* by James Michener. Love his books, I recall you also like his books.

In the event of my death, I wish to be cremated and my ashes spread in the Flint Hills. It's nice to know where you will be and in God's hand.

I wish you luck on work and everyday life. Tell Darian, hi for me. God Bless.

Love,
Dad

OCTOBER

Dad had written: "Remember, I love you, you will always be my little girl, my tomboy and best friend. Many-many good memories of you and family. Keep faith in the good: life, hope and love."

Crying out sobs, those words breached my hardened heart. *"And now these three remain: faith, hope and love. But the greatest of these is love."*[1]

On the evening of October 9, Darian and I sat down to watch a movie on network TV: *The Hunt for the BTK Killer.* I had to look away during the violent parts, and I still cringe when I see the actor who portrayed my dad in anything else, but it was also surreal stress relief. It was so off in some places about my home and my mom, and so telling in other parts, especially about my dad's oddities, that there wasn't anything to do but laugh.

Most inappropriate laughter ever.

The best scene was my dad in his brown compliance officer uniform sitting at a counter in a café, ordering milk with his lunch and specifically making a point to ask the waitress for ice. I have no idea how the movie people knew that Dad liked to drink milk with ice in it. But it was brilliant—and I fell over laughing till my sides hurt.

In the fall we adopted two kittens from a rescue. We called the gray fuzz ball who curled up in our arms and purred, Hamlet. Molly was a black-and-orange tortie clinging vertically to her cage, clearly in need of relocation. Hamlet quickly became Hammy, and Molly zipped around our new home, chirping at us and the birds at the feeders I had hung on the patio.

Those kittens were life. They brought joy into our broken hearts, gave us purpose.

Some parts of teaching had gotten easier, but mainly it was exhausting—and a few unexpected aspects downright terrified me.

The school staff parked in a fenced-in lot, but two teachers still had their nice SUVs stolen during school hours. I was just driving the Tempo but grew leery walking to my car on the afternoons I stayed late.

Once there was a threat of school violence, and we gathered for a staff meeting. I realized I didn't have a key to lock my classroom door, nor was there any sort of lockdown plan. Contemplating how to push a desk and chairs in front of my door and where to tuck children tied my guts in knots.

As a student teacher, I'd gone through training—but everything had changed inside me since then. Violence. Trauma. Crime. Death. It altered me. I wasn't the same person, and I couldn't wrap my head around needing to implement my own school safety plan.

Not long after that, I fell asleep one warm afternoon coming home from school, stuck in bumper-to-bumper stalled traffic on I-96. I was startled awake by a honk behind me and drove the next thirty minutes with cold air blasting, shaking my head to clear it. The next morning, driving to school in the early light, tears rolling down my face, I asked God for help.

God? If I'm supposed to stay, I will. If I'm not, can you send a sign?

That afternoon the principal told me they needed to let me go—I was part of a dozen staff let go in those first months.

That was quick, God.

I replied, "I was thinking of quitting anyway."

I packed up my things, alternating between anger at myself for putting myself into a hopeless position and crying out of sadness to have to leave the kids and my classroom. Another first-grade teacher tried to console me, and while talking to her, it all tumbled out.

Shaking, on edge, about to break, I asked sharply, "Do you want to know who my father is?" Without waiting for an answer, I googled my dad and tapped on the screen at the picture of him in the orange jumpsuit.

"Oh. I saw something about him on TV. No wonder you're struggling. You need time to rest and heal."

Yes, yes, I do.

I went home, crashed on the floor, and sobbed for hours while the kittens kept watch over me and my broken spirit.

I'd tried with everything I had in me—with everything I knew—to be a good teacher to those kids. I failed them. *Failed myself.*

A few weeks later, in the middle of the night, I found Hammy curled up in his turquoise-blue bed with blood coming out of his nose and mouth. I slept by him the rest of the night and took him to the vet as soon as it opened. They ran a simple test, and the results came back positive for feline leukemia virus. It was fatal, with an average lifespan of three years.

Devastated, I called Darian and drove home to pick up Molly to have her tested too. She was a positive carrier also.

The vet told me some people choose to put a cat down once they know it's carrying a fatal disease, but he also said, "These guys don't know they will die, and they aren't dying today."

We weren't about to put down our kittens. I took them home and sprawled out on the living room floor again, sobbing.

Not dying today. I thought a lot about those words.

You can lie on this floor and cry all you want, but these two little guys—and you—aren't dying today.

I grew a bit stronger after that.

November 17

Dear Kerri and Darian,

Warm Greeting from me. Hopefully warm, for I know it is probably cold winter by now.

I just watched our Kansas sunset, they are so beautiful in the winter; with shades of purple, pink and cream and the sun a giant orange ball. Have a west window, looks past home. Can watch the birds at times and the seasons change, that really helps in spirit.

Kerri, you were always like that, watched and appreciated nature to its fullest. So many people never slow down to enjoy life so simple, beautiful treasures.

My hope is you will write me someday. My love as a Dad is still there, and you don't know how many times I think about you, Darian, Mom and Brian; every day. If betrayal is what is keeping you from writing, please forgive me.

So, proud of your brother, a Navy man now! He wrote a long letter, telling of his coast to coast adventures. Hold him in your thoughts and prayers. I know he was reporting to his sub soon.

One thing I do is study the bible and work toward Christian light. This is the only way God can forgive me. I have asked him to be in between me and the victims. They are gone, I'm so sorry and ask him to explain.

I gave confession before the sentencing, trial day.

But, I'm working with God, Christian pen-pals, and hopefully toward that light. It is my dear hope, I can meet you, Mom, Brian, and rest of relatives on the "other side of the river," that final day for me.

Please take care, best of holiday to you and Darian.

God Bless, Love to you both,

Dad!

NOVEMBER

We nursed Hammy back to health, and Molly never got sick as a kitten. In November, I went back to substitute teaching—it was flexible and I could rest on the days I didn't have it in me to face the world.

My night terrors were a constant companion, and one night, trying to flee whatever was trying to kill me, I jumped out of bed, fell into a laundry basket, and twisted my left knee. My left knee had been bum since 1998, when I jumped to make an Ultimate Frisbee catch and instead collided with a dumb boy.

I ended up limping to an orthopedist—who sent me to physical therapy and told me I might need surgery.

Hey, God, you up there?

Quiet, easy, restful life?

Okay?

December 17

Kerri,

I know this cannot be a very, "Merry Christmas" or a "Happy Holiday" due to my and family circumstances. You are deeply hurt and may never understand or come to term with things.

Want you to know I have found Peace with God, and someday we will meet again, on the other side of the River.

You will always be and remember[ed] dearly in my heart and love.

I have two great kids, and so glad you met Darian. It was great in memories all of us met for Christmas 2004. That was a special year, thanks for coming home. Please spend extra time, with Mom this year. It will be rough on her. Her world, she deeply love[d] is gone.

Hope things are okay there. Snowing here today! Blessed and better 2006.

Love,
Dad

CHAPTER 40

A Desert Is a Great Place to Hide

FEBRUARY 25, 2006
PHOENIX, ARIZONA

Time was forever marked: before February 25—after February 25.

Before Dad. After Dad.

It had been a year. We had made it; we had survived.

I woke up the morning of February 25, 2006, to bright sunshine filtering through my cousin Andrea's windows. Darian and I were in Phoenix, sleeping on the fold-out couch in her living room. My knee ached, my stomach stung with trepidation—remembering—but my heart was okay. The house was full of noise, the best kind, and my mom was waking up in the guest room next to us.

Life. Hope. Peace.

Darian was in search of peace too. His grandma Pearl passed away the day before we flew out, the result of a stroke the summer before. We were glad we had made it to New York the past few years to see her.

The family wanted to be together for the anniversary—and far away from any news crews—so my mom and grandparents drove to Phoenix to gather with a bunch of other folks we were related to. Darian and I flew in from Detroit.

Earlier in the week, Darian and I drove north to tour the Hoover Dam, just as I had with my dad when we were out west in 1986. We took dirt roads to the far western edge of the Grand Canyon, and I breathed deep as we watched the hazy orange sun set on reddish-purple slopes that overlooked the Colorado River.

Dad and I would have floated right by here if we had made it on that rafting trip we were dreaming about.

While Darian and I traveled along Route 66, I filled the car with stories about my old life with my father. Another piece of me came back to life among the stark sand flats, warm ridges, and dark mountains. It's the most at home I had felt in a year.

On the morning of the anniversary, my cousin gave Mom and me silver cross necklaces; I promptly put mine on. Longing for quiet, Darian, Mom, and I took off on our own, heading north.

In Sedona, we climbed up a steep stone walkway to the spectacular Chapel of the Holy Cross, which juts out from massive red rocks overlooking the desert. We were among many tourists, but when I entered the sanctuary, a peace I hadn't known in a long time descended upon me.

Home.

God.

Rows of red votive candles flickered light onto the orange-brown stone walls, and I could have stood under the massive stone cross looking out at the rising buttes in the distance the rest of my days.

God?

More days like this.

We wandered through shops and an art market and drove north through Coconino National Forest along the Oak Creek Canyon, catching glimpses of water tumbling down through its copper-colored narrows. High up on a mountain road we stopped at a pullout, and Darian and I walked out to the edge to look out over a valley of pines.

Dad should be here. He would have loved this.

As I let out a breath, I realized that even on one of the best days, I'd been on edge, anticipating something terrible. My body, my lungs, my bones—all felt the weight of the day, knew what it was.

We drove back to Phoenix late that afternoon and met a table full of family for dinner. It had been a good day, but as the evening progressed, a sadness descended on me and I cried. I was embarrassed to cry in a restaurant in front of a bunch of my family.

In low voices, they inquired after me, and I said, "Dad . . . miss him. It's been a lot today . . ."

Grief. Funny thing, how it came and went.

I missed my father. That was one of the first times I'd admitted that. Was it okay to admit I missed a serial killer? That I loved one?

I didn't miss a serial killer, didn't love one—I missed my dad. I loved my dad.

I had no idea what anyone around that table, people I also loved, thought about me.

But that was it. That day he was just my dad, whom I loved and missed. It was always going to be that simple and that hard.

JUNE
DETROIT

I don't recall receiving any letters from my dad in the spring of 2006, but one arrived four days before my twenty-eighth birthday. There wasn't anything damaging in the letter, but it set me off into a fit of ire. It wasn't what the letter said—it was the absence of what it should have.

Hovering under the surface of my anger was a cesspool of pitch-black pain I rarely acknowledged. Grief came with no rhyme or reason. Mine didn't fall neatly into the stages you hear about: denial, anger, bargaining, depression, acceptance. Mine bounced around like a pinball, setting off whatever it felt like, whenever it felt like it.

Awakened by a night terror and unable to get back to sleep, I hobbled out of bed to my computer, propped my leg up on an overturned Rubbermaid bin, and typed a letter to my father for the first time in almost a year.

I'd been in a black hinged knee brace since March, after having surgery on the ligaments to realign my kneecap. The day after the surgery, it felt like my knee was on fire—the worst physical pain I'd ever suffered. When I called the surgeon about increasing my pain meds, he said, "Oh yeah, these types of surgeries hurt like a son of a gun."

Hammy and Molly found it great fun to run up and down my foam-braced leg that first week. I could barely make it to the bathroom and back on crutches. Darian left lunch, drinks, and ice packs in the cooler next to the couch before leaving in the mornings. He brought home a three-disc set of the Jurassic Park movies to cheer me up and set up a patio chair in the tub before helping me bathe.

For better or for worse. In sickness and in health. Love never fails.

I slowly regained strength and ability with physical therapy and time, but it took several more months before I was fully healed. I eventually became pain-free, except when it stormed, after aching for eight years.

There were lessons in that: time, I needed more time. Therapy, I guess, was a lesson I could heed, too, but I didn't want to go back to get my head shrunk again. Even though I knew I probably should. Instead, writing an angry letter would have to suffice.

I didn't mail the letter. I didn't want to hurt my dad.

June 2006

Dad,

It's four flipping a.m. and I just composed the 1200th opening lines to you while lying next to my slumbering husband. I can't get back to sleep, so I decided to go ahead, get up, drink a cold glass of milk (no ice), and type out what I was just yelling at you in my head.

Except typing it seems so mundane, so normal, when all I really want to do is grab a can of red paint and throw my words onto the semi-clean beige wall in front of me and tell you off.

Go ahead and write it down and say . . . what? Should I tell you I grew up adoring you, you were the sunshine of my life, the apple of my eye and all that other greeting-card crap? It's true, even if it is coming out jaded and bitter now—but really, who could blame me. Hey, it's okay to yell at your father all you want when he's a serial killer.

Should I tell you in one breath I want to tell you I want nothing more to do with you and you can just rot in hell? Being called a "social contact" by her father in front of the whole world will do that to a girl.

Or maybe I should tell you in the very next breath, I miss you. I saw *Cars* tonight, the new movie by Pixar. In it, there's a scene where they are driving along Interstate 40, coming down into the orangey-red vistas and buttes of the New Mexico desert. I thought of you and our trips out west. I remembered how much you wanted to drive old Route 66, and I just wished you were sitting next to me in that theater, sharing a tub of buttered popcorn.

But you're not. You're sitting in your concrete room. (What you like to call it: your room! Hello! It's a jail cell, not a room! Like you're staying at some inn where they serve you breakfast in bed, with a fresh-cut flower on the tray—instead of where you really are, where they serve you ground-up mush on a cold metal tray that slips through a crack in the door.)

And you won't ever be sitting next to anyone ever again.

That tub of buttered popcorn reminds me sometimes I just want to go out and buy the biggest buttery tub I can find and wave it in your face and say, "Ha, you won't ever have this again," and ask, "Was it worth it?" Eating a really good hamburger makes me want to do that also. Does that make me a bad person—to enjoy eating a really good hamburger and getting pleasure from the thought you won't ever get to?

Or should you know in the next breath I want to ask if you're staying warm at night, did you get some house slippers and an extra blanket or two?

Are you lonely? I'm so sorry you're alone in that small, cold, concrete cell, and sometimes I just wish I could give you a hug.

But most [of] the time I just feel like a part of a quote by Elie Wiesel I read a while back: "The opposite of love is not hate, it's indifference."[1] I used to love you, but now I'm the opposite of that, it's not that I hate you, it's just I don't care.

—Your lovingly indifferent
daughter

AUGUST 2006
LAS VEGAS, NEVADA

In August I flew out to Las Vegas, spending a few days with Darian, who was there on a business trip. I tried my hand at the slots, while Darian watched me toss his twenty dollars away. We walked around the strip at night and I marveled at how much it had changed since I had visited Circus Circus with my folks on our trip out west in 1986.

We had separate flights coming home, and I flew over the Grand Canyon and the Rockies, catching glimpses of them through the clouds.

Flying over two of my favorite places prompted me to try to listen to John Denver's *Greatest Hits* album on my MP3 player. I hadn't listened to much music since losing my dad, and I hadn't gone near any that reminded me of him.

As soon as the first notes hit, I burst into tears.

It was my favorite album when I was young. Dad would drop

the record on the turntable and dance around to "Take Me Home, Country Roads." He'd spin with his brown house slippers on, snapping his fingers in time. I'd giggle so hard my sides would hurt, watching him being a goof.

"Sunshine on My Shoulders."

We had taken several trips to Colorado when I was a kid, staying in a cabin in Lake City and fishing for trout at a nearby stream. I can still picture my dad in his green-and-white plaid shirt with the sleeves rolled up, patiently casting colorful flies into the sparkling water, the sun bouncing off his shoulders.

"Rocky Mountain High."

We had gone jeeping just once, near Ouray, driving up Engineer Mountain. My door popped off the rental when we hit a rut in the road, startling me. Dad chuckled as he worked the door back on. We drove above the tree line and came upon snow in a high valley, even though it was summer and we were in shorts. The sun, brilliant and bright under a startling clear-blue sky, was so close I wanted to reach up and touch it.

I had a memory for every song on that album. The immense loss I'd suffered hit hard.

I was missing him so much it hurt to breathe.

As memories flowed through my ears, another sliver of pain was pulled from my soul. Thousands of feet above the mountains I loved, with my head up against the cool window, I gained another piece of myself back.

Thousands more to go.

NOVEMBER 2006
DETROIT

In the fall, I started subbing for a nearby district. I only had to drive a few miles some days, and I was able to string together more days of work—it was the happiest I'd been at a job. We also replaced the sputtering Corsica with Grandma Pearl's huge silver Mercury Grand Marquis. Uncle John drove it over to us one weekend.

He was Darian's height, and his sole goal in life seemed to be to try to figure out how to make us laugh. We took him to dinner at our favorite Italian restaurant, and he crashed on our floor next to the cats, who thought highly of him. We dropped him off the next day at the airport to fly back to New York.

Mid-November, we went back to church. When I stepped through the spinning doors into a brightly lit lobby, I felt peace and knew I'd come home. God had been waiting for us.

In the auditorium, there were cupholders for lattes from the café, and Coldplay's "Fix You" was blasting out from the stage.

Tears ran down my face at church for the next several weeks as I heard our pastor preach on mercy and God's never-ending love. As more shattered pieces of my spirit mended, I found grace once more, grace I was sure had been lost forever.

CHAPTER 41

PTSD Blows Chunks

JUNE 2007

D arian saw the agent out the door and I stood up and took the picture of my dad and mom off the wall. I propped the picture up against the wall on the floor of my closet."

"Good. That's when it ends—when the agent leaves. I think we will just need to go through it one more time," the calm female voice said. We were in a small, peaceful room. There was gentle instrumental music playing softly, and I was sitting on a couch (not an eggplant one).

"All right, breathe in and out slowly, like we have practiced. Now, tell me again."

I slowly opened my eyes and looked at her with uncertainty, brushing tears away from my face, twisting a crumbling wet tissue around my fingers. "Do I have to?"

"Yes. This is how we get it to stop looping. Now, tell me again."

It was midmorning in June 2007, and I was sitting on my therapist's couch. For the past four months, every week, I'd been seeing a psychologist, a trauma specialist. She was helping me.

We were chasing after the big one today: the loop that wouldn't stop replaying in my brain, starting from when I noticed the beat-up old car by the dumpster till the man with the badge left my apartment. Again and again.

From when I noticed the beat-up old car . . .

For two years and four months, again and again.

. . . till the man with the badge left.

It was preventing me from living.

It was an intense memory, with a reddish-gray hue around it, like an aura. Strong. And I was full of fear. I was stuck in 2005, on February 25. I couldn't shake it. Couldn't escape it. Couldn't get out from under it. It was killing me.

I looked fine on the outside if you hadn't known me before. But I wasn't fine. My back was hunched over, my chest was tight—squeezed. It was hard for me to look in other people's eyes, didn't want to. Balled up tight within myself, shutting down, sleeping a lot, moving slow, gray-murky—nothing. Then seething with red-hot anger, wanting to lash out at nothing and everything. Hating myself. Wanting it to end, all of it.

Trauma.

It had changed me physically, emotionally, spiritually. It wouldn't leave. Again and again, on replay, I experienced the day the world broke out from under my feet, and nothing had been the same or ever would be again.

It's called posttraumatic stress disorder.

I'd been diagnosed four months before, when I finally decided to drag my butt back into therapy. I don't exactly know why I landed back on a therapist's couch. I wanted to point to the past year and a half as evidence I was coping. Although I guess switching jobs, trying to outrun grief in the desert, and sobbing in restaurants, airplanes, and churches might say otherwise. Oh, and the angry letter. And the stupid loop that wouldn't go away.

Or maybe it was due to the umpteen thoughts spinning in my head, like how Dad committed his first murders a few months before turning twenty-nine, and I was turning twenty-nine soon, and maybe something would change in me too?

When I brought it up, Darian said, "No. Come on, you don't flip a switch one day and become a serial killer."[1]

Yeah. But what if you do?

I guess one could also argue I'd been struggling with depression and anxiety for several years, but I definitely wasn't going to admit that out loud.

Yeah, that too.

———

Back in February, a couple of weeks before the second anniversary of the arrest, I ended up in a hospital after days of unexplained nausea and pain near my stomach. The ER served me two disgusting bottles of chalky-tasting barium so I'd light up like a Christmas tree for my CT scan. They didn't find anything conclusive but kept me overnight on appendix watch, with a young roommate who wouldn't stay off her cell phone. Thanks to the fancy drinks, I spent most of the night in the bathroom, clutching an IV pole, getting revenge on the roommate.

The next morning, a priest came by and asked if he could pray for me. I mumbled my assent and sobbed while his words rested over me. What I really needed was an exorcism.

Not long after the hospital stay, I got on the internet, googled trauma therapists, found one with a nearby office, and—fighting against everything in me—forced myself to go. With my stomach in knots and a great desire to flee, I sat in the therapist's waiting room and marked the dumb "thoughts of suicide" box again.

Dang tiny judgmental boxes. Dang therapist offices.

"I need help."

"That's why I'm here."

"Yeah, well, I've got an unusual thing going. And I've got privacy issues." I said this to the nice lady with the yellow legal pad and pen who was patiently listening, perched on a chair by the door. The door I was eyeing as if something bad was going to burst through any second.

"I will be the only one who sees your files; I'll lock them in my cabinet, okay?"

"Okay. My mom's doctors do the same for her, back in Wichita. That's where I'm from . . ."

"So what's going on?"

"Well, uh, you see, my dad, is . . . is, uh, in jail. He's in for murder."

The therapist didn't flinch.

"He's known as B . . . T . . . K. Maybe you've heard of him? We were in the news a while back. My maiden name is Rader. Dad is . . ."

Still no flinching. And she was trying to look me in the eyes even though I was doing my best to dodge hers.

"I don't like saying B . . . T . . . K."

"Why not?"

Oh heck, this one means business.

"'Cause of what it stands for, and because that's not my dad, the man I knew."

I told her, "There's something stuck in my head. Like a loop. I don't understand it. I think I'm going crazy. It's from the day my dad was arrested. I've got bad stranger danger: men in uniforms, maintenance men, delivery men. Even seeing a police officer causes me to jump and can send me into some kind of hyperalert. Like I'm waiting for great harm to happen to me. Bracing for it.

"My stomach has been hurting bad—I ended up in the hospital from it a few weeks ago. And my chest is tight all the time, like it's being squeezed. I'm not working much, sleeping a lot. And sometimes I'm very angry. I don't like it. I've got bad night terrors—like, full-on haunting me. I've had them since I was a little girl.

"I don't want to live like this anymore. Can you help me?"

"Yes," she said. "It sounds like you might be dealing with anxiety and depression. Very common, especially with trauma. Your chest being squeezed can come from anxiety—we can work on some techniques to help with breathing. Sometimes we sleep a lot because it blocks out the pain for a while. Yes?"

Right. Anxiety and depression. Someone finally called it that out loud. Off and on since Michelle—my first year of college. It took ten years, but now it had a name.

"And a body can often react—know things, feel things the mind doesn't or isn't ready to face yet. Your stomach could be reacting to an old memory, old trauma."

Oh.

"The anniversary of my dad's arrest just passed." I got a small smile of understanding from my therapist with that admission.

"Also, it sounds like what you're describing—the thing stuck in your head—is posttraumatic stress disorder. PTSD for short. And certain memories, situations, strangers, could be triggering you. Your night terrors could be from PTSD or they could be a more general sleep disorder."

"Oh, PTSD, so that's what's wrong. I didn't know it had a name. I thought I was going crazy."

"Nope. I can help you."

"But no one died, like with my cousin's accident. That was in 1996. It got stuck for a while replaying in my head, my first year in college."

"Were you in the accident?"

"No. Just told about it, read about it. I could picture it, though. Imagine it, you know? That's what got stuck."

"How did you get unstuck?"

"I went to see a counselor on campus. She had me go through the day my cousin died in detail, desensitizing myself. Told me the replaying of the accident was a common reaction to trauma."

"Right. Desensitizing to trauma—smart. It sounds as if your mind—your body—perceived the visit by the FBI agent as a threat. And you understandably went into shock, hearing such devastating news. That's all trauma."

She paused to let me absorb that.

"What your father did, what you know about it—all that's traumatic. What you've been through since he was arrested—all trauma, and it sounds like it could go back into your childhood?"

"Yeah." I mumbled this quietly, dropping my head.

"Let's take some time getting to know one another. We'll let you get comfortable here, get comfortable with me, and when you're ready, we will work on it. I can help you. I have been able to help others."

Help. She kept saying that word—when I had no desire to ever utter it myself: *I need help.*

⸺

Therapy came with homework. Requests I'd grimace and roll my eyes at.

I was supposed to be walking regularly, to help my body fight off what it was under attack from. Walking outside was a chilly option in early March, and being alone outside could increase my anxiety, so I tried walking at the mall. I did walk a few times, following the snazzily dressed power walkers, but my instincts to be a bum overrode my attempts to exercise. Even stopping at the cookie kiosk wasn't enough of an incentive.

I went to a psychiatrist, who placed me on an antidepressant and a sleeping pill. But the sleeping pill made me see floaty things and caused me to walk into walls, which was less than helpful.

I told my mom I'd gone back to therapy and she said, "PTSD. That's what my therapist said I have too. From the day your father was arrested."

We experienced the same trauma, sixteen hours apart.

Mom had been embroiled in the lawsuit, a lawyer working for her pro bono. The lawsuit against her got tossed out. Even with it cleared, Mom still couldn't find a buyer for the house, till someone anonymously stepped forward and paid off her mortgage, donating the house to Park City to be torn down. It was a stunning, immensely kind, and generous thing for someone to do for my family.

We were thankful Mom didn't have to make the mortgage payments anymore, but it was sad to know the house was going to be knocked down. This was better, though, than folks filming third-rate horror films in it or taking it apart in pieces and hocking them on eBay.

On March 7, two days before my dad's sixty-second birthday, our old home was bulldozed. Thirty-four years of memories, gone like that. The land was supposed to be turned into an entrance to the park, but it never was. The next time I was in Kansas I drove by it slowly but didn't stop. My trees were the only things left standing.

APRIL

In the spring, I was subbing in a sixth-grade classroom and went to use the copy machine during my planning period. Standing in the office were detectives with shiny badges on their hips and guns in holsters.

Trying to hide my fear, I made my copies and tried not to stare. One of the detectives noticed my face and gently said, "It's okay. We found a note threatening violence at the school but we stopped it in plenty of time."

I went back to the class and taught the rest of the afternoon, attempting to squelch the rampant rumors flying around my room and to keep my own fears in check. I went home and thought I was okay.

I wasn't.

A few days later, after accepting a sub job at the same building, I didn't go. I didn't call anyone to explain my PTSD. I didn't even call in absent till after the day was over—making up a lame excuse on an answering machine.

I lay in my bed, frozen, full of fear for hours, ransacking my brain, and feeling terrible for not showing up. I was never actually told I lost my job—I just didn't ever accept any more sub jobs with that district.

At my next therapy session, I broke down in sobs, telling my therapist about the badges, the guns, and being unable to return to my job.

Trauma. It was real.

CHAPTER 42

Therapy Might Just
Save Your Life

In May, ten years after committing my life to Christ in the canyon, I stood in front of an auditorium of cheering people and watched Darian be baptized. Then he stood and watched me do the same. I wore a black T-shirt and shorts and the tiny silver cross earrings my aunt Donna had given me for confirmation fifteen years before. It felt right—I'd come full circle.

"'Today, if you hear his voice, do not harden your hearts as you did in the rebellion.'"[1]

When I went under the clear water, an immense warmth of knowing hit me square in the chest—home.

God.

I came up from the water with a huge grin on my face.

A peace, a hope, a future.

My baptism stood as a mark of remembrance—of what God had seen me through. It also stood as a testament to the future I desired: God's path always under my feet. And to join the church and community we were coming to know and care about.

JUNE

On the day before my twenty-ninth birthday, a BTK book was released. Written by four *Wichita Eagle* journalists, it was about my dad's crimes and the decades-long investigation around them.

Happy birthday to me.

Like the biggest idiot ever, I preordered it from Amazon. For the next many years, Amazon asked if I would like to see more books like the book about my dad with graphics on the cover of folks being tortured.

I should have realized ordering from Amazon would trigger this. The company had already been asking for the past three years if I would like to purchase more garden tools like the ones I ordered back in 2004 and shipped for Father's Day.

No. I don't believe so. Can't ship tools to prison.

When the book arrived, a few days after my birthday, I casually flipped through it. Big mistake. Nice pictures of smiling people my dad later murdered. Crime scene photos. Photos from court. Dad in bondage. I found my name in the index: Rader, Kerri. I tried to read small sections, but I quickly snapped the book closed and shut down.

It all was swirling inside me—my head, my guts, my heart.

I took the book into therapy and shook it slightly at my therapist; red-faced and livid, I read sections to her. When I got home, I turned the book so I couldn't read the spine and stuck it on my bookshelf.

A session or two later we tackled the loop, using exposure therapy: telling the story out loud and telling it again and again in detail, till it stopped having such a hold on me.

"You're safe here. Breathe, in and out. Again. Breathe. Good. Now, tell me again, from the start."

"On February twenty-fifth, I woke up late . . ."

That was the last time I ever had to tell it to her.

We got it. It was gone. From that day on, what happened on February 25 didn't hold the same power over me. It settled into its correct place. My therapist was a God-sent genius.

JULY

After the loop was vanquished, I went off my antidepressant. It had helped me, but now Darian and I wanted to try to get pregnant—I didn't have much desire while on it.

I told Darian we needed to start trying because it took my mom three years with each kid. Two weeks later, we were pregnant.

I calculated the math, bought pee-sticks, and took the test. Lying sprawled out on the floor next to the kitchen with a dumbfounded grin on my face, I pressed my hands lightly over my belly.

Pregnant.

Wow.

The cats thought I'd finally lost it. So did Darian when he arrived home and I flung a pee-stick in his face.

"I thought you said it could take years of trying?"

Yeah, well. Surprise!

As soon as I knew I was expecting, I ran out and bought maternity clothes—I was sure I was already showing.

Not long after we found out about the baby, Molly fell ill. We took her to an emergency vet and were told her feline leukemia had caught up with her—Molly's bone marrow was shutting down. We brought her home and I made a space for her in our linen closet, a spot she had never wanted to rest in before. For the next few days, we quietly walked by and lay next to her on the hallway floor, as Hammy stayed near—both cats sleeping curled up on our bath towels.

Less than a week after she had fallen ill, we took her to our vet, said goodbye, and let her slip away. Grief crippled me once more.

Too much loss, too much death.

AUGUST

I spent six months in therapy, working through chunks of my pain, talking a lot about growing up with my father. I told the story of Dad screaming in a rage at Mom in Jackson Hole, Wyoming, in August 1995.

We were visiting the Tetons, and Mom fell off a path, twisting her ankle and scraping her knee. Dad went ballistic. I don't ever remember seeing him that insane: yelling at her, blaming her for falling and ruining his day.

With blood running down Mom's leg, Brian and I helped her up and got her to a forest ranger's cabin, where she lay down on a first-aid cot. I sat with her, and I remember the ranger looking kindly at us and eyeing my dad cautiously. Dad was pacing outside, red-faced and steamed.

Later Dad apologized and took us to a fancy restaurant for lunch, a place my mom liked. Mom hung back at the hotels even more that trip. I figured she needed to rest her leg and wanted to read—she wasn't much into exploring with us adventurous souls anyway. I remember Dad asking me later in the trip, "I'm not sure what's wrong with your mom. Do you think it's because of her falling?" I don't remember what I said to him, but in 2015 she told me, "Your father ruined my trip."

Looking back, I wonder if the ranger thought my dad was an abuser. He looked at him—through him—in a way other people didn't. It hurt me then, and it hurts now, thinking about that day.

Working through these incidents, I realized I suffered emotional abuse from my dad, likely my whole life—Mom and Brian too. Brian had been physically abused also. I knew this—inside me. It wasn't easy to hear it said out loud, even from my own voice, but at least now I could work at coming to terms with it.

I'd been an abuse victim since I was little. I've been a trauma victim since the day I found out I was a crime victim. I've been a crime victim since before I was born.

Crime. Abuse. Trauma.

Victim.

Me?

Me.

Anxiety, depression, PTSD.

Me.

My therapist encouraged me to write my father, but I dragged my feet. Once I found out I was pregnant, I was torn. I wanted him to know he was going to be a grandfather, but I was growing protective of my baby and, frankly, of myself.

I still had a lot of hurt inside me, and I should've stayed in therapy to keep removing the pain. But I didn't have it in me to keep going. I couldn't handle dissecting myself and holding my pregnancy together at the same time. I left therapy after writing my father for the first time in two years.

August 8, 2007

Dear Dad,

I know it's been a very long time since I've written.

I didn't write because I was very angry about your "social contacts" and "pawns in your game" comments at your sentencing, among many other things. Your words and actions have hurt, and I'm still conflicted on how much contact I want to have with you.

You were a good Dad most of the time and raised us well, and we do not know what to believe—who you were to us, or who you were to others. Maybe you were trying to protect us in court when you made those harsh comments. I don't really know. You could've chosen to leave us at any time, but you didn't. You took care of us, did things with us, so I hope you really didn't mean what you said.

Mom chooses not to write you because she cannot have you be a part of her life anymore. She reads your letters though, and I don't think she minds hearing from you. I do not know why other family and friends do not write, but you need to respect their decision to not communicate. Everyone handles things differently.

Grandma Dorothea is fading more every month; she has lost a lot of her memory and is unable to write. It is hard to get her out of the home now, so I don't think she will be able to visit you again.

Brian is doing well and underway until late fall.

Darian and I found out two weeks ago that we're expecting our first child! I am due in the spring. We are making plans for the future and all our family is excited.

I was glad to hear you have a Bible and you are studying it. Philippians is my favorite book, Paul wrote it from prison, and I think it might bring you some comfort. I know God forgives all sins; all you need to do is ask.

It's not your fault if you were abused or hurt as a child, but you're still responsible for your actions as an adult regardless of what may or may not have happened to you.

I'm coming to terms with a lot that has transpired these past two years. I'm starting to move on or "come back" to who I was before.

I have been enjoying watching the birds at our home. We had 18 different species visit our birdfeeder this summer. I have your bird books to identify them with, and several of your camping and hiking books.

I also planted flowers in hanging and patio boxes this summer. Some of them are doing better than others; this is my first-year planting flowers, and I'm still learning what grows best here. I planted mine a little early, even in the summer, it can get cool here in the evenings.

I will try to write again soon.

Love,

Kerri

Not long after I sent the letter letting Dad know I was expecting, something deep within me shifted, and I decided to protect my unborn child like both our lives depended on it. I covered my growing belly with my hands as I thought about my dad, and the pain seared straight through to my uterus—where I felt slight, fluttering kicks of hope.

Dad murdered Nancy Fox when Mom was three months pregnant with me. Dad murdered part of a family: a father, mother, and two children. Orphaning three children. Dad murdered three mothers in front of their children. Daughters, sisters, mothers, grandmothers.

Seven families destroyed. And my family too.

Unable (again) to wrap my head around what my dad did, I cut off all communication with him.

CHAPTER 43

Laugh or Cry to Survive

AUGUST 2007

Over the past six months, I'd grown to trust my therapist and the steady process of directed healing—enough that I willingly unbandaged my wounds.

My mind was healed from the worst of my PTSD and my night terrors lessened. My chest was less compressed; my stomach no longer ached. I was walking a little taller, a little straighter. But with the baby growing inside me, I wanted to securely wrap the remaining pain within me and set it far away from the increasing signs of life I was feeling.

I was shutting down again after we worked so hard in therapy.

Come back some other time—I have a baby inside me, and my dad's insanity ain't coming anywhere near her.

The baby was just a tiny peanut, but that peanut was mine, and I loved him or her fiercely. I'd do anything to protect the baby—even from myself. And my heart was hardening again toward my father—I didn't want Mom to mail his latest letter. "Hold it," I told her. "I'll read it next time I'm home. Maybe."

My father left me—he had forsaken me. His baby girl. But God had taught me in the canyon—and told me repeatedly since—*I will never leave you nor forsake you.*[1] And I was his daughter too. God had been with me from the very beginning, before I was knitted in my mother's womb.[2]

My earthly father had left me. But God, my Father up above, had never left. He had always been right by my side—through all of it. Even when my heart was hard, shut down, and far from forgiving my father.

SEPTEMBER

Life was expanding exponentially since we joined our church. Dad and what we endured was still one side. But new friends, lunch on Sundays with a group from the couples' class, and my growing belly were now on the other side. Though trying to walk in faith, being in community after Dad, after trauma, after grief, was like putting on new clothes that didn't comfortably fit yet.

Our friends back home, who knew Darian and me before my dad's arrest, knew what we endured. We didn't have to explain it to them, didn't have to tell them our backstory. Didn't have to answer odd questions. They just held it, walking alongside us.

It was harder with people coming into our lives in Michigan. There was a learning curve on how to share about my father. On whether to mention him at all.

SURVIVOR'S TIP:

What not to say to someone who is suffering:

- This is God's will for your life.
- God will only give you what you can handle.
- You need to pray more.
- You must be sinning.
- You need to stop living in the past.
- Everything happens for a reason!
- Choose hope!

Darian said later: "There are two kinds of friends. The kind when we told them about Kerri's dad, they'd say, 'That's super weird, but it doesn't change the way we think about you guys.' And then there's the other kind, who perhaps think this thing defines you."[3] The ones who accepted us for ourselves were a gift of grace from God.

Early on, it was often easier to say nothing. Or remain vague during prayer request time instead of dropping a bombshell on a table of women gathered on Tuesdays doing a six-week Bible study. Especially when you were new, already felt like you stuck out like the oddest sort of Christian, and, in our huge church, wouldn't necessarily run into these women again.

At the most, I'd say, "I'm not in contact with my father, *estranged* is the word, I think." If asked why, I'd answer, "Oh, he's in prison." I'd get the perplexed grief face—the one folks do at funerals. They'd say, "I'm sorry," and stop asking questions. If they kept asking, they might have gotten tumbling-out answers they likely hadn't wanted in the first place.

Other times, it was hard to hold back when I wanted to shout to the rafters, "I'm not okay!" In one group, a woman shared that the worst day of her life had been due to a broken dishwasher flooding her kitchen. I left the room quickly, hoping I could reach the restroom before the tears rolled down. I could have shared about the worst day of my life, but where would I even begin?

On braver days, I would say, "I've been through some hard things I wasn't sure I'd survive, but God did and *is* seeing me through." I noticed even that little bit of testimony would resonate with the people around whatever table I was at.

OCTOBER

In the fall, we moved to a bigger apartment within the same complex after realizing we needed more room with the baby coming. It had its own entrance and a large picture window Hammy loved to look out of.

We had our eighteen-week ultrasound, but our baby wouldn't

cooperate to show us the goods. So we went with neutrals: Darian painted the nursery golden yellow, put up large Winnie-the-Pooh stickers on the walls, and hung moon-and-star lamps.

In October, my grandma Dorothea died. I was sad she wouldn't get to meet her great-grandbaby. It was hard to lose her, but I was thankful she wasn't suffering anymore. She was now at peace and with Grandpa.

I decided to be brave and talk about my dad with our couples' small group at our last Sunday-evening gathering before Christmas. My voice shook slightly, and I glanced at the carpet a lot, but I let these people more fully into our lives.

One of my all-time favorite photos is from Christmas Day 2007: lounging on Aunt Sharon's couch in my red turtleneck maternity sweater, lying up against my mom, my hands on my expanding belly. Uncle John was staying with Darian's folks, and I laughed, seeing him down on the floor losing tug-of-war to their dog, Skipper.

On our way back to Michigan, Darian and I were delayed at O'Hare. In the terminal, I propped my swollen feet up on the chair across from me, sipped a latte, and delightedly watched my belly move.

MARCH 2008

"So, uh, I've got to go to the hospital." It was early March, and I was standing in my OB's parking lot, wigging out on the phone with Darian. The baby wasn't due for three weeks, but I was showing signs of preeclampsia.

I battled all-day sickness early on and gestational diabetes the past few months. In the early months, all the good foods made me throw up. In the late months, all the good foods made my sugars high. It was a lousy way to be pregnant.

I spent a good part of my third trimester on the couch craving carbs, watching *Friends* episodes on DVD, and figuring out a name for the baby, who liked rolling in my tummy like an acrobat.

I survived the last weeks with doctors' orders to lie on my left side as much as I could, with the baby now kicking me square in the ribs.

"Do I need to go with you to the hospital?" Poor man, whose wife made the oddest, most abrupt phone calls.

"Uh, yeah. There could be a baby today. We need to take my bag with us."

"Oh! On my way!"

We grabbed my bag and pillows, told Hammy we would see him soon, went through the Arby's drive-through and then on to the hospital. (Survivor's tip: if the last meal you are going to eat outside of hospital food for a week is Arby's, rethink your life choices.)

When we reached labor and delivery, my blood pressure was so high they almost delivered via C-section. But I talked them into letting me lie on my left side to see if I could get my numbers lower. It worked.

There were times I wished I let them do the C.

I'd studied my five-hundred-page pregnancy book intently over the past months but was still taken aback by having to stay in the hospital for an extended period, constantly hooked up to a gently whooshing machine. I also wasn't so keen on having to collect my pee for twenty-four hours in a plastic bottle that was on ice in the bathroom.

I also was freaking out that the baby would be born on my dad's birthday.

I was relieved when March 10 arrived and I was still pregnant, and even more relieved to see my mom, who flew in weeks early to be with us.

I had a high-tech 3D ultrasound and got to see our baby in magical clarity. The tech printed off pictures, marking the photos *Baby Girl!*

She had big, peaceful eyes and looked straight at us as if saying: *We're going to survive this together—you and me.*

An amniocentesis followed the ultrasound to determine if our baby girl's lungs were developed enough for her to be delivered. I lay there terrified while they pushed a gigantic needle into my belly, wishing I could hold Darian's hand. Instead, they had him sit in the corner, blocking his view of what they were doing to his very pregnant wife.

When it was determined she was ready, I was induced.

I was in labor thirty-seven hours with nothing to eat and only ice chips—that I secretly let melt—to drink. Somewhere in there was: throwing up, an epidural that didn't do anything, oxygen in my nose, two hours of pushing while Darian held one of my legs and a nurse the other, trying not to scream cuss words in front of my mom and failing miserably, our baby girl's head turned opposite, an episiotomy, and, finally, our baby girl, Emilie.

She was seven pounds, seven ounces, had brown hair and big brown eyes, and came out strong, fighting—like her mama. A new life. Tiny fingers of hope wrapped around one of mine. Eyes full of nothing but love. An utter gift straight down from the heavens above.

God?

Thank you and amen.

I held her for a few minutes, bawling, mesmerized. Then I handed her over to her dad, who was grinning from ear to ear and promptly called her Peaches. I so wished I could have handed her to my dad too.

I was flat-out exhausted but somehow found the strength to call in a breakfast order off the nondiabetic menu.

A feast for the ages arrived shortly after; it even included a donut.

Emilie and I stayed two days, and then like that, Darian and I were home with a newborn baby, two weeks before she even was supposed to be due.

MAY

My mom stayed for two weeks, and when she left I cried, "Please don't leave me with a baby!"

Within a month, I was capable enough to fly to Wichita by myself with my peanut girl. We took a rare nonstop flight, which she slept through in its entirety, fortunately, wrapped in her brown-and-green blanket, sucking peacefully on her green pacifier.

I held her in my arms and zoned out with headphones in, my head pressed up against the windowpane, her bottle ready in the seat pocket in front of me, a diaper bag turned travel bag under my feet. What a leap life had taken in three years!

It was wonderful to be able to hand her to my family and see people's faces light up, especially after everything we had been through.

I was grateful to have lots of extra hands offering to hold, feed, and change her. But it also ached to hand her over: *Here, you can see her for a little while, but I'm going to need her back because she needs, and I need, and* . . . I needed the help, but I had the idea that since I was her mom, I was supposed to be the one to take care of her, no matter how little she slept on her own, no matter how much she wanted to sleep on me.

I think Wichita triggered my PTSD, and it compounded with my weeks of lack of solid sleep, which began my tumble down into places I didn't want to go. And wouldn't admit to anyone that I was falling into. I'd do anything to protect her—even from myself.

Em and I flew back to Michigan late in the afternoon on Mother's Day. She was fussy, and I, weary and wiped out, picked an awful fight with Darian within minutes of arrival.

After hours of nonstop wailing at the top of her lungs, and my anxious self frantically trying to get Em to settle, we took her to the hospital, thinking the flight had harmed her ears. They told us she was fine, and she finally fell asleep while we rocked her in a dimly lit emergency room.

———

Two days later, Darian and I, still raw and sore from my first crazy Mother's Day, received a heartbreaking phone call from his father—Uncle John had committed suicide.

Trauma and grief—it knew no bounds, no end.

Shocked, torn to pieces again, Darian and I stumbled through the next few days, scrambling to pack our and the baby's things to meet Dave in New York. I went to the county office to pick up Em's certified birth certificate so we could cross the Canadian border with her. We set out in the early morning, stopping at several travel plazas to change—and tickle the feet of—our sleepy girl to get her to wake up enough to eat. We arrived late that night.

Much to the distress of her wiped-out parents, Em spent part of her first night in the hotel joyfully making all sorts of happy squeals and kicking her long legs up and down on her jungle-themed Pack 'n Play.

We spent a week with Darian's father, helping out around Uncle John's home, while Em sat in her blue bouncer, reaching for the stars that hung down in front of her, trying hard to bring smiles to our grief-stricken faces. Darian's dad told us later that bringing Em made all the difference in the world.

———

I was strong for Darian, Dave, and Em the week we were in New York. But time and I would drift after we left. I have no recollection of our trip back to Michigan. I would lose recollection of a lot of things in the coming months.

In hindsight, we know it was my old brute, anxiety, colliding with my newer one, PTSD, combined with postpartum depression—two words that still make my heart seize in fear. The simplest tasks became overwhelming, and Darian scrambled, trying to take care of me and Em. I didn't tell him or anyone else I was drowning in a pit of blackness.

CHAPTER 44

Grit Your Teeth and Keep Going

MARCH 2009

I can open Em's baby book now and show you carefully marked-down milestones met with glee: rolling over, sitting up, crawling, standing, first steps. That her first words were: *ma-ma, da-da, kit-ty, hi, bye.*

I can show you photos of her first baths in a small tub we set next to our kitchen sink—she crying and I fretting at first. Later photos show her happily splashing and Darian and I laughing as she grew to love the water. There are photos of her first messy tries at baby cereal-mush, and neater attempts at flavored puffs, then Cheerios by the fistful. I can tell you about her snoozing in her jungle swing as it serenaded her with gentle sounds of birds and monkeys and later her jump-jumping in her Jumperoo.

I can walk you through her quickly changing wardrobes. Summer trips to the Detroit Zoo, pushing a stroller, Em kicking out her chubby legs in a flowered onesie. A sweltering July evening at a wedding in Kansas, and Em fussing so much in the frilly yellow dress my mom bought her that I let her sit happily in just her diaper for the reception.

I can point to pictures in the fall at her dedication, her in a periwinkle-blue dress with a large colorful butterfly on it, sitting on my lap, Darian scrunched next to us. I can show you photos of her wearing "my first" bibs at Halloween, Thanksgiving, and Christmas.

I could tell you about her first birthday at Red Robin, Em in a sparkly cone hat surrounded by our friends, and the teddy bear cake a dear friend baked and lovingly decorated for her.

I could hand you her baby book and you would know this was a happy baby, who was well taken care of and loved beyond all reason.

What you wouldn't see, and I wouldn't tell you about, is all the dark days.

The in-between.

There are no pictures of the long, lonely hours, and weeks, and months, of caring for a baby who needed to fall asleep on her often-struggling mom. All the baby wanted was me, and all I wanted was to sleep because sleep alleviated all worry, all pain, all suffering—it was respite from the dark drowning place inside my suffocating chest.

There's no record of the daily phone calls and texts from Darian: "What can I bring you for lunch? What can I pick up for dinner?"

Taco Bell, no, Wendy's—how about pizza?

I didn't often have it in me to drive down the street to the grocery store or put together whatever had been bought when one of us actually made it there for more than diapers, formula, and tiny jars of baby food that sometimes splattered our ceiling.

There are no pictures of me propped up against the tall arm of our eggplant couch with spit-up cloths draped over my arms grown strong from holding Em, sometimes for hours, so she'd sleep. And trying ever so gingerly to lay her down in her crib, tiptoeing away, only to hear the wail that sent dread right down to the pit of my soul.

There's no record of the middle-of-the-night feedings, praying, pleading, that she would go back to sleep, and my creeping fears I'd finally gone crazy.

The darkness had come, worse than before, because I now perceived myself as the threat. Crime, abuse, trauma—these corrupting things happened to me. They weren't still in my home but were connected to my anxiety, depression, and PTSD. And those beasts were still festering inside me.

I tried to push it all away, far away, from myself and the baby, but it just balled up into a pit of red, angry, pulsating despair. It didn't discriminate, and it wouldn't leave.

I didn't tell our family doctor at Em's well-baby visits nor did I mention it to my OB at my own checkups. I didn't tell the women I knew well in my small group.

We're good, doing fine, nothing to see here.

I didn't tell my table at MOPS in the fall. I was thankful to drop Em off in the nursery for a two-hour break, but was in no condition to handle a packed room of women in colorful T-shirts running around, excited for motherhood, with chipper music blasting.

This is not going to work.

I wouldn't try again for four years.

I didn't tell Darian, who begged me to let him help more, whom I answered back in anger. I just carried on—one dragging foot in front of the other, one diaper, one bottle, one day at a time.

She needs me, and I need her, and I can't tell them—any of them—because they will think I'm a bad mother.

———

I don't know when the worst of it lifted.

Maybe it was the night I sat in our dark living room, imagining frightening shapes crawling on the walls, and remembered that once before I'd fought off the darkness with bits and pieces from the Psalms. "The LORD is my light and my salvation—whom shall I fear?"[1]

And maybe it wasn't just that I remembered it, but something within my spirit prompted me to utter it out loud. It was crazy, wasn't it? To talk to myself?

But the darkness receded as I spoke it quietly under my breath, and I didn't feel so crazy after that. "The LORD is the stronghold of my life—of whom shall I be afraid?"[2]

APRIL 2009

I don't know how Em, Darian, and I got through that first year. I should have told my doctors, told my husband. Asked for help. Gone back to therapy. Taken medicine. Hired my mom to stay with us full-time. Hindsight.

In April, thirteen months after Em was born, she and I took two flights to Wichita so she could stay with my mom for a week while I took two more flights to Fort Lauderdale to meet Darian for a six-day cruise. We jokingly called it our six-year honeymoon—the one that came after Dad, after Uncle John, after the first year of having a baby.

We lounged on the quiet third deck near the rolling water, and I line-danced at night on the lido deck, drink in hand, while Darian watched and tried to steer me in the right direction—the one everyone else was facing.

Darian and I kayaked in Key West, with me in the front and him steering from behind. Later we would say that was proof our marriage could withstand anything. We went on a historical tour of Jamaica and snorkeled in the Caymans, where we visited a reef full of colorful fish and brushed up against stingrays.

We had been through so much, but the day I got to swim in the bright-blue Caribbean will always stand out as one of the best days—a day I came back to life.

CHAPTER 45

Put Your Armor On

APRIL 2010

A move to a quieter place, with large windows that let in lots of light, helped the fog to continue to lift. Around the age of two, Emilie was finally able to fall asleep on her own and usually slept through the night, granting us and our home a good deal of grace.

My prayer for a peaceful little life was being answered, but it was never far from me—who I was in regard to my father. I was the daughter of a serial killer, and I didn't know anyone else like me.

In the spring of 2010, I took a tentative step into social media after repeatedly asking Darian if I should join Facebook. An ordinary thing for most felt like an act of courage to me.

Darian and I decided not to share family photos on Facebook, but not openly sharing photos led to more headaches. A few times, I logged on only to find myself tagged in photos from a gathering with friends. I had to email the friend, asking they remove the photo. Inevitably they would ask, "Why?"

"Go google me."

About fifteen minutes later, I'd get a reply. "Oh."

You'd think five years out from my dad's arrest, I wouldn't have to fight so hard to have a life.

SURVIVOR'S TIP

What not to say to a serial killer's daughter:

- OMG, no way, he did what?
- Did you know you're on Google?
- Do you think you will murder anyone?
- Do you have a serial-killer gene?
- They say traits skip a generation. Aren't you worried about your kids?
- Please stop talking. You're going to give me nightmares.
- Aren't you over that yet?
- Your dad should fry.

That spring, I remember sinking down in my chair at Tuesday Bible study as a woman mentioned visiting a prison: orange jumpsuits; high, barbed-wire walls; armed guards; shuffling, shackled prisoners.

My innards tied tight, my face flushed, my hands shook. The room spun, bright white, blazing. My chest squeezed—I couldn't breathe.

It was February 25 . . . I woke up late . . . There was a knock . . .

I stood up and fled to the bathroom before the group could see tears streaking down my panic-stricken face.

The loop was supposed to be gone—we had gotten it in therapy three years ago.

I paced back and forth in the bathroom, taking big gulps of air, trying to get control of my very out-of-control insides. I was having a PTSD-fueled panic attack.

God?

My hands in balled-up fists, I went back toward the room and ran into a couple of women in the hall who asked, "Are you okay?"

My whole body shaking, I ruptured loose. "No. Not at all."

Agitated, my mouth flying fast, I told them who I was—who my dad was, and why I was flipping out on a Tuesday morning.

Breathe.

They listened kindly and went on their way.

"The LORD is my light and my salvation—whom shall I fear?"[1]

I picked up Em from the nursery, tucked her into her car seat, handed her a bowl of fish crackers and a spill-proof cup, kissed her forehead, sat down, and slumped onto the steering wheel.

Breathe.

"The LORD is the stronghold of my life—of whom shall I be afraid?"[2]

You'd think five years out, I wouldn't have to fight so hard to stay alive.

I didn't go back to my group that season; with the PTSD, it was too much to think about the room.

In 2007, not long after buying the *Eagle*'s BTK book, I had set it facing backward on a shelf. When we moved, I tucked it away in a tote box. Sometime after my PTSD flashback, I dug out the book and chucked it into the trash.

Gone and good riddance, Dad!

I then dug through my photo albums, removed all the photos I had of my father, placed them in a plastic bag, grabbed the litter scoop, tossed clumps on them, and threw them away in the trash.

Goodbye, Dad.

You wouldn't think—five years out—I'd still be this angry.

MARCH 2011

"Do we have kids?" I asked this in an IV-induced haze to a bemused Darian, who was sitting in a hospital chair next to a snow-clad frozen window in March 2011.

He gave this a good comedic pause, his eyes twinkling, waiting to answer. "Yes. We have a daughter at home; she's three." He pointed to my massive belly. "We also have a son."

I giggled. "Do we own an apple orchard?"

"No. Please shush and try to rest."

"Please shush"—I was only having the man's baby.

It had only taken a few months of Emilie sleeping through the night to desire to have another baby—and to get pregnant. I spent the first half of my second pregnancy throwing up, eating Eggo waffles by the boxful, and unsure if I should laugh or cry when Em greeted Darian in the evenings with "Mama bleh all over herself."

In the fall, my nausea subsided and we found out we were having a boy. He was more than willing to show us the goods at his ultrasound. We shopped for shades of blue, and Darian set up the jungle swing and the bouncer with the dangling star arch and put the crib back together.

Thinking the baby would come early, my mom flew to Detroit in late February. She ended up staying with us a month as my dad's birthday safely passed and we celebrated Em's third birthday. Two weeks past due, the boy still refusing to come out, I waddled into the hospital for an induction and promptly was asked, "Labor and delivery?"

Five hours later, on my hands and knees in intense pain, my OB gave me the good drugs while we waited for an epidural. After the epidural kicked in, I zoned out to "Moon River," sung by Frank Sinatra, playing on repeat for hours in my ears.

"It's time to push." I was woken up by my OB who was checking on my progress. *Those were some good drugs.*

Thirty minutes later, after pushing, letting the cuss words fly, going on oxygen, and having another episiotomy, our baby boy was out.

Why don't I hear crying?

My heart stopped.

The doctor quickly swiped our baby's mouth, turned him upside down, and gave him a hearty pat on the back.

"Wahh!"

It was the best sound I've ever heard. Our son, Ian, was born a scrapper like his mama. When they weighed him, Darian asked, "Is that nine pounds, *point* fifteen ounces?"

No. Can we call it ten pounds?

A few minutes later, Ian let the world know he was going to be a handful when the nurse didn't get a diaper on him quick enough and he doused all his official paperwork in a large arc of pee.

On the night Ian was born, I was handed a large bundle with blue eyes and strawberry-blond hair who wanted to tuck as tight as he could into me and chug on a bottle for as long as anyone would let him. On the night Ian was born, another piece of my heart came back to life.

God?

Thank you and amen.

I was terrified that with Ian's birth I'd fall back into the same pit I landed in with Emilie's birth, even finally bringing myself to be upfront about my previous struggles. Darian steadily responded, "You've got to let me do more, get up at night with him."

And my OB gently said, "We will watch you and can get you help. Medication, if we need to."

Okay. That wasn't so scary telling them.

Fear and panic tried to creep in the first day I was on my own with two, when Ian woke up wailing at the top of his lungs and Em tugged on my T-shirt, asking for "Cheerios, juice, and George." But Darian had already set her breakfast out and had a bottle ready for the boy, and soon enough we were watching a curious monkey get into all sorts of trouble on Netflix.

Thank you, good, good man.

Early on, I could feel the dark weight attempting to come down on me, especially on long afternoons trying to get everyone in the house to nap. But a friend reassured me all women go through baby blues and she'd check in often to see if it lifted. She checked in, and it lifted within a few weeks.

Thank you, God.

MARCH 2012

Ian had been born to a more stable mama: instead of life ceasing with his birth, he joined right into our ongoing one. His eyes turned brown, his hair turned sandy blond, and his name might as well have been "Joy."

He was rolling over before I blinked and flipped himself out of his swing within his first month. So we moved him to a blanket under a jungle arch that squawked and roared. He was crawling by six months and walking by ten. The crib came down and gates went up. Darian anchored the furniture, installed extra baby-proof outlet covers, and I braced for the next crash.

Please, God. Let him make it to two.

In the spring of 2012, Darian and I took another step toward normalcy, sharing pictures of ourselves and our kids on Facebook.

I returned to MOPS and led a women's Bible study, *James: Mercy Triumphs*, by Beth Moore.[3] I felt God nudging me through the study, asking: *What good is your faith? What is your life?*

Faith testifies.

That spring, I heard Priscilla Shirer speak on spiritual warfare—the Enemy. I pulled Rebecca aside; she was one of our mentors, full of warmth and laughter. I whispered to her, "Is there really something to calling out the Devil, the Enemy?"

Rebecca and I talked about how to rebuke, out loud, the fallen enemy, who "prowls around . . . looking for someone to devour."[4]

"Oh," I said. "I've been doing that for years. 'The LORD is my light and my salvation—whom shall I fear?'"[5]

She smiled knowingly and gave a nod.

A month later, leaders asked for a handful of women who would stand up and give their testimony around themes. One was armor: warfare, battles.

I felt God's nudging: *You could testify to that.*

No, no. My head internally shook side to side as my heart sped up.

God's nudging grew louder. *It's time.*

My heart was now about to come out of my chest, but I knew—there was no point in arguing with him. His knocking would get louder till I gave in.

A few weeks later, I nervously sat across from Rebecca at a coffeehouse.

This is gonna sting.

I quietly uttered, "My dad is a serial killer" and scrunched up my face, waiting for it.

What met me was grace upon grace. My voice grew stronger under Rebecca's gentle prompting and I poured it all out—why I thought I had something to testify to.

Yes, dear girl, you do.

In the middle of August, I stood up in front of a room full of women at my church and shared my story. Even though my stomach rolled loops and my paper rattled in my shaking hands, my voice carried strong and the room sat still. I told them:

We live on a battlefield, in a fallen world, where bad things can happen to good people. My dad made terrible choices with lifelong generational impacting consequences—he cost ten their lives. Where was God then?

But maybe I am letting evil win if I stay curled up in my hole, shut down in my ball of fear, hiding under my self-created armor of humor and sarcasm, walking around like nothing fazes me when sometimes it truly feels like I'm dying inside.

We live in a fallen world but we don't have to live like fallen people. Whatever you're going through, you can get through. The Enemy is going to try to drag as many people down with him as he can. Until Jesus returns and defeats him forever, we need to put on our God-given armor and go out into this world and fight the fight God has put before us.

"Therefore put on the full armor of God, so that when the day of evil comes, you may be able to stand your ground, and after you have done everything, to stand."[6]

CHAPTER 46

Try to Forgive

In the fall, our life continued to grow busier with Em starting preschool. While Em was in school, Ian, who was one and a half, tagged along on errands and to the gym that offered free childcare while I attempted to work out.

The worst of my PTSD had been conquered, Darian and I were raising two amazing kids, I was leading at my church, and I'd stood up and testified about God, who had seen me through so much.

On the outside, I looked well. But on the inside, I was still festering. My wounds were seeping underneath the bandages I wound tightly around them. I'd figured with enough time and distance from my father, I would heal.

But I was still angry, still hurting. Anger, pain—they wouldn't leave. I was holding on to them, keeping them tucked near me, to protect my heart from being broken again.

And holding on to them was hardening me. It was easier to be hard than to love because love hurt too much, cost too much. It was easier to push my father far away than to let him stay in my life, because letting him in my life meant loving him.

And to love him meant to forgive him . . . and I hadn't forgiven.

313

OCTOBER

"You have a stress fracture at the top of your tibia."

Oh.

I was on the phone with my orthopedic doctor's office, who had called me with my MRI results. A few weeks ago, I'd been jogging on the treadmill at the gym, pushing myself even though my leg had been aching, when I felt a sharp, stinging pain under my knee. Since then, I'd been on crutches and crawling around on my rear in the house after the kids.

"We want you to stay off it as much as possible; pain is your cue to stop weight-bearing."

Pain is your cue.

I ached all the time, and now I was grounded: no weekday meet-ups with church friends, no running errands, no outrunning the deep ache still inside me. The busyness that masked my deep, searing wounds slammed to a sudden halt.

I spent the next several weeks stuck on the couch, stewing over my latest predicament, bawling in pain as I tried to keep my toddler son out of trouble, and wrestling with God.

Quiet, peaceful, easy little life, God. Remember?

But God lets nothing go to waste.

We need to work on your forgiveness problem—we've got nothing but time.

I don't wanna, God.

Do it anyway.

I am a daughter of God, and I was supposed to forgive my father. But I was so hard-hearted that if I knew our pastor was going to preach on forgiveness, I'd skip the service or walk out when he hit that part.

I told the women at church: I hadn't forgiven my father. But I also told them of God's unending capacity to forgive: he forgives as far as the east is from the west.[1]

God calls us to forgive, and I truly believe all people can be forgiven for their sins. I'd written my dad back in 2005: "God is with you, he will never leave you nor forsake you.[2] He has loved you even before you were created, he loves you no matter what, and will forgive all your sins if you ask for forgiveness."

In Isaiah, we read: "Wash yourselves and be clean! Get your sins out of my sight. Give up your evil ways . . . 'Come now, let's settle this,' says the LORD. 'Though your sins are like scarlet, I will make them as white as snow. Though they are red like crimson, I will make them as white as wool.'"[3]

My father had written after his sentencing he asked God for forgiveness. So even though most people look at me skeptically, my father will be in heaven someday if he has accepted Jesus Christ—who died on the cross for everyone—including him.

I spoke of God's unending ability to forgive—to love. But I was stubbornly holding out on doing it myself. I didn't know if I could forgive my dad.

God? Are you asking me to forgive him or to write him also—let him back into my life? I don't know if I can—I don't know if I can trust him.

You can trust me—I'm your Father too.

But *my* father hurt me.

Yes. Remember Joseph?

We had been studying the life of Joseph in Genesis over the fall in my couples' small group. Joseph's brothers desired to murder him; they threw Joseph into a cistern before selling him into slavery. Over the next two decades, under the watchful, guiding hand of God, under immensely difficult circumstances, Joseph trusted and relied on God, rising to power within Egypt, overseeing the harvest and storage of grain.

When a famine hit, Joseph's brothers came to Egypt seeking aid. With his family standing before him, seeking shelter, seeking life, Joseph declared: "You intended to harm me, but God intended it for good to accomplish what is now being done, the saving of many lives."[4]

Joseph's declaration to his family struck me square in my heart. Treated with depravity, discarded, sold, Joseph stood up to evil, clung to God, rose above his suffering, and lavished grace upon his tormenters—his family—saving their lives.

My identity didn't belong to my broken father on earth. My identity was meant to rest in the arms of God—my heavenly Father. Who never fails and never gives up. God was asking me to trust and follow him.

You have a dad problem—which is a trust and obedience problem. You trusted your earthly father, who hurt you, so now you're holding out on me. You've been holding out on me for seven years. Let's fix that. You have a forgiveness problem, which is a love problem—which is a God problem.

I love you, God.

Then show me—do it.

DECEMBER

Softening over the fall, I asked Mom to mail me all of Dad's letters from the past five years, and I read through them all.

On a late winter evening, I was driving back from the theater after seeing a movie with a friend, and forgiveness toward my father unexpectedly washed over me while I was sitting at a red light. I was sobbing so hard, I had to pull the car over.

White-hot cleansing light overwhelmed my soul—setting me free. It wasn't from me—it was from God.

When I got home, I hurried upstairs and burst into our office, telling Darian I'd forgiven my father. I then sat down and wrote him for the first time in five years. After filling pages full of the past years, I finished my letter:

Wanted to make sure you heard from me; I hope you get this before Christmas. I miss you and think often of all the good times. I wonder about you a lot, how you are.

My prayer since 2005 has been for a quiet, peaceful life, and God has answered in abundance. I have a wonderful husband, two amazing kids.

I have come to terms with what happened with you and laid it to rest. I'm never going to understand it, but I forgive you.

I'm sorry, and I miss you.

I don't know if I will ever be able to make it for a visit but know I love you and hope to see you in heaven someday.

"Be strong and courageous. Do not be afraid or terrified because of them, for the LORD your God goes with you; he will never leave you nor forsake you."[5]

I realized my letter was filled with news of grandkids my dad won't ever meet and my life he won't ever get to be a part of again. I know now he cost himself this life—the one he lost—when he decided to take others' lives from them.

On the Good Days

I'd been holding on too tightly to the bandages I wrapped around my wounds years ago, wearing my armor to protect my heart from getting hurt again. I wasn't just holding out on my dad and myself, I was holding out on God. I was rotting within, so I forgave my dad for myself.

After I forgave my father, the rot was removed, the hardness lifted, and I came back to myself—the old me I thought was long lost, gone forever.

God led me through the canyon, one foot in front of the other, and God saw me minute by minute, hour by hour, day by day, through all that followed.

One foot in front of the other, I continued forward after forgiveness. I began to unwrap the bandages, letting light and air in so my wounds could truly heal, rather than just be protected. Two years after forgiving my dad, I gave my first interview to the *Eagle*.

I began to share the story of my life, who my father was to me, and who God is to all of us. In the summer that followed, I shared my story with thousands at my church; my pastor tied my story to Joseph's, whom he called an unlikely hero.

There have been massive struggles since forgiving my dad too. Return trips to therapy, suppressed trauma finally finding the light, almost nightly battles with night terrors, and PTSD that can still rear its ugly head. Anxiety can still seize me, and depression can still send me to the bottom of despair. But God has walked by my side through all of it—seeing me through, just as he did from the very beginning.

I'm now able to say—without shame or fear—I'm a trauma, crime, and abuse victim. I live with anxiety, depression, and PTSD.

What's in my past is what it is; it can't be changed—Dad murdered ten people and devastated countless lives. Yet on the days when I'm not wrestling with hard, terrible truths, I will tell you: I love my dad—the one I mainly knew. I miss him.

On the good days, memories fill my soul.

When I was a little girl, I would slip my tiny feet into Dad's brown leather boots with zippers on the side and stomp around, making a racket on our white kitchen tile. I'd usually fall over giggling, and Dad would chuckle too. He'd set me back up with an "ups-a-daisy," his calloused, working-man hands gently placed under my arms. He'd tug on one of my pigtails, call me Sunshine, and send me on my way, barefoot, my yellow gingham sundress swishing around me.

On the good days—I'm as near as I can be to being healed. On the good days, I think of writing my dad—sharing the latest about my life.

Acknowledgments

It started with the question, "What's next?" And that led to the best agent in the world, Doug Grad. Thank you, Doug, for your belief in me, unending patience, and years of work, to get this greenhorn scaling glaciers. L. Kelly, girls got to have each other's backs and you've had mine. Thank you for getting my heart and head going again and showing me what was possible if I only moved out of the rocks.

A huge thank you to Nelson Books and Brian Hampton, for taking a chance on me and to Jenny Baumgartner, my editor with the patience and faith of a saint. Jenny, thank you for enduring my false starts, my stalls, my breakdowns, and my many months and words over. Thank you for your friendship and kindness. We got through it together and for that, I will always be grateful.

A big thanks to Belinda Bass, Brigitta Nortker, and the Thomas Nelson design team for a fantastic looking book and your hard work. Thank you to Jamie Chavez, for your careful work in editing. You cleaned up my mess and challenged me to be better. Thank you to Stephanie Tresner and Sara Broun from Nelson Books and Sarah Miniaci and Michela DellaMonica from Smith Publicity, for working hard to get this book out to the masses and bearing the load for me.

Thank you to my family for trusting me to tell our story that spans decades. Darian, Emilie, and Ian, thank you for enduring years of living non-stop with a stumbling writer and loving me through it all.

Notes

Chapter 3: Hope for Happily Ever After
1. Katherine Ramsland, *Confession of a Serial Killer: The Untold Story of Dennis Rader, the BTK Killer* (Lebanon, NH: ForeEdge, 2016), 52.
2. Ramsland, *Confession of a Serial Killer*, 4.
3. Ramsland, 24.
4. Ramsland, 92.
5. Ramsland, 104.
6. "The State of Kansas vs. Dennis Rader," (18th Judicial District Court, Sedgwick County, Kansas, August 17, 2005), 67.

Breaking News
1. Roy Wenzl et al., *Bind, Torture, Kill: The Inside Story of BTK, the Serial Killer Next Door* (New York: HarperCollins, 2007), 75.

Chapter 4: Weave Among the Pines Like a Tomboy
1. Katherine Ramsland, *Confession of a Serial Killer: The Untold Story of Dennis Rader, the BTK Killer* (Lebanon, NH: ForeEdge, 2016), 5.

Chapter 7: Allow Yourself to Grieve
1. Heb. 3:15.

Chapter 8: Attempt to Outrun What Haunts You
1. John 14:2–3.

Chapter 10: Know and Respect Your Limitations . . . Yeah, Right
1. "Warning, Heat Kills!" is paraphrased by Kerri Rawson, based off signs posted at the Hermit trail head and handouts given to Dennis Rader from the National Park Service in May 1997.
2. Sarah Bohl Gerke, "Hermit Trail," Nature, Culture, and History at the Grand Canyon, Arizona State University, 2008, accessed July 27,

2018, http://www.grcahistory.org/sites_rimtoriverandinnercanyon
_hermittrail.html.

Chapter 11: Miscalculations of the Ego Can Be Deadly
1. Stephen Whitney, *A Field Guide to the Grand Canyon*, 2nd ed.
(Seattle: Mountaineers, 1996), 168.

Chapter 18: Make a Place of Your Own
1. Ps. 27:1.

Chapter 19: Head Down the Wedding Aisle, Even If You Have to Hobble
1. 1 Cor. 13:6–8.

Chapter 21: Don't Say Goodbye—Say See Ya in a While
1. Roy Wenzl et al., *Bind, Torture, Kill: The Inside Story of BTK, the Serial Killer Next Door* (New York: HarperCollins, 2007), 222.

Breaking News
1. Roy Wenzl et al., *Bind, Torture, Kill: The Inside Story of BTK, the Serial Killer Next Door* (New York: HarperCollins, 2007), 266.

Chapter 24: Don't Google for an Alibi
1. Roy Wenzl et al., *Bind, Torture, Kill: The Inside Story of BTK, the Serial Killer Next Door* (New York: HarperCollins, 2007), 54.
2. Ps. 23:1–3, 4, 6 ESV.
3. Wenzl et al., *Bind, Torture, Kill*, 287.
4. Wenzl et al., 290.

Chapter 25: Media Circuses Belong in Big Tops, Not Apartments
1. Roy Wenzl et al., *Bind, Torture, Kill: The Inside Story of BTK, the Serial Killer Next Door* (New York: HarperCollins, 2007), 292.
2. "Report: Daughter of BTK Suspect Alerted Police," CNN, February 26, 2005, www.cnn.com/2005/US/02/26/btk.investigation.

Chapter 26: Respite Can Be Found Thousands of Feet in the Air
1. "Local Kansas Man, Church Leader and 'Guy Next Door,' Arrested in Decades-Old 'BTK Killings' Case," NBC, February 27, 2005, www.nbclearn.com/portal/site/k-12/flatview?cuecard=47773.
2. Ps. 18:2.

3. Ps. 27:1.

Chapter 27: There Is Safety in Numbers

1. Roy Wenzl et al., *Bind, Torture, Kill: The Inside Story of BTK, the Serial Killer Next Door* (New York: HarperCollins, 2007), 297.
2. Wenzl et al., *Bind, Torture, Kill*, 297.
3. Wenzl et al., 297.
4. Ps. 27:1.
5. Ps. 27:1.

Chapter 28: Maybe Love Is Enough

1. Excerpts seen here are taken from longer originals and have been lightly edited.
2. John 1:5.
3. To maintain accuracy, spelling and grammatical errors in Dennis Rader's and Kerri Rawson's letters have not been corrected intentionally, unless required for meaning.

Chapter 29: Leave the Crime Solving to the Experts

1. Katherine Ramsland, *Confession of a Serial Killer: The Untold Story of Dennis Rader, the BTK Killer* (Lebanon, NH: ForeEdge, 2016), 212.

Chapter 30: Light Will Overcome the Darkness

1. Ps. 27:1.
2. Ps. 18:2.
3. Ps. 27:1.
4. John 1:5.
5. Song 2:4.

Chapter 33: Most Folks Are Good and Intend You No Harm

1. Roy Wenzl, "BTK's Daughter: Stephen King 'Exploiting My Father's 10 Victims and Their Families' with Movie," *Wichita Eagle*, September 25, 2014, www.kansas.com/news/local/article2251870.html.

Chapter 34: Fight for Those You Love

1. Ps. 27:1.

Breaking News

1. "Breaking News: Guilty Ten Times Over" is written by Kerri Rawson and based off information obtained from: Roy Wenzl et al., *Bind,*

Torture, Kill: The Inside Story of BTK, the Serial Killer Next Door (New York: HarperCollins, 2007), 302.

Chapter 37: Truth and Justice Can Hurt

1. Roy Wenzl et al., *Bind, Torture, Kill: The Inside Story of BTK, the Serial Killer Next Door* (New York: HarperCollins, 2007), 360.
2. Roy Wenzl, "When Your Father Is the BTK Serial Killer, Forgiveness Is Not Tidy," *Wichita Eagle*, February 21, 2015, www.kansas.com /news/special-reports/btk/article10809929.html.
3. Katherine Ramsland, *Confession of a Serial Killer: The Untold Story of Dennis Rader, the BTK Killer* (Lebanon, NH: ForeEdge, 2016), 85.
4. Ramsland, *Confession of a Serial Killer*, 116.

Chapter 38: 175 Years Is a Long Time

1. Roy Wenzl et al., *Bind, Torture, Kill: The Inside Story of BTK, the Serial Killer Next Door* (New York: HarperCollins, 2007), 313.
2. Wenzl et al., *Bind, Torture, Kill*, 313.

Chapter 39: Keep Faith in the Good

1. 1 Cor. 13:13.

Chapter 40: A Desert Is a Great Place to Hide

1. From an article in *US News & World Report*, October 27, 1986, quoted in "Elie Wiesel," Wikiquote, accessed April 5, 2018, en.wikiquote.org /wiki/Elie_Wiesel.

Chapter 41: PTSD Blows Chunks

1. Roy Wenzl, "When Your Father Is the BTK Serial Killer, Forgiveness Is Not Tidy," *Wichita Eagle*, February 21, 2015, www.kansas.com /news/special-reports/btk/article10809929.html

Chapter 42: Therapy Might Just Save Your Life

1. Heb. 3:15.

Chapter 43: Laugh or Cry to Survive

1. Deut. 31:6.
2. Ps. 139:13.
3. Roy Wenzl, "When Your Father Is the BTK Serial Killer, Forgiveness Is Not Tidy," *Wichita Eagle*, February 22, 2015, www.kansas.com /news/special-reports/btk/article10809929.html.

Chapter 44: Grit Your Teeth and Keep Going

1. Ps. 27:1.
2. Ps. 27:1.

Chapter 45: Put Your Armor On

1. Ps. 27:1.
2. Ps. 27:1.
3. Beth Moore and Melissa Moore, *James: Mercy Triumphs* (Nashville: LifeWay Press, 2011).
4. 1 Peter 5:8.
5. Ps. 27:1.
6. Eph. 6:13.

Chapter 46: Try to Forgive

1. Ps. 103:12.
2. Deut. 31:6.
3. Isa. 1:16, 18 NLT.
4. Gen. 50:20.
5. Deut. 31:6.

About the Author

Kerri Rawson is the daughter of Dennis Rader, better known to the world as the serial killer BTK. Since her father's arrest, Kerri has been an advocate for victims of abuse, crime, and trauma, sharing her journey of hope, healing, faith, and forgiveness. She lives with her husband, two children, and two cats in Michigan.